501
Algebra Questions

501

Algebra Questions

LEARNINGEXPRESS ®

NEW YORK

Library of Congress Cataloging-in-Publication Data:
Recco, William.
    501 algebra questions / William Recco.—1st ed.
        p. cm.
    ISBN 1-57685-424-8 (pbk.)
    1. Algebra. I. Title: Five hundred one algebra questions. II. Title:
Five hundred and one algebra questions. III. Title.
    QA152.2 .R42 2002
    512—dc21

                                                    2002004440

Printed in the United States of America
9 8 7 6 5
First Edition

ISBN 1-57685-424-8

For more information or to place an order, contact LearningExpress at:
    55 Broadway
    8th Floor
    New York, NY 10006

Or visit us at:
    www.learnatest.com

The LearningExpress Skill Builder in Focus Writing Team is comprised of experts in test preparation, as well as educators and teachers who specialize in language arts and math.

LearningExpress Skill Builder in Focus Writing Team

Brigit Dermott
Freelance Writer
English Tutor, New York Cares
New York, New York

Sandy Gade
Project Editor
LearningExpress
New York, New York

Kerry McLean
Project Editor
Math Tutor
Shirley, New York

William Recco
Middle School Math Teacher, Grade 8
New York Shoreham/Wading River School District
Math Tutor
St. James, New York

Colleen Schultz
Middle School Math Teacher, Grade 8
Vestal Central School District
Math Tutor
Vestal, New York

Contents

Contents

Introduction

This book is designed to provide you with review and practice for algebra success! It is not intended to teach common algebra topics. Instead, it provides 501 problems so you can flex your muscles and practice a variety of mathematical and algebraic skills. *501 Algebra Questions* is designed for many audiences. It's for anyone who has ever taken a course in algebra and needs to refresh and revive forgotten skills. It can be used to supplement current instruction in a math class. Or, it can be used by teachers and tutors who need to reinforce student skills. If at some point you feel you need further explanation about some of the algebra topics highlighted in this book, you can find them in the LearningExpress publication *Algebra Success in 20 Minutes a Day*.

How To Use This Book

First, look at the table of contents to see the types of algebra topics covered in this book. The book is organized into twenty chapters with a variety of arithmetic, algebra, and word problems. The structure follows a common sequence of concepts introduced in basic algebra courses. You may want to follow the sequence, as each succeeding chapter builds on skills taught in previous chapters. But if your skills are just rusty, or if you are using this book to supplement top-ics you are currently learning, you may want to jump around from topic to topic.

Chapters are arranged using the same method. Each chapter has an introduction describing the mathematical concepts covered in the chapter. Second, there are helpful tips on how to practice the problems in each chapter. Last, you are pre-sented with a variety of problems that generally range from easier to more difficult problems and their answer explanations. In many books, you are given one model problem and then asked to do many problems following that model. In this book, every problem has a complete step-by-step explanation for the solutions. If you find yourself getting stuck solving a problem, you can look at the answer explanation and use it to help you understand the problem-solving process.

As you are solving problems, it is important to be as organized and sequential in your written steps as possible. The purpose of drills and practice is to make you pro-ficient at solving problems. Like an athlete preparing for the next season or a musi-cian warming up for a concert, you become skillful with practice. If after completing all the problems in a section you feel that you need more practice, do the problems over. It's not the answer that matters most—it's the process and the reasoning skills that you want to master.

You will probably want to have a calculator handy as you work through some of the sections. It's always a good idea to use it to check your calculations. If you have difficulty factoring numbers, the multiplication chart on the next page may help you. If you are unfamiliar with prime numbers, use the list on the next page so you won't waste time trying to factor numbers that can't be factored. And don't forget to keep lots of scrap paper on hand.

Make a Commitment

Success does not come without effort. Make the commitment to improve your alge-bra skills. Work for understanding. *Why* you do a math operation is as important as *how* you do it. If you truly want to be successful, make a commitment to spend the time you need to do a good job. You can do it! When you achieve algebra suc-cess, you have laid the foundation for future challenges and success. So sharpen your pencil and practice!

Multiplication Table

×	2	3	4	5	6	7	8	9	10	11	12
2	4	6	8	10	12	14	16	18	20	22	24
3	6	9	12	15	18	21	24	27	30	33	36
4	8	12	16	20	24	28	32	36	40	44	48
5	10	15	20	25	30	35	40	45	50	55	60
6	12	18	24	30	36	42	48	54	60	66	72
7	14	21	28	35	42	49	56	63	70	77	84
8	16	24	32	40	48	56	64	72	80	88	96
9	18	27	36	45	54	63	72	81	90	99	108
10	20	30	40	50	60	70	80	90	100	110	120
11	22	33	44	55	66	77	88	99	110	121	132
12	24	36	48	60	72	84	96	108	120	132	144

Commonly Used Prime Numbers

2	3	5	7	11	13	17	19	23	29
31	37	41	43	47	53	59	61	67	71
73	79	83	89	97	101	103	107	109	113
127	131	137	139	149	151	157	163	167	173
179	181	191	193	197	199	211	223	227	229
233	239	241	251	257	263	269	271	277	281
283	293	307	311	313	317	331	337	347	349
353	359	367	373	379	383	389	397	401	409
419	421	431	433	439	443	449	457	461	463
467	479	487	491	499	503	509	521	523	541
547	557	563	569	571	577	587	593	599	601
607	613	617	619	631	641	643	647	653	659
661	673	677	683	691	701	709	719	727	733
739	743	751	757	761	769	773	787	797	809
811	821	823	827	829	839	853	857	859	863
877	881	883	887	907	911	919	929	937	941
947	953	967	971	977	983	991	997	1009	1013

501
Algebra Questions

Working With Integers

For some people, it is helpful to try to simplify expressions containing signed numbers as much as possible. When you find signed numbers with addition and subtraction operations, you can simplify the task by changing all subtraction to addition. Subtracting a number is the same as adding its opposite. For example, subtracting a three is the same as adding a negative three. Or subtracting a negative fourteen is the same as adding a positive fourteen. As you go through the step-by-step answer explanations, you will begin to see how this process of using only addition can help simplify your understanding of operations with signed numbers. As you begin to gain confidence, you may be able to eliminate some of the steps by doing them in you head and not having to write them down. After all, that's the point of practice! You work at the problems until the process becomes automatic. Then you own that process and you are ready to use it in other situations.

The **Tips for Working with Integers** section below gives you some simple rules to follow as you solve problems with integers. Refer to them each time you do a problem until you don't need to look at them. That's when you can consider them yours.

You will also want to review the rules for Order of Operations with numerical expressions. You can use a memory device called a mnemonic to help you remember a set of instructions. Try remembering the word **PEMDAS**. This nonsense word helps you remember to:

P   do operations inside *Parentheses*
E   evaluate terms with *Exponents*
M D   do *Multiplication* and *Division* in order from left to right
A S   *Add* and *Subtract* terms in order from left to right

Tips for Working with Integers

Addition
    Signed numbers the same? Find the SUM and use the same sign. Signed numbers different? Find the DIFFERENCE and use the sign of the larger number. (The larger number is the one whose value without a positive or negative sign is greatest.)
    Addition is commutative. That is, you can add numbers in any order and the result is the same. As an example, **3 + 5 = 5 + 3**, or **−2 + −1 = −1 + −2**.

Subtraction
    Change the operation sign to addition, change the sign of the number following the operation, then follow the rules for addition.

Multiplication/Division
    Signs the same? Multiply or divide and give the result a **positive** sign. Signs different? Multiply or divide and give the result a **negative** sign.
    Multiplication is commutative. You can multiply terms in any order and the result will be the same. For example: **(2 · 5 · 7) = (2 · 7 · 5) = (5 · 2 · 7) = (5 · 7 · 2)** and so on.

Evaluate the following expressions.

1. $27 + {}^-5$

2. ${}^-18 + {}^-20 - 16$

3. ${}^-11 - {}^-8$

4. $33 + {}^-16$

5. $8 + {}^-4 - 12$

6. $38 \div {}^-2 + 9$

7. ${}^-25 \cdot {}^-3 + 15 \cdot {}^-5$

8. ${}^-6 \cdot {}^-3 \cdot {}^-2$

9. $24 \cdot {}^-8 + 2$

10. $2 \cdot {}^-3 \cdot {}^-7$

11. ${}^-15 + 5 + {}^-11$

12. $(49 \div 7) - (48 \div {}^-4)$

13. $5 + {}^-11 - 3 + 8$

14. ${}^-(5 \cdot 3) + (12 \div {}^-4)$

15. $({}^-18 \div 2) - (6 \cdot {}^-3)$

16. $23 + (64 \div {}^-16)$

17. $2^3 - ({}^-4)^2$

18. $(3 - 5)^3 + (18 \div 6)^2$

19. $24 + (9 + {}^-6)^3$

20. $(3^2 + 6) \div ({}^-24 \div 8)$

21. A scuba diver descends 80 feet, rises 25 feet, descends 12 feet, and then rises 52 feet where he will do a safety stop for five minutes before surfacing. At what depth did he do his safety stop?

22. A digital thermometer records the daily high and low temperatures. The high for the day was +3° C. The low was −10° C. What was the difference between the day's high and low temperatures?

23. A checkbook balance sheet shows an initial balance for the month of $300. During the month, checks were written in the amounts of $25, $82, $213, and $97. Deposits were made into the account in the amounts of $84 and $116. What was the balance at the end of the month?

24. A gambler begins playing a slot machine with $10 in quarters in her coin bucket. She plays 15 quarters before winning a jackpot of 50 quarters. She then plays 20 more quarters in the same machine before walking away. How many quarters does she now have in her coin bucket?

25. A glider is towed to an altitude of 2,000 feet above the ground before being released by the tow plane. The glider loses 450 feet of altitude before finding an updraft that lifts it 1,750 feet. What is the glider's altitude now?

Answers

Numerical expressions in parentheses like this [ ] are operations performed on only part of the original expression. The operations performed within these symbols are intended to show how to evaluate the various terms that make up the entire expression.

Expressions with parentheses that look like this ( ) contain either numerical substitutions or expressions that are part of a numerical expression. Once a single number appears within these parentheses, the parentheses are no longer needed and need not be used the next time the entire expression is written.

When two pair of parentheses appear side by side like this ( )( ), it means that the expressions within are to be multiplied.

Sometimes parentheses appear within other parentheses in numerical or algebraic expressions. Regardless of what symbol is used, ( ), { }, or [ ], perform operations in the innermost parentheses first and work outward.

<u>Underlined</u> expressions show the original algebraic expression as an equation with the expression equal to its simplified result.

1. The signs of the terms are different, so find the difference
    of the values. $[27 - 5 = 22]$
    The sign of the larger term is positive, so the sign of
    the result is positive. $\underline{27 + {}^-5 = {}^+22}$

2. Change the subtraction sign to addition by
    changing the sign of the number that follows it. ${}^-18 + {}^-20 + ({}^-16)$
    Since all the signs are negative, add the
    absolute value of the numbers. $[18 + 20 + 16 = 54]$
    Since the signs were negative, the result
    is negative. ${}^-18 + {}^-20 + {}^-16 = {}^-54$
    The simplified result of the numeric expression
    is as follows: $\underline{{}^-18 + {}^-20 - 16 = {}^-54}$

3. Change the subtraction sign to addition by
    changing the sign of the number that follows it. ${}^-11 + {}^+8$
    Signs different? Subtract the absolute value of
    the numbers. $[11 - 8 = 3]$
    Give the result the sign of the larger term. ${}^-11 + {}^+8 = {}^-3$
    The simplified expression is as follows: $\underline{{}^-11 - {}^-8 = {}^-3}$

4. Signs different? Subtract the value of the numbers. $[33 - 16 = 17]$
    Give the result the sign of the larger term. $\underline{33 + {}^-16 = {}^+17}$

5. Change the subtraction sign to addition by changing
   the sign of the number that follows it. $8 + {}^-4 + {}^-12$
   With three terms, first group like terms and add. $8 + ({}^-4 + {}^-12)$
   Signs the same? Add the value of the terms and
      give the result the same sign. $[({}^-4 + {}^-12) = {}^-16]$
   Substitute the result into the first expression. $8 + ({}^-16)$
   Signs different? Subtract the value of the numbers. $[16 - 8 = 8]$
   Give the result the sign of the larger term. $8 + ({}^-16) = {}^-8$
   The simplified result of the numeric expression
      is as follows: $\underline{8 + {}^-4 - 12 = {}^-8}$

6. First divide. Signs different? Divide and give the
      result the negative sign. $[(38 \div {}^-2) = {}^-19]$
   Substitute the result into the expression. $({}^-19) + 9$
   Signs different? Subtract the value of the numbers. $[19 - 9 = 10]$
   Give the result the sign of the term with the
      larger value. $({}^-19) + 9 = {}^-10$
   The simplified result of the numeric expression
      is as follows: $\underline{38 \div {}^-2 + 9 = {}^-10}$

7. First perform the multiplications.
   Signs the same? Multiply the terms and give
      the result a positive sign. $[{}^-25 \cdot {}^-3 = {}^+75]$
   Signs different? Multiply the terms and give
      the result a negative sign. $[15 \cdot {}^-5 = {}^-75]$
   Now substitute the results into the original
      expression. $({}^+75) + ({}^-75)$
   Signs different? Subtract the value of the
      numbers. $[75 - 75 = 0]$
   The simplified result of the numeric
      expression is as follows: $\underline{25 \cdot 3 + 15 \cdot 5 = 0}$

8. Because all the operators are multiplication, you
      could group any two terms and the result would
      be the same. Let's group the first two terms. $({}^-6 \cdot {}^-3) \cdot {}^-2$
   Signs the same? Multiply the terms and give
      the result a positive sign. $[6 \cdot 3 = {}^+18]$
   Now substitute the result into the original
      expression. $({}^+18) \cdot {}^-2$
   Signs different? Multiply the terms and give
      the result a negative sign. $({}^+18) \cdot {}^-2 = {}^-36$
   The simplified result of the numeric expression
      is as follows: $\underline{{}^-6 \cdot {}^-3 \cdot {}^-2 = {}^-36}$

9. Group the terms being multiplied and evaluate. $(24 \cdot {}^-8) + 2$
   Signs different? Multiply the terms and give the
      result a negative sign. $[24 \cdot {}^-8 = {}^-192]$
   Substitute. $({}^-192) + 2$
   Signs different? Subtract the value of the terms. $[192 - 2 = 190]$
   Give the result the sign of the term with the
      larger value. $({}^-192) + 2 = {}^-190$
   The simplified result of the numeric expression
      is as follows: $\underline{24 \cdot {}^-8 + 2 = {}^-190}$

10. Because all the operators are multiplication, you
       could group any two terms and the result would be
       the same. Let's group the last two terms. $2 \cdot ({}^-3 \cdot {}^-7)$
    Signs the same? Multiply the terms and give the
       result a positive sign. $[({}^-3 \cdot {}^-7) = {}^+21]$
    Substitute. $2 \cdot ({}^+21)$
    Signs the same? Multiply the terms and give the
       result a positive sign. $2 \cdot ({}^+21) = {}^+42$
    The simplified result of the numeric expression is
       as follows: $\underline{2 \cdot {}^-3 \cdot {}^-7 = {}^+42}$

11. Because all the operators are addition, you could
       group any two terms and the result would be the
       same. Or you could just work from left to right. $({}^-15 + 5) + {}^-11$
    Signs different? Subtract the value of the numbers. $[15 - 5 = 10]$
    Give the result the sign of the term with the
       larger value. $[({}^-15 + 5) = {}^-10]$
    Substitute. $({}^-10) + {}^-11$
    Signs the same? Add the value of the terms
       and give the result the same sign. $[10 + 11 = 21]$
    $({}^-10) + {}^-11 = {}^-21$

    The simplified result of the numeric expression
       is as follows: $\underline{{}^-15 + 5 + {}^-11 = {}^-21}$

12. First evaluate the expressions within the
       parentheses. $[49 \div 7 = 7]$
    Signs different? Divide and give the result
       a negative sign. $[48 \div {}^-4 = {}^-12]$
    Substitute into the original expression. $(7) - ({}^-12)$
    Change the subtraction sign to addition
       by changing the sign of the number that
       follows it. $7 + {}^+12$
    Signs the same? Add the value of the terms
       and give the result the same sign. $7 + {}^+12 = {}^+19$
    The simplified result of the numeric
       expression is as follows: $\underline{(49 \div 7) - (48 \div {}^-4) = {}^+19}$

13. Change the subtraction sign to addition by
changing the sign of the number that follows it. $5 + {}^-11 + {}^-3 + 8$
Now perform additions from left to right. $(5 + {}^-11) + {}^-3 + 8$
Signs different? Subtract the value of the numbers
and give the result the sign of the higher value
number. $[11 - 5 = 6]$
     $[5 + {}^-11 = {}^-6]$

Substitute. $({}^-6) + {}^-3 + 8$
Add from left to right. $({}^-6 + {}^-3) + 8$
Signs the same? Add the value of the terms and
give the result the same sign. $[{}^-6 + {}^-3 = {}^-9]$
Substitute. $({}^-9) + 8$
Signs different? Subtract the value of the
numbers and give the result the sign of the
higher value number. $[9 - 8 = 1]$
     $({}^-9) + 8 = {}^-1$

The simplified result of the numeric expression
is as follows: $5 + {}^-11 - 3 + 8 = {}^-1$

14. First evaluate the expressions within the
parentheses. $[5 \cdot 3 = 15]$
Signs different? Divide and give the result
a negative sign. $[12 \div {}^-4 = {}^-3]$
Substitute the values into the original
expression. ${}^-(15) + ({}^-3)$
Signs the same? Add the value of the terms
and give the result the same sign. $[15 + 3 = 18]$
     ${}^-(15) + ({}^-3) = {}^-18$

The simplified result of the numeric
expression is as follows: ${}^-(5 \cdot 3) + (12 \div {}^-4) = {}^-18$

15. First evaluate the expressions within the
parentheses. $[(^-18 \div 2)]$
Signs different? Divide the value of the
terms and give the result a negative sign. $[18 \div 2 = 9]$
                                                                          $[(^-18 \div 2 = ^-9)]$

Signs different? Multiply the term values
and give the result a negative sign. $(6 \cdot ^-3)$
                                                                          $[6 \cdot 3 = 18]$
                                                                          $(6 \cdot ^-3) = ^-18$

Substitute the values into the original
expression. $(^-9) - (^-18)$
Change subtraction to addition and change
the sign of the term that follows. $(^-9) + (^+18)$
Signs different? Subtract the value of the
numbers and give the result the sign of the
higher value number. $[18 - 9 = 9]$
                                                                          $(^-9) + (^+18) = ^+9$

The simplified result of the numeric
expression is as follows: $(^-18 \div 2) - (6 \cdot ^-3) = ^+9$

16. Evaluate the expressions within the parentheses. $(64 \div ^-16)$
Signs different? Divide and give the result
a negative sign. $[64 \div 16 = 4]$
                                                                          $(64 \div ^-16 = ^-4)$

Substitute the value into the original expression. $23 + (^-4)$
Signs different? Subtract the value of the
numbers and give the result the sign of the
higher value number. $[23 - 4 = 19]$
                                                                          $23 + (^-4) = ^+19$

The simplified result of the numeric expression
is as follows: $23 + (64 \div ^-16) = ^+19$

17. The order of operations tells us to evaluate the
terms with exponents first. $[2^3 = 2 \cdot 2 \cdot 2 = 8]$
                                                                          $[(^-4)^2 = (^-4) \cdot (^-4)]$

Signs the same? Multiply the terms and give
the result a positive sign. $[4 \cdot 4 = 16]$
                                                                          $[(^-4)^2 = ^+16]$

Substitute the values of terms with exponents
into the original expression. $2^3 - (^-4)^2 = (8) - (^+16)$
Change subtraction to addition and change
the sign of the term that follows. $8 + ^-16$
Signs different? Subtract the value of the
numbers and give the result the sign of the
higher value number. $[16 - 8 = 8]$
                                                                          $8 + ^-16 = ^-8$

The simplified result of the numeric expression
is as follows:

$$2^3 - (^-4)^2 = ^-8$$

18. First evaluate the expressions within the
parentheses.

$$[3 - 5]$$

Change subtraction to addition and change
the sign of the term that follows.

$$[3 + (^-5)]$$

Signs different? Subtract the value of the
numbers and give the result the sign of the
higher value number.

$$[5 - 3 = 2]$$
$$[3 - 5 - ^-2]$$
$$[18 \div 6 = 3]$$

Substitute the values of the expressions in
parentheses into the original expression.

$$(^-2)^3 + (3)^2$$

Evaluate the terms with exponents.

$$[(^-2)^3 = ^-2 \cdot ^-2 \cdot ^-2]$$
$$[(^-2 \cdot ^-2) \cdot ^-2 = (^+4) \cdot ^-2]$$

Signs different? Multiply the value of the
terms and give the result a negative sign.

$$[(^+4) \cdot ^-2 = ^-8]$$
$$[(3)^2 = 3 \cdot 3 = 9]$$

Substitute the values into the expression.

$$(^-2)^3 + (3)^2 = ^-8 + 9$$

Signs different? Subtract the value of the
numbers and give the result the sign of the
higher value number.

$$9 - 8 = ^+1$$

The simplified result of the numeric
expression is as follows:

$$(3 - 5)^3 + (18 \div 6)^2 = ^+1$$

19. First evaluate the expression within the parentheses.

$$[9 + ^-6]$$

Signs different? Subtract the value of the numbers
and give the result the sign of the higher value
number.

$$[9 - 6 = 3]$$
$$[9 + ^-6 = ^+3]$$

Substitute the value into the expression.

$$24 + (^+3)^3$$

Evaluate the term with the exponent.

$$[(^+3)^3 = 3^3 = 27]$$

Substitute the value into the expression.

$$24 + (27) = 51$$

The simplified result of the numeric expression is
as follows:

$$24 + (9 + ^-6)^3 = 51$$

20. First evaluate the expressions within the
parentheses.

$$[3^2 + 6 = (9) + 6 = 15]$$

Signs different? Divide and give the result
the negative sign.

$$[^-24 \div 8 = ^-3]$$

Substitute values into the original expression.

$$(15) \div (^-3)$$

Signs different? Divide the value of the
terms and give the result a negative sign.

$$[15 \div 3 = 5]$$
$$(15) \div (^-3) = ^-5$$

The simplified result of the numeric
expression is as follows:

$$(3^2 + 6) \div (^-24 \div 8) = ^-5$$

21. If you think of distance above sea level as a positive number, then you must think of going below sea level as a negative number. Going up is in the positive direction, while going down is in the negative direction. Give all the descending distances a negative sign and the ascending distances a positive sign.

The resulting numerical expression would be as follows: $^-80 + {}^+25 + {}^-12 + {}^+52$

Because addition is commutative, you can associate like-signed numbers. $(^-80 + {}^-12) + ({}^+25 + {}^+52)$

Evaluate the numerical expression in each parentheses. $[^-80 + {}^-12 = {}^-92]$
$[^+25 + {}^+52 = {}^+77]$

Substitute the values into the numerical expression. $(^-92) + ({}^+77)$

Signs different? Subtract the value of the numbers and give the result the sign of the higher value number. $[92 - 77 = 15]$

The diver took his rest stop at $^-15$ feet.

22. You could simply figure that $^+3°C$ is 3° above zero and $^-10°C$ is 10° below. So the difference is the total of $3° + 10° = 13°$.
Or you could find the difference between $^+3°$ and $^-10°$.
That would be represented by the following equation. $^+3° - {}^-10° = {}^+3° + {}^+10° = {}^+13°$

23. You can consider that balances and deposits are positive signed numbers while checks are deductions, represented by negative signed numbers.

An expression to represent the activity during the month would be as follows: $300 + {}^-25 + {}^-82 + {}^-213 + {}^-97 + {}^+84 + {}^+116$

Because addition is commutative, you can associate like signed numbers. $(300 + {}^+84 + {}^+116) + (^-25 + {}^-82 + {}^-213 + {}^-97)$

Evaluate the numbers within each parentheses. $[300 + {}^+84 + {}^+116 = {}^+500]$
$[(^-25 + {}^-82 + {}^-213 + {}^-97 = {}^-417]$

Substitute the values into the revised expression. $(^+500) + (^-417) = {}^+83$

The balance at the end of the month would be $83.

24. You first figure out how many quarters she starts
with. Four quarters per dollar gives you $4 \cdot 10$
$= 40$ quarters. You can write an expression that
represents the quarters in the bucket and the
quarters added and subtracted. In chronological
order, the expression would be as follows: $\quad 40 - 15 + 50 - 20$

Change all operation signs to addition and
the sign of the number that follows. $\quad\quad 40 + {}^-15 + 50 + {}^-20$

Because addition is commutative, you can
associate like-signed numbers. $\quad\quad (40 + 50) + ({}^-15 + {}^-20)$

Use the rules for adding integers with like
signs. $\quad\quad\quad\quad\quad\quad\quad [40 + 50 = 90]$
$\quad\quad\quad\quad\quad\quad\quad\quad\quad\quad\quad\quad [{}^-15 + {}^-20 = {}^-35]$

Substitute into the revised expression. $\quad\quad (90) + ({}^-35)$

Signs different? Subtract the value of the
numbers and give the result the sign of the
higher value number. $\quad\quad\quad\quad\quad [90 - 35 = 55]$

The simplified result of the numeric
expression is as follows: $\quad\quad\quad\quad \underline{40 + {}^-15 + 50 + {}^-20 = 55}$

25. As in problem 21, ascending is a positive number while descending is a negative number. You can assume ground level is the zero point.

An expression that represents the problem
is as follows: $\quad\quad\quad\quad\quad\quad\quad {}^+2{,}000 + {}^-450 + {}^+1{,}750$

Because addition is commutative, you can
associate like-signed numbers. $\quad\quad ({}^+2{,}000 + {}^+1{,}750) + {}^-450$

Evaluate the expression in the parentheses. $\quad [{}^+2{,}000 + {}^+1{,}750 = {}^+3{,}750]$

Substitute into the revised equation. $\quad\quad ({}^+3{,}750) + {}^-450$

Signs different? Subtract the value of the
numbers and give the result the sign of the
higher value number. $\quad\quad\quad\quad\quad [3{,}750 - 450 = 3{,}300]$

The simplified result of the numeric
expression is as follows: $\quad\quad\quad\quad ({}^+3{,}750) + {}^-450 = {}^+3{,}300$

Working with Algebraic Expressions

This chapter contains 25 algebraic expressions; each can contain up to five variables. Remember that a variable is just a letter that represents a number in a mathematical expression. When given numerical values for the variables, you can turn an algebraic expression into a numerical one.

As you work through the problems in this chapter, you are to substitute the assigned values for the variables into the expression and evaluate the expression. You will be evaluating expressions very much like the previous numerical expressions. The answer section contains complete explanations of how to go about evaluating the expressions. Work on developing a similar style throughout, and you will have one sure way of solving these kinds of problems. As you become more familiar and comfortable with the look and feel of these expressions, you will begin to find your own shortcuts.

Read through the **Tips for Working with Algebraic Expressions** before you begin to solve the problems in this section.

Tips for Working With Algebraic Expressions

- Substitute assigned values for the variables into the expression.
- Use PEMDAS to perform operations in the proper order.
- Recall and use the **Tips for Working with Integers** from Chapter 1.

■ Evaluate the following algebraic expressions when

$a = 3$
$b = {}^-5$
$x = 6$
$y = \frac{1}{2}$
$z = {}^-8$

26. $4a + b$

27. $3x \div z$

28. $2ax - z$

29. $5ab + xy$

30. $4b^2 - az$

31. $7x \div 2yz$

32. $bx + z \div y$

33. $8y - 3ab$

34. $a(b + z)^2$

35. $2(a^2 + 2y) \div b$

36. $a^3 + 24y - 3b$

37. $2x - b + az$

38. $3b^2 - 2b + 12$

39. $5xy \div 2b$

40. $7x + \frac{12}{x} - z$

41. $2z^2 \div y$

42. $bx(z + 3)$

43. $6y(z \div y) + 3ab$

44. $2bx \div (z - b)$

45. $12ab \div y$

46. $y\{(\frac{x}{2} - 3) - 4a\}$

47. $10b^3 - 4b^2$

48. $8y(a^3 - 2y)$

49. $z^2 - 4a^2y$

50. $3x^2b(5a - 3b)$

Answers

Numerical expressions in parentheses like this [ ] are operations performed on only part of the original expression. The operations performed within these symbols are intended to show how to evaluate the various terms that make up the entire expression.

Expressions with parentheses that look like this ( ) contain either numerical substitutions or expressions that are part of a numerical expression. Once a single number appears within these parentheses, the parentheses are no longer needed and need not be used the next time the entire expression is written.

When two pair of parentheses appear side by side like this ( )( ), it means that the expressions within are to be multiplied.

Sometimes parentheses appear within other parentheses in numerical or algebraic expressions. Regardless of what symbol is used, ( ), { }, or [ ], perform operations in the innermost parentheses first and work outward.

<u>Underlined</u> expressions show the original algebraic expression as an equation with the expression equal to its simplified result.

$a = 3$
$b = {}^-5$
$x = 6$
$y = \frac{1}{2}$
$z = {}^-8$

26. Substitute the values for the variables into the expression. $\qquad$ $4(3) + ({}^-5)$
Order of operations tells you to multiply first. $\qquad$ $[4(3) = 12]$
Substitute. $\qquad$ $(12) + ({}^-5)$
Signs different? Subtract the value of the numbers. $\qquad$ $[12 - 5 = 7]$
Give the result the sign of the larger value. (No sign
  means $^+$) $\qquad$ $^+7$
The value of the expression is as follows: $\qquad$ $\underline{4a + b = {}^+7}$

27. Substitute the values for the variables into the
    expression. $\qquad$ $3(6) \div ({}^-8)$
PEMDAS: Multiply the first term. $\qquad$ $[3(6) = 18]$
Substitute. $\qquad$ $(18) \div ({}^-8)$
Signs different? Divide and give the result the
  negative sign. $\qquad$ $[18 \div 8 = 2\frac{2}{8} = 2\frac{1}{4}]$
  $({}^-2\frac{1}{4})$
The value of the expression is as follows: $\qquad$ $\underline{3x \div z = {}^-2\frac{1}{4} \text{ or } {}^-2.25}$

28. Substitute the values for the variables into the expression. $\qquad$ $2(3)(6) - ({}^-8)$
Multiply the factors of the first term. $\qquad$ $[2(3)(6) = 36]$
Substitute. $\qquad$ $(36) - ({}^-8)$
Change the operator to addition and the sign of the
  number that follows. $\qquad$ $(36) + ({}^+8)$
Signs the same? Add the value of the terms and give the
  result the same sign. $\qquad$ $[36 + 8 = 44]$

The simplified value of the expression is as follows:

$$\begin{array}{c} (^+44) \\ \underline{2ax - z = {}^+44} \end{array}$$

29. Substitute the values for the variables into the expression.

$5(3)(^-5) + (6)(\tfrac{1}{2})$

Evaluate the first term of the expression.

$[5(3)(^-5) = 15(^-5)]$

Signs different? Multiply the terms and give the result a negative sign.

$[15(^-5) = {}^-75]$

Evaluate the second term of the expression.

$[(6)(\tfrac{1}{2}) = 3]$

Substitute the equivalent values into the original expression.

$(^-75) + (3)$

Signs different? Subtract the value of the numbers.

$[75 - 3 = 72]$

Give the result the sign of the larger value.

$(^-72)$

The simplified value of the expression is as follows:

$\underline{5ab + xy = {}^-72}$

30. Substitute the values for the variables into the expression.

$4(^-5)^2 - (3)(^-8)$

PEMDAS: Evaluate the term with the exponent.

$[(^-5)^2 = (^-5) \cdot (^-5)]$

Signs the same? Multiply the terms and give the result a positive sign.

$[5 \cdot 5 = 25 = {}^+25]$

Substitute.

$[4('25) = 100]$

Now evaluate the other term.

$[(3)(^-8)]$

Signs different? Multiply and give the result a negative sign.

$[3 \cdot {}^-8 = {}^-24]$

Substitute the equivalent values into the original expression.

$(100) - (^-24)$

Change the operator to addition and the sign of the number that follows.

$100 + {}^+24 = 124$

The simplified value of the expression is as follows:

$\underline{4b^2 - az = 124}$

31. Substitute the values for the variables into the expression.

$7(6) \div 2(\tfrac{1}{2})(^-8)$

PEMDAS: Multiply the terms in the expression.

$[7 \cdot 6 = 42]$
$[\{2(\tfrac{1}{2})\}(^-8) = (1)(^-8) = {}^-8]$

Substitute the equivalent values into the original expression.

$(42) \div (^-8)$

Signs different? Divide and give the result a negative sign.

$[42 \div 8 = 5.25]$
$(42) \div (^-8) = {}^-5.25$

The simplified value of the expression is as follows:

$\underline{7x \div 2yz = {}^-5.25}$

32. Substitute the values for the variables into
    the expression.

$(^-5)(6) + (^-8) \div (\frac{1}{2})$

Group terms using order of operations.

$(^-5)(6) + \{(^-8) \div (\frac{1}{2})\}$

PEMDAS: Multiply or divide the terms in
    the expression.

$[(^-5)(6)]$

Signs different? Multiply and give the result
    a negative sign.

$[5 \cdot 6 = 30]$
$[(^-5)(6) = ^-30]$

Consider the second term.

$[(^-8) \div (\frac{1}{2})]$

Signs different? Divide and give the result
    a negative sign.

$[8 \div \frac{1}{2}]$

To divide by a fraction, you multiply by
    the reciprocal.

$[8 \div \frac{1}{2} = 8 \cdot \frac{2}{1} = 8 \cdot 2 = 16]$
$[(^-8) \div (\frac{1}{2}) = ^-16]$

Substitute the equivalent values into the
    original expression.

$(^-30) + (^-16)$

Signs the same? Add the value of the terms
    and give the result the same sign.

$[30 + 16 = 46]$
$(^-30) + (^-16) = ^-46$

The simplified value of the expression
    is as follows:

$\underline{bx + z \div y = ^-46}$

33. Substitute the values for the variables into the
    expression.

$8(\frac{1}{2}) - 3(3)(^-5)$

Evaluate the terms on either side of the
    subtraction sign.

$[8 \cdot \frac{1}{2} = 4]$
$[3(3)(^-5) = 3 \cdot 3 \cdot ^-5]$

Positive times positive is positive. Positive times
    negative is negative.

$[9 \cdot ^-5 = ^-45]$

Substitute the equivalent values into the original
    expression.

$(4) - (^-45)$

Change the operator to addition and the sign
    of the number that follows.

$(4) - (^-45) = 4 + {}^+45$
$4 + {}^+45 = {}^+49$

The simplified value of the expression is as
    follows:

$\underline{8y - 3ab = {}^+49}$

34. Substitute the values for the variables into the
    expression.

$3((^-5) + (^-8))^2$

PEMDAS: You must add the terms inside the
    parentheses first.

$[(^-5) + (^-8)]$

Signs the same? Add the value of the terms and
    give the result the same sign.

$[5 + 8 = 13]$
$[(^-5) + (^-8) = ^-13]$

Substitute into the original expression. $\quad 3(^-13)^2$

Next you evaluate the term with the exponent. $\quad [(^-13)^2 = ^-13 \cdot ^-13]$

Signs the same? Multiply the terms and give the
result a positive sign. $\quad [13 \cdot 13 = {}^+169]$

Substitute the equivalent values into the original
expression. $\quad 3(169) = 507$

The simplified value of the expression is as follows: $\quad \underline{a(b + z)^2 = 507}$

35. Substitute the values for the variables into the
expression. $\quad 2((3)^2 + 2(\frac{1}{2})) \div (^-5)$

Look first to evaluate the term inside the bold
parentheses. $\quad [(3)^2 + 2(\frac{1}{2})]$

The first term has an exponent. Evaluate it. $\quad [(3)^2 = 3 \cdot 3 = 9]$

Evaluate the second term. $\quad [2(\frac{1}{2}) = 1]$

$\quad [(3)^2 + 2(\frac{1}{2}) = 9 + 1 = 10]$

Substitute into the original numerical
expression. $\quad 2(10) \div (^-5)$

Evaluate the first term. $\quad [2(10) = 20]$

Substitute into the numerical expression. $\quad (20) \div (^-5)$

Signs different? Divide and give the result a
negative sign. $\quad [20 \div 5 = 4]$

$\quad (20) \div (^-5) = {}^-4$

The simplified value of the expression is as
follows: $\quad \underline{2(a^2 + 2y) \div b = {}^-4}$

36. Substitute the values for the variables into the
expression. $\quad (3)^3 + 24(\frac{1}{2}) - 3(^-5)$

Evaluate the term with the exponent. $\quad [(3)^3 = 3 \cdot 3 \cdot 3 = 27]$

Evaluate the second term. $\quad [24(\frac{1}{2}) = 12]$

Evaluate the third term. $\quad [3(^-5)]$

Signs different? Multiply and give the result a
negative sign. $\quad [3 \cdot 5 = 15]$

$\quad [3(^-5) = {}^-15]$

Substitute the equivalent values into the original
expression. $\quad (27) + (12) - (^-15)$

Change the subtraction to addition and the sign
of the number that follows. $\quad (27) + (12) + ({}^+15)$

Signs the same? Add the value of the terms and
give the result the same sign. $\quad 27 + 12 + 15 = 54$

The simplified value of the expression is as
follows: $\quad \underline{a^3 + 24y - 3b = {}^+54}$

37. Substitute the values for the variables into the
expression.

$$^-2(6) - (^-5) + (3)(^-8)$$

Evaluate first and last terms. Positive times
negative results in a negative.

$$[^-2(6) = ^-2 \cdot 6 = ^-12]$$
$$[(3)(^-8) = 3 \cdot ^-8 = ^-24]$$

Substitute the equivalent values into the original
expression.

$$(^-12) - (^-5) + (^-24)$$

Change the subtraction to addition and the
sign of the number that follows.

$$^-12 + (^+5) + ^-24$$

Commutative property of addition allows
grouping of like signs.

$$(^-12 + ^-24) + (^+5)$$

Signs the same? Add the value of the terms
and give the result the same sign.

$$[^-12 + ^-24 = ^-36]$$
$$(^-36) + (^+5)$$

Substitute.

Signs different? Subtract and give the result
the sign of the higher value number.

$$[36 - 5 = 31]$$
$$(^-36) + (^+5) = ^-31$$

The simplified value of the expression is as
follows:

$$\underline{^-2x - b + az = ^-31}$$

38. Substitute the values for the variables into the
expression.

$$3(^-5)^2 - 2(^-5) + 12$$

PEMDAS: Evaluate the term with the exponent
first.

$$[(^-5)^2 = ^-5 \cdot ^-5 = ^+25]$$

Substitute the value into the numerical
expression.

$$3(^+25) - 2(^-5) + 12$$

PEMDAS: Evaluate terms with multiplication
next.

$$[3(^+25) = 75]$$
$$[2(^-5) = ^-10]$$

Substitute the values into the numerical
expression.

$$(75) - (^-10) + 12$$

Change the subtraction to addition and the
sign of the number that follows.

$$(75) + (^+10) + 12$$

Add terms from left to right. All term signs are
positive, a result of addition $^+$.

$$75 + 10 + 12 = 97$$

The simplified value of the expression is as
follows:

$$\underline{3b^2 - 2b + 12 = 97}$$

39. Substitute the values for the variables into the
expression.

$$5(6)(\tfrac{1}{2}) \div 2(^-5)$$

Consider the two terms on either side of
the division sign.

Evaluate the first term by multiplying.

$$[5 \cdot 6 \cdot \tfrac{1}{2} = (5 \cdot 6) \cdot \tfrac{1}{2} = 15]$$

Evaluate the second term.

$$[2(^-5) = ^-10]$$

Substitute the values into the original numerical expression.	$(15) \div (^-10)$
Signs different? Divide and give the result a negative sign.	$[15 \div 10 = 1\frac{1}{2}]$ $(15) \div (^-10) = ^-1\frac{1}{2}$
The simplified value of the expression is as follows:	$5xy \div 2b = ^-1\frac{1}{2}$ or $^-1.5$

40.

Substitute the values for the variables into the expression.	$7(6) + \frac{12}{(6)} - (^-8)$
Evaluate the first term.	$[7(6) = 7 \cdot 6 = 42]$
Evaluate the second term.	$[\frac{12}{(6)} = 12 \div 6 = 2]$
Substitute the values into the original numerical expression.	$(42) + (2) - ^-8$
Change the subtraction to addition and the sign of the number that follows.	$42 + 2 + ^-8$
Add terms from left to right.	$42 + 2 + ^-8 = 52$
The simplified value of the expression is as follows:	$7x + \frac{12}{x} - z = 52$

41.

Substitute the values for the variables into the expression.	$2(^-8)^2 \div (\frac{1}{2})$
First, evaluate the term with the exponent.	$[2(^-8)^2 = 2 \cdot (^-8) \cdot (^-8)]$
Multiply from left to right.	$[\{2 \cdot (^-8)\} \cdot (^-8)]$
Signs different? Multiply and give the result a negative sign.	$[2 \cdot (^-8) = ^-16]$
Signs the same? Multiply and give the result a positive sign.	$[(^-16) \cdot (^-8) = ^+128]$
Substitute the values into the original numerical expression.	$(^+128) \div \frac{1}{2}$
Change division to multiplication and change the value to its reciprocal.	$(^+128) \cdot 2 = 256$
The simplified value of the expression is as follows:	$2z^2 \div y = 256$

42.

Substitute the values for the variables into the expression.	$(^-5)(6)((^-8) + 3)$
First, evaluate the expression inside the parentheses.	$[(^-8) + 3]$
Signs different? Subtract and give the result the sign of the higher value number.	$[8 - 3 = 5]$ $[(^-8) + 3 = ^-5]$
Substitute the result into the numerical expression.	$(^-5)(6)(^-5)$
Multiply from left to right. Negative times positive equals negative.	$[^-5 \cdot 6 = ^-30]$
Signs the same? Multiply and give the result a positive sign.	$(^-30) \cdot ^-5 = ^+150$
The simplified value of the expression is as follows:	$bx(z + 3) = ^+150$

43. Substitute the values for the variables into the expression.

$$6(\tfrac{1}{2})(^-8 \div \tfrac{1}{2}) + 3(3)(^-5)$$

First evaluate the expression inside the parentheses.

Division by a fraction is the same as multiplication by its reciprocal.

$$[^-8 \div \tfrac{1}{2} = ^-8 \cdot \tfrac{2}{1} = ^-16]$$

Substitute the result into the numerical expression.

$$6(\tfrac{1}{2})(^-16) + 3(3)(^-5)$$

Evaluate the first term in the expression.

$$[6(\tfrac{1}{2})(^-16) = 6 \cdot \tfrac{1}{2} \cdot ^-16]$$
$$[3 \cdot ^-16 = ^-48]$$

Evaluate the second term in the expression.

$$[3(3)(^-5) = 3 \cdot 3 \cdot ^-5]$$
$$[9 \cdot ^-5 = ^-45]$$

Substitute the result into the numerical expression.

$$(^-48) + (^-45)$$

Signs the same? Add the value of the terms and give the result the same sign.

$$^-48 + ^-45 = ^-93$$

The simplified value of the expression is as follows:

$$\underline{6y(z \div y) + 3ab = ^-93}$$

44. Substitute the values for the variables into the expression.

$$2(^-5)(6) \div ((^-8) - (^-5))$$

First evaluate the expression inside the parentheses.

$$[(^-8 - ^-5)]$$

Change the subtraction to addition and the sign of the number that follows.

$$[^-8 + 5]$$

Signs different? Subtract and give the result the sign of the higher value number.

$$[8 - 5 = 3]$$
$$[^-8 + {}^+5 = ^-3]$$

Substitute the results into the numerical expression.

$$2(^-5)(6) \div (^-3)$$

Multiply from left to right.

$$[2 \cdot ^-5 \cdot 6 = ^-60]$$

Substitute the result into the numerical expression.

$$(^-60) \div ^-3$$

Signs the same? Divide and give the result a positive sign.

$$[60 \div 3 = 20]$$
$$(^-60) \div ^-3 = 20$$

The simplified value of the expression is as follows:

$$\underline{2bx \div (z - b) = 20}$$

45. Substitute the values for the variables into the
expression.

$$12(3)(^-5) \div (\tfrac{1}{2})$$

Evaluate the first term. Multiply from left
to right.

$$[12 \cdot 3 \cdot {}^-5 = 36 \cdot {}^-5]$$

Signs different? Multiply the numbers and give
the result a negative sign.

$$[36 \cdot 5 = 180]$$
$$[36 \cdot {}^-5 = {}^-180]$$

Substitute the result into the numerical
expression.

$$(^-180) \div (\tfrac{1}{2})$$

Division by a fraction is the same as multiplication
by its reciprocal.

$$^-180 \cdot (\tfrac{2}{1}) = {}^-180 \cdot 2$$

Signs different? Multiply numbers and give the
result a negative sign.

$$[180 \cdot 2 = 360]$$
$$^-180 \cdot 2 = {}^-360$$

The simplified value of the expression is
as follows:

$$\underline{12ab \div y = {}^-360}$$

46. Substitute the values for the variables into the
expression.

$$(\tfrac{1}{2}) \{((\tfrac{(6)}{2}) - 3) - 4(3)\}$$

Evaluate the expression in the innermost
parentheses.

$$[(\tfrac{(6)}{2} - 3) = \tfrac{6}{2} - 3]$$

PEMDAS: Division before subtraction.

$$[\tfrac{6}{2} - 3 = 3 - 3 = 0]$$

Substitute the result into the numerical
expression.

$$(\tfrac{1}{2})\{(0) - 4(3)\}$$

Evaluate the expression inside the parentheses.

$$[\{0 - 4(3)\} = 0 - 4 \cdot 3]$$

PEMDAS: Multiply before subtraction.

$$[0 - 4 \cdot 3 = 0 - 12]$$

Change subtraction to addition and the sign
of the term that follows.

$$[0 - 12 = 0 + {}^-12 = {}^-12]$$

Substitute the result into the numerical
expression.

$$(\tfrac{1}{2})\{{}^-12\} = \tfrac{1}{2} \cdot {}^-12$$

Signs different? Multiply numbers and give
the result a negative sign.

$$[\tfrac{1}{2} \cdot 12 = 6]$$
$$\tfrac{1}{2} \cdot {}^-12 = {}^-6$$

The simplified value of the expression is as
follows:

$$\underline{y\{(\tfrac{x}{2} - 3) - 4a\} = {}^-6}$$

47. Substitute the values for the variables into the expression.

$10(^-5)^3 - 4(^-5)^2$

Evaluate the first term.

$[10(^-5)^3 = 10 \cdot {^-5} \cdot {^-5} \cdot {^-5}]$

Multiply from left to right.

$[10 \cdot {^-5} = (^-50)]$
$[(^-50) \cdot {^-5} = {^+250}]$
$[{^+250} \cdot {^-5} = {^-1250}]$

Evaluate the second term in the numerical expression.

$[4(^-5)^2 = 4 \cdot {^-5} \cdot {^-5}]$

Multiply from left to right.

$[4 \cdot {^-5} = {^-20}]$
$[{^-20} \cdot {^-5} = {^+100}]$

Substitute the results into the numerical expression.

$^-1250 - {^+100}$

Change subtraction to addition and the sign of the term that follows.

$^-1250 + {^-100}$

Same signs? Add the value of the terms and give the result the same sign.

$[1250 + 100 = 1350]$
$10(^-5)^3 - 4(^-5)^2 = {^-1350}$

The simplified value of the expression is as follows:

$\underline{10b^3 - 4b^2 = {^-1,350}}$

48. Substitute the values for the variables into the expression.

$8(\frac{1}{2})((3)^3 - 2(\frac{1}{2}))$

Evaluate the expression in the innermost parentheses.

$((3)^3 - 2(\frac{1}{2})) = (3^3 - 2 \cdot \frac{1}{2})$

Evaluate the first term. Multiply from left to right.

$[3^3 = 3 \cdot 3 \cdot 3 = 9 \cdot 3 = 27]$

Evaluate the second term.

$[2 \cdot \frac{1}{2} = 1]$

Substitute the results into the numerical expression in the parentheses.

$[(27) - (1)]$

Subtract.

$[27 - 1 = 26]$

Substitute the result into the original expression.

$8(\frac{1}{2})(26)$

Multiply from left to right.

$[8 \cdot \frac{1}{2} = 4]$
$[4 \cdot 26 = 104]$

The simplified value of the expression is as follows:

$\underline{8y(a^3 - 2y) = 104}$

49. Substitute the values for the variables into the
    expression.

    Evaluate the first term.

    Signs the same? Multiply and give the result
      a positive sign.

    Evaluate the second term.

    Multiply from left to right.

$(^-8)^2 - 4(3)^2(\frac{1}{2})$
$[(^-8)^2 = ^-8 \cdot {}^-8]$

$[^-8 \cdot {}^-8 = 64]$
$[4(3)^2(\frac{1}{2}) = 4 \cdot 3 \cdot 3 \cdot \frac{1}{2}]$
$[4 \cdot 3 = 12]$
$[12 \cdot 3 = 36]$
$[36 \cdot \frac{1}{2} = 18]$

    Substitute the results into the numerical
      expression.

    Yes, you can just subtract.

    The simplified value of the expression is
      as follows:

$(64) - (18)$
$64 - 18 = 46$

$z^2 - 4a^2y = 46$

50. Substitute the values for the variables
    into the expression.

    PEMDAS: Evaluate the expression
      in the parentheses first.

$3(6)^2(^-5)(5(3) - 3(^-5))$

$[(5(3) - 3(^-5)) = 5 \cdot 3 - 3 \cdot {}^-5]$
$[5 \cdot 3 - 3 \cdot {}^-5 = 15 - {}^-15]$

    Change subtraction to addition and
      the sign of the term that follows.

    Substitute the result into the
      numerical expression.

    PEMDAS: Evaluate terms with
      exponents next.

    Substitute the result into the
      numerical expression.

    Multiply from left to right.

    Signs different? Multiply the values
      and give a negative sign.

$[15 + {}^+15 = 30]$

$3(6)^2(^-5)(30)$

$[(6)^2 = 6 \cdot 6 = 36]$

$3(36)(^-5)(30)$
$[3(36) = 108]$

$[(108) \cdot (^-5) = ^-540]$
$[(^-540) \cdot (30) = ^-16,200]$
$3(6)^2(^-5)(5(3) - 3(^-5)) = ^-16,200$

    The simplified value of the expression
      is as follows:

$3x^2b(5a - 3b) = ^-16,200$

3

Combining Like Terms

In this chapter, you will practice simplifying algebraic expressions. As you do this, you will recognize and combine terms with variables that are alike and link them to other terms using the arithmetic operations.

You should know that

- the numbers in front of the variable or variables are called coefficients.
- a coefficient is just a factor in an algebraic term, as are the variable or variables in the term.
- like terms can have different coefficients, but the configuration of the variables must be the same for the terms to be alike. For example, $3x$ and ^-4x are like terms but are different from $7ax$ or $2x^3$.

You can think of an algebraic term as a series of factors with numbers, and you can think of variables as factors. When the variables are given number values, you can multiply the factors of a term together to find its value, as you did in Chapter 2. When you have terms that are alike, you can add or subtract them as if they were signed numbers. You may find that combining like terms may be easier if you do addition by changing all subtraction to addition of the following term with its sign changed. This strategy will continue to be shown in the answer explanations. But as you either know or are beginning to see, sometimes it's easier to just subtract.

You will also use the important commutative and associative properties of addition and multiplication. Another important and useful property is the distributive property. See the **Tips for Combining Like Terms**.

Tips for Combining Like Terms

Distributive Property of Multiplication
The distributive property of multiplication tells you how to multiply the terms inside a parentheses by the term outside the parentheses. Study the following general and specific examples.

$a(b + c) = ab + ac$
$a(b - c) = ab - ac$
$(b + c)a = ba + ca$
$4(6 + 3) = 4 \cdot 6 + 4 \cdot 3 = 24 + 12 = 36$
$(^-5 + 8)3 = ^-5 \cdot 3 + 8 \cdot 3 = ^-15 + 24 = 9$
$7(10 + 3) = 7 \cdot 10 + 7 \cdot 3 = 70 + 21 = 91$
$3(x + 2y) = 3 \cdot x + 3 \cdot 2y = 3x + 6y$
$a(b - 5d) = a \cdot b - a \cdot 5d = ab - 5ad$

Numerical examples of the commutative properties for addition and multiplication were given in the **Tips for Working with Integers**. Now look at the following examples:

Commutative Property of Addition

$a + b = b + a$

This equation reminds us that terms being combined by addition can change their location (commute), but the value of the expression remains the same.

Commutative Property of Multiplication

$x \cdot y = y \cdot x$

This equation reminds us that the order in which we multiply expressions can change without changing the value of the result.

Associative Property of Addition

$$(q + r) + s = q + (r + s)$$

This equation reminds us that when you are performing a series of additions of terms, you can associate any term with any other and the result will be the same.

Associative Property of Multiplication

$$(d \cdot e) \cdot f = d \cdot (e \cdot f)$$

This equation reminds us that you can multiply three or more terms in any order without changing the value of the result.

Identity Property of Addition

$$n + 0 = n$$

Identity Property of Multiplication

$$n \cdot 1 = n$$

Term Equivalents

$$x = 1 \cdot x$$

For purposes of combining like terms, a variable by itself is understood to mean one of that term.

$$n = {}^{+}n$$

A term without a sign in front of it is considered to be positive.

$$a + {}^{-}b = a - {}^{+}b = a - b$$

Adding a negative term is the same as subtracting a positive term. Look at the expressions on either side of the equal signs. Which one looks simpler? Of course, it's the last, $a - b$. Clarity is valued in mathematics. Writing expressions as simply as possible is always appreciated.

While it may not seem relevant yet, as you go through the practice exercises you will see how each of these properties will come into play as we simplify algebraic expressions by combining like terms.

Simplify the following expressions by combining like terms.

51. $3a + 4a + 9a$

52. $7a + 6b + 3a$

53. $4x + 2y - x + 3y$

54. $27 - 3m + 12 - 5m$

55. $3h + 5 + 2w - 3 + h$

56. $4(x + 2y) + 2(x + y)$

57. $2(3a + 4b) + 7(a - b)$

58. $11(4m + 5) + 3(^-3m + 8)$

59. $64 + 5(n - 8) + 12n - 24$

60. $4(x + y - 4) + 6(2 - 3y)$

61. $^-7(a + b) + ^+12a - 16b$

62. $14 + 9(2w + 7) - 2(6 - w)$

63. $8s - 3r + 5(2r - s)$

64. $6(3m - 12) - 4(9m + 8)$

65. $5(15 - 2j) + 11(7j - 3)$

66. $a(a + 4) + 3a^2 - 2a + 10$

67. $9(x - 6) + x(3 - x)$

68. $3r^2 + r(2 - r) + 6(r + 4)$

69. $2x - x(5 + y) + 3xy + 4(2x - y)$

70. $^-7(c - 2d) + 21c - 3(d - 5)$

71. $5(3x - y) + x(5 + 2y) - 4(3 + x)$

72. $6(m - 3n) + 3m(n + 5) - 2n(3 - m)$

73. $9(2x - t) + 23xt + x(^-4 + 5t)$

74. $4\{2a(a + 3) + 6(4 - a)\} + 5a^2$

75. $8(2a - b - 3c) + 3(2a - b) - 4(6 - b)$

Answers

Numerical expressions in parentheses like this [ ] are operations performed on only part of the original expression. The operations performed within these symbols are intended to show how to evaluate the various terms that make up the entire expression.

   Expressions with parentheses that look like this ( ) contain either numerical substitutions or expressions that are part of a numerical expression. Once a single number appears within these parentheses, the parentheses are no longer needed and need not be used the next time the entire expression is written.

   When two pair of parentheses appear side by side like this ( )( ), it means that the expressions within are to be multiplied.

   Sometimes parentheses appear within other parentheses in numerical or algebraic expressions. Regardless of what symbol is used, ( ), { }, or [ ], perform operations in the innermost parentheses first and work outward.

   Underlined expressions show the simplified result.

51. Use the associative property of addition. $(3a + 4a) + 9a$
   Add like terms. $[3a + 4a = 7a]$
   Substitute the results into the original expression. $(7a) + 9a$
   Add like terms. $7a + 9a = 16a$
   The simplified result of the algebraic expression is: $\underline{3a + 4a + 9a = 16a}$

52. Use the commutative property of addition to
   move like terms together. $7a + 3a + 6b$
   Use the associative property for addition. $(7a + 3a) + 6b$
   Add like terms. $[(7a + 3a) = 10a]$
   Substitute. $(10a) + 6b$
   The simplified result of the algebraic
   expression is: $\underline{7a + 6b + 3a = 10a + 6b}$

53. Change subtraction to addition and
   change the sign of the term
   that follows. $4x + 2y + (^-x) + 3y$
   Use the commutative property of
   addition to move like terms together. $4x + (^-x) + 2y + 3y$
   Use the associative property
   for addition. $(4x + {}^-x) + (2y + 3y)$
   Add like terms. $[4x + {}^-x = {}^+3x = 3x]$
   $[2y + 3y = 5y]$

   Substitute the results into the
   expression. $(4x + {}^-x) + (2y + 3y) = (3x) + (5y)$
   The simplified algebraic
   expression is: $\underline{4x + 2y - x + 3y = 3x + 5y}$

54. Change subtraction to addition
and change the sign of the term
that follows. $27 + -3m + 12 + {}^-5m$

Use the commutative property
for addition to put like terms
together. $27 + 12 + {}^-3m + {}^-5m$

Use the associative property
for addition. $(27 + 12) + ({}^-3m + {}^-5m)$

Add like terms. $[27 + 12 = 39]$
                                              $[{}^-3m + {}^-5m = {}^-8m]$

Substitute the results into the
expression. $(27 + 12) + ({}^-3m + {}^-5m) = (39) + ({}^-8m)$

Rewrite addition of a negative
term as subtraction of a positive
term by changing addition to
subtraction and changing the
sign of the following term. $39 - {}^+8m = 39 - 8m$

The simplified algebraic
expression is: $\underline{27 - 3m + 12 - 5m = 39 - 8m}$

55. Change subtraction to addition and change the
sign of the term that follows. $3h + 5 + 2w + ({}^-3) + h$

Use the commutative property for addition
to put like terms together. $3h + h + 2w + 5 + {}^-3$

Use the associative property for addition. $(3h + h) + 2w + (5 + {}^-3)$

Add like terms. $[(3h + h) = 4h]$
                                              $[(5 + {}^-3) = 2]$

Substitute the result into the expression. $(4h) + 2w + (2)$

The simplified algebraic expression is: $\underline{4h + 2w + 2}$

56. Use the distributive property of multiplication
on the first expression. $[4(x + 2y) = 4 \cdot x + 4 \cdot 2y]$
                                              $[4x + 8y]$

Use the distributive property of multiplication
on the second expression. $[2(x + y) = 2 \cdot x + 2 \cdot y]$
                                              $[2x + 2y]$

Substitute the results into the expression. $(4x + 8y) + (2x + 2y)$

Use the commutative property of addition
to put like terms together. $(4x + 2x + 8y + 2y$

Use the associative property for addition. $(4x + 2x) + (8y + 2y)$

Add like terms. $[4x + 2x = 6x]$
                                              $[8y + 2y = 10y]$

Substitute the results into the expression. $(6x) + (10y)$

The simplified algebraic expression is: $\underline{6x + 10y}$

57. Use the distributive property of multiplication on the first term.

$[2(3a + 4b) = 2 \cdot 3a + 2 \cdot 4b]$
$[6a + 8b]$

Use the distributive property of multiplication on the second term.

$[7(a - b) = 7 \cdot a - 7 \cdot b]$
$[7a - 7b]$

Substitute the results into the expression.

$(6a + 8b) + (7a - 7b)$
$6a + 8b + 7a - 7b$

Change subtraction to addition and change the sign of the term that follows.

$6a + 8b + 7a + (^-7b)$

Use the commutative property for addition to put like terms together.

$6a + 7a + 8b + (^-7b)$

Use the associative property for addition.

$(6a + 7a) + (8b + {}^-7b)$

Add like terms.

$[6a + 7a = 13a]$

Signs different? Subtract the value of the terms.

$[8b + {}^-7b = b]$

Substitute the result into the expression.

$(13a) + (b)$

The simplified algebraic expression is:

$\underline{13a + b}$

58. Use the distributive property of multiplication on the first term.

$[11(4m + 5) = 11 \cdot 4m + 11 \cdot 5]$
$[44m + 55]$

Use the distributive property of multiplication on the second term.

$[3(^-3m + 8) = 3 \cdot {}^-3m + 3 \cdot 8]$
$[^-9m + 24]$

Substitute the result into the expression.

$(44m + 55) + (^-9m + 24)$
$44m + 55 + {}^-9m + 24$

Use the commutative property for addition to put like terms together.

$44m + {}^-9m + 55 + 24$

Use the associative property for addition.

$(44m + {}^-9m) + (55 + 24)$

Add like terms.

$[44m + {}^-9m = 35m]$
$[55 + 24 = 79]$

Substitute the result into the expression.

$(35m) + (79)$

The simplified algebraic expression is:

$\underline{35m + 79}$

59. Use the distributive property of multiplication on the second term.

$[5(n - 8) = 5 \cdot n - 5 \cdot 8]$
$[5n - 40]$

Substitute the result into the expression.

$64 + (5n - 40) + 12n - 24$

Parentheses are no longer needed.

$64 + 5n - 40 + 12n - 24$

Change subtraction to addition and change the sign of the term that follows.

$64 + 5n + {}^-40 + 12n + {}^-24$

Use the commutative property for
   addition to put like terms together. $5n + 12n + 64 + {}^-40 + {}^-24$
Use the associative property for
   addition. $(5n + 12n) + (64 + {}^-40 + {}^-24)$
Add like terms. $[5n + 12n = 17n]$
Add like terms. $[64 + {}^-40 + {}^-24 = 64 + ({}^-40 + {}^-24)]$
       $[64 + {}^-64 = 0]$

Substitute the results into the
   expression. $(17n) + (0)$
The simplified algebraic
   expression is: $\underline{17n}$

60. Use the distributive property of
   multiplication on the first term. $[4(x + y - 4) = 4 \cdot x + 4 \cdot y - 4 \cdot 4]$
       $[4 \cdot x + 4 \cdot y - 4 \cdot 4 = 4x + 4y - 16]$

Use the distributive property of
   multiplication on the
   second term. $[6(2 - 3y) = 6 \cdot 2 - 6 \cdot 3y = 12 - 18y]$
Substitute the results into the
   expression. $(4x + 4y - 16) + (12 - 18y)$
Parentheses are no longer needed. $4x + 4y - 16 + 12 - 18y$
Use the commutative property for
   addition to put like terms
   together.
Change subtraction to addition
   and change the sign of the
   terms that follow. $4x + 4y + {}^-18y + {}^-16 + 12$
Use the associative property for
   addition. $4x + (4y + {}^-18y) + ({}^-16 + 12)$
Add like terms. $[4y + {}^-18y = {}^-14y]$
       $[{}^-16 + 12 = 12 + {}^-16 = {}^-4]$

Substitute the results into the
   expression. $4x + ({}^-14y) + ({}^-4)$
Rewrite addition of a negative term
   as subtraction of a positive term
   by changing addition to subtraction
   and changing the sign of the
   following term.
The simplified algebraic
   expression is: $\underline{4x - 14y - 4}$

61. Use the distributive property of multiplication
on the first term. $[^-7(a + b) = ^-7 \cdot a + ^-7 \cdot b]$
Substitute the results into the expression. $(^-7a + ^-7b) + 12a - 16b$
Parentheses are no longer needed. $^-7a + ^-7b + 12a - 16b$
Use the commutative property for addition
to put like terms together. $12a + ^-7a + ^-7b - 16b$
Change subtraction to addition and
change the sign of the terms that follow. $12a + ^-7a + ^-7b + ^-16b$
Use the associative property for addition. $(12a + ^-7a) + (^-7b + ^-16b)$
Add like terms. $[12a + ^-7a = 5a]$
$[^-7b + ^-16b = ^-23b]$

Substitute the results into the expression. $(5a) + (^-23b)$
Adding a negative term is the same as
subtracting a positive term. $\underline{5a - 23b}$

62. Change subtraction to addition and
change the sign of the terms that follow. $14 + 9(2w + 7) + ^-2(6 + ^-w)$
Use the distributive property of
multiplication on the second term. $[9(2w + 7) = 9 \cdot 2w + 9 \cdot 7]$
$[9 \cdot 2w + 9 \cdot 7 = 18w + 63]$

Use the distributive property of
multiplication on the third term. $[^-2(6 + ^-w) = ^-2 \cdot 6 + ^-2 \cdot ^-w]$
Notice the result of multiplication
for opposite and like-signed terms. $[^-2 \cdot 6 + ^-2 \cdot ^-w = ^-12 + ^+2w]$
Substitute the results into the original
expression. $14 + (18w + 63) + (^-12 + ^+2w)$
Parentheses are no longer needed. $14 + 18w + 63 + ^-12 + ^+2w$
Use the commutative property of
addition to put like terms together. $18w + ^+2w + 14 + 63 + ^-12$
Use the associative property for
addition. $(18w + ^+2w) + (14 + 63 + ^-12)$
Add like terms. $[18w + ^+2w = 20w]$
Add from left to right. $[14 + 63 + ^-12 = 77 + ^-12 = 65]$
Substitute the results into the
expression. $(20w) + (65)$
Parentheses are no longer needed. $\underline{20w + 65}$

501 Algebra Questions

63. Change subtraction to addition and change
the sign of the terms that follow. $\qquad$ $8s + {}^-3r + 5(2r + {}^-s)$
Use the distributive property of
multiplication on the third term. $\qquad$ $[5(2r + {}^-s) = 5 \cdot 2r + 5 \cdot {}^-s]$
$\qquad$ $[5 \cdot 2r + 5 \cdot {}^-s = 10r + {}^-5s]$

Substitute the results into the expression. $\qquad$ $8s + {}^-3r + (10r + {}^-5s)$
Parentheses are no longer needed. $\qquad$ $8s + {}^-3r + 10r + {}^-5s$
Use the commutative property of addition
to put like terms together. $\qquad$ $8s + {}^-5s + 10r + {}^-3r$
Use the associative property for addition. $\qquad$ $(8s + {}^-5s) + (10r + {}^-3r)$
Add like terms. $\qquad$ $[8s + {}^-5s = 3s]$
$\qquad$ $[10r + {}^-3r = 7r]$

Substitute the results into the expression. $\qquad$ $(3s) + (7r)$
Parentheses are no longer needed. $\qquad$ $\underline{3s + 7r}$

64. Change subtraction to addition and change
the sign of the terms that follow. $\qquad$ $6(3m + {}^-12) + {}^-4(9m + 8)$
Use the distributive property of
multiplication on the first term. $\qquad$ $[6(3m + {}^-12) = 6 \cdot 3m + 6 \cdot {}^-12]$
$\qquad$ $[6 \cdot 3m + 6 \cdot {}^-12 = 18m + {}^-72]$

Use the distributive property of
multiplication on the second term. $\qquad$ $[{}^-4(9m + 8) = {}^-4 \cdot 9m + {}^-4 \cdot 8]$
$\qquad$ $[{}^-4 \cdot 9m + {}^-4 \cdot 8 = {}^-36m + {}^-32]$

Substitute the results into the
expression. $\qquad$ $(18m + {}^-72) + ({}^-36m + {}^-32)$
Parentheses are no longer needed. $\qquad$ $18m + {}^-72 + {}^-36m + {}^-32$
Use the commutative property of
addition to put like terms together. $\qquad$ $18m + {}^-36m + {}^-72 + {}^-32$
Use the associative property for
addition. $\qquad$ $(18m + {}^-36m) + ({}^-72 + {}^-32)$
Add terms using the rules for terms
with different signs. $\qquad$ $[18m + {}^-36m = {}^-18m]$
Add terms using the rules for terms
with the same signs. $\qquad$ $[{}^-72 + {}^-32 = {}^-104]$
Substitute the results into the
expression. $\qquad$ $({}^-18m) + ({}^-104)$
Parentheses are no longer needed. $\qquad$ ${}^-18m + {}^-104$
Adding a negative term is the same as
subtracting a positive term. $\qquad$ ${}^-18m - {}^+104$
Use the commutative property
of addition. $\qquad$ ${}^-104 + {}^-18m$
Change addition to subtraction and
change the sign of the term
that follows. $\qquad$ ${}^-104 - ({}^+18m)$
Either of the last two expressions is
correct, but the second is the simpler. $\qquad$ $\underline{{}^-104 - 18m}$

65. Change subtraction to addition and
change the sign of the terms that follow. $5(15 + {}^-2j) + 11(7j + {}^-3)$
Use the distributive property of
multiplication on the first term.

$[5(15 + {}^-2j) = 5 \cdot 15 + 5 \cdot {}^-2j]$
$[5 \cdot 15 + 5 \cdot {}^-2j = 75 + {}^-10j]$

Use the distributive property of
multiplication on the second term.

$[11(7j + {}^-3) = 11 \cdot 7j + 11 \cdot {}^-3]$
$[11 \cdot 7j + 11 \cdot {}^-3 = 77j + {}^-33]$

Substitute the results into the
expression.

$(75 + {}^-10j) + (77j + {}^-33)$

Parentheses are no longer needed. $75 + {}^-10j + 77j + {}^-33$

Use the commutative property of
addition to put like terms together. $77j + {}^-10j + 75 + {}^-33$

Use the associative property for
addition. $(77j + {}^-10j) + (75 + {}^-33)$

Add terms using the rules for terms
with different signs. $[77j + {}^-10j = {}^+67j]$

Add terms using the rules for terms
with different signs. $[75 + {}^-33 = {}^+42]$

Substitute the results into the
expression. $(67j) + (42)$

Parentheses are no longer needed. $\underline{67j + 42}$

66. Change subtraction to addition and change
the sign of the terms that follow. $a(a + 4) + 3a^2 + {}^-2a + 10$

Use the distributive property of
multiplication on the first term. $[a(a + 4) = a \cdot a + a \cdot 4]$

Use the commutative property for
multiplication for the second term. $[a \cdot a + a \cdot 4 = a^2 + 4a]$

Substitute the results into the expression. $(a^2 + 4a) + 3a^2 + {}^-2a + 10$

Parentheses are no longer needed. $a^2 + 4a + 3a^2 + {}^-2a + 10$

Use the commutative property of addition
to put like terms together. $a^2 + 3a^2 + 4a + {}^-2a + 10$

Use the associative property for addition. $(a^2 + 3a^2) + (4a + {}^-2a) + 10$

Add the first term using the rules for
terms with the same signs. $[a^2 + 3a^2 = 4a^2]$

Add the second term using the rules for
terms with different signs. $[4a + {}^-2a = 2a]$

Substitute the results into the expression. $(4a^2) + (2a) + 10$

Parentheses are no longer needed. $\underline{4a^2 + 2a + 10}$

67. Change subtraction to addition and change
the sign of the terms that follow.

$9(x + {}^-6) + x(3 + {}^-x)$

Use the distributive property of
multiplication on the first term.

$[9(x + {}^-6) = 9 \cdot x + 9 \cdot {}^-6]$
$[9 \cdot x + 9 \cdot {}^-6 = 9x + {}^-54]$

Use the distributive property of
multiplication on the second term.

$[x(3 + {}^-x) = x \cdot 3 + x \cdot {}^-x]$
$[x \cdot 3 + x \cdot {}^-x = 3x + {}^-x^2]$

Substitute the results into the expression.
Parentheses are no longer needed.
Use the commutative property of addition
to put like terms together.
Use the associative property for addition.
Add terms in parentheses using the rules
for terms with the same signs.
Change addition to subtraction and change
the sign of the term that follows
Use the commutative property of addition
to put the terms in exponential order.

$(9x + {}^-54) + (3x + {}^-x^2)$
$9x + {}^-54 + 3x + {}^-x^2$

$9x + 3x + {}^-54 + {}^-x^2$
$(9x + 3x) + {}^-54 + {}^-x^2$

$(12x) + {}^-54 + {}^-x^2$

$12x - ({}^+54) + {}^-x^2$

$\underline{{}^-x^2 + 12x - 54}$

68. Change subtraction to addition and change
the sign of the terms that follow.

$3r^2 + r(2 + {}^-r) + 6(r + 4)$

Use the distributive property of
multiplication on the second term.

$[r(2 + {}^-r) = r \cdot 2 + r \cdot {}^-r]$
$[r \cdot 2 + r \cdot {}^-r = 2r + {}^-r^2]$

Use the distributive property of
multiplication on the third term.

$[6(r + 4) = 6 \cdot r + 6 \cdot 4]$
$[6 \cdot r + 6 \cdot 4 = 6r + 24]$

Substitute the results into the expression.
Remove the parentheses.
Use the commutative property of addition
to put like terms together.
Use the associative property for addition.
Add the first term using the rules for
terms with different signs.

$3r^2 + (2r + {}^-r^2) + (6r + 24)$
$3r^2 + 2r + {}^-r^2 + 6r + 24$

$3r^2 + {}^-r^2 + 2r + 6r + 24$
$(3r^2 + {}^-r^2) + (2r + 6r) + 24$

$[3r^2 + {}^-r^2 = 2r^2]$

Add the second term using the rules for
terms with the same signs.
Substitute the results into the expression.
Remove the parentheses.

$[2r + 6r = 8r]$
$(2r^2) + (8r) + 24$
$\underline{2r^2 + 8r + 24}$

69. Change subtraction to addition and
the sign of the terms that follow. $2x + {}^-x(5 + y) + 3xy + 4(2x + {}^-y)$
Use the distributive property of
multiplication on the second term. $[{}^-x(5 + y) = {}^-x \cdot 5 + {}^-x \cdot y]$
Use the rules for multiplying
signed terms. $[{}^-x \cdot 5 + {}^-x \cdot y = {}^-5x + {}^-xy]$
Use the distributive property of
multiplication on the fourth term. $[4(2x + {}^-y) = 4 \cdot 2x + 4 \cdot {}^-y]$
Use the rules for multiplying
signed terms. $[4 \cdot 2x + 4 \cdot {}^-y = 8x + {}^-4y]$
Substitute the results into the
expression. $2x + ({}^-5x + {}^-xy) + 3xy + (8x + {}^-4y)$
Remove the parentheses. $2x + {}^-5x + {}^-xy + 3xy + 8x + {}^-4y$
Use the associative and commutative
properties for addition. $(2x + {}^-5x + 8x) + ({}^-xy + 3xy) + ({}^-4y)$
Add the first set of terms using the
rules for terms with different signs. $[2x + {}^-5x + 8x = 5x]$
Add the second set of terms using the
rules for terms with different signs. $[{}^-xy + 3xy = 2xy]$
Substitute the results into the
expression. $({}^-5x) + (2xy) + ({}^-4y)$
Remove the parentheses. $\underline{5x + 2xy - 4y}$

70. Change subtraction to addition and the
sign of the terms that follow. ${}^-7(c + {}^-2d) + 21c + {}^-3(d + {}^-5)$
Use the distributive property of
multiplication on the first term. $[{}^-7(c + {}^-2d) = {}^-7 \cdot c + {}^-7 \cdot {}^-2d]$
Use the rules for multiplying
signed terms. $[{}^-7 \cdot c + {}^-7 \cdot {}^-2d = {}^-7c + {}^+14d]$
Use the distributive property of
multiplication on the third term. $[{}^-3(d + {}^-5) = {}^-3 \cdot d + {}^-3 \cdot {}^-5]$
Use the rules for multiplying
signed terms. $[{}^-3 \cdot d + {}^-3 \cdot {}^-5 = {}^-3d + {}^+15]$
Substitute the results into the
last expression. $({}^-7c + {}^+14d) + 21c + ({}^-3d + {}^+15)$
Remove the parentheses. ${}^-7c + {}^+14d + 21c + {}^-3d + {}^+15$
Use the commutative property of
addition to move terms together. $21c + {}^-7c + {}^+14d + {}^-3d + {}^+15$
Use the associative property for
addition. $(21c + {}^-7c) + ({}^+14d + {}^-3d) + {}^+15$
Combine like terms using addition
rules for signed numbers. $(14c) + (11d) + 15$
Remove the parentheses. $\underline{14c + 11d + 15}$

71. Change subtraction to addition and
the sign of the terms that follow. $5(3x + {}^-y) + x(5 + 2y) + {}^-4(3 + x)$
Use the distributive property of
multiplication on the first term. $[5(3x + {}^-y) = 5 \cdot 3x + 5 \cdot {}^-y]$
Use the rules for multiplying
signed terms. $[5 \cdot 3x + 5 \cdot {}^-y = 15x + {}^-5y]$
Use the distributive property of
multiplication on the second term. $[x(5 + 2y) = x \cdot 5 + x \cdot 2y]$
Use the rules for multiplying
signed terms. $[x \cdot 5 + x \cdot 2y = 5x + 2xy]$
Use the distributive property of
multiplication on the third term. $[{}^-4(3 + x) = {}^-4 \cdot 3 + {}^-4 \cdot x]$
Use the rules for multiplying
signed terms. $[{}^-4 \cdot 3 + {}^-4 \cdot x = {}^-12 + {}^-4x]$
Substitute the results into the
original expression. $(15x + {}^-5y) + (5x + 2xy) + ({}^-12 + {}^-4x)$
Remove the parentheses. $15x + {}^-5y + 5x + 2xy + {}^-12 + {}^-4x$
Use the commutative property of
addition to move like terms
together. Use the associative
property for addition. $(15x + 5x + {}^-4x) + {}^-5y + 2xy + {}^-12$
Combine like terms using addition
rules for signed numbers. $(16x) + {}^-5y + 2xy + {}^-12$
Adding a negative term is the same
as subtracting a positive term. $(16x) - ({}^+5y) + 2xy - ({}^+12)$
Remove the parentheses. $\underline{16x - 5y + 2xy - 12}$

72. Change subtraction to addition
and the sign of the terms
that follow. $6(m + {}^-3n) + 3m(n + 5) + {}^-2n(3 + {}^-m)$

Use the distributive property
of multiplication on the
first term. $[6(m + {}^-3n) = 6 \cdot m + 6 \cdot {}^-3n]$

Use the rules for multiplying
signed terms. $[6 \cdot m + 6 \cdot {}^-3n = 6m + {}^-18n]$

Use the distributive property
of multiplication on the
second term. $[3m(n + 5) = 3m \cdot n + 3m \cdot 5]$

Use the rules for multiplying
signed terms. $[3m \cdot n + 3m \cdot 5 = 3mn + 15m]$

Use the distributive property
of multiplication on the
third term. $[{}^-2n(3 + {}^-m) = {}^-2n \cdot 3 + {}^-2n \cdot {}^-m]$

Use the rules for multiplying
signed terms. $[{}^-2n \cdot 3 + {}^-2n \cdot {}^-m = {}^-6n + {}^+2mn]$

Substitute the results into
the original expression. $(6m + {}^-18n) + (3mn + 15m) + ({}^-6n + {}^+2mn)$

Remove the parentheses. $6m + {}^-18n + 3mn + 15m + {}^-6n + {}^+2mn$

Use the commutative property
of addition to move like terms
together. Use the associative
property for addition. $(6m + 15m) + (3mn + {}^+2mn) + ({}^-6n + {}^-18n)$

Combine like terms using
addition rules for
signed numbers. $(21m) + (5mn) + ({}^-24n)$

Adding a negative term is
the same as subtracting a
positive term. $\underline{21m + 5mn - 24n}$

73. Change subtraction to addition and the
sign of the terms that follow. $9(2x + {}^-t) + 23xt + x({}^-4 + 5t)$

Use the distributive property of
multiplication on the first term. $[9(2x + {}^-t) = 9 \cdot 2x + 9 \cdot {}^-t]$

Use the rules for multiplying
signed terms. $[9 \cdot 2x + 9 \cdot {}^-t = 18x + {}^-9t]$

Use the distributive property of
multiplication on the third term. $[x({}^-4 + 5t) = x \cdot {}^-4 + x \cdot 5t]$

Use the rules for multiplying
signed terms. $[x \cdot {}^-4 + x \cdot 5t = {}^-4x + 5xt]$

Substitute the results into the
expression. $(18x + {}^-9t) + 23xt + ({}^-4x + 5xt)$

Remove the parentheses. $18x + {}^-9t + 23xt + {}^-4x + 5xt$

Use the commutative property of
    addition to move like terms together. $18x + {}^-4x + {}^-18t + 23xt + 5xt$
Use the associative property for
    addition. $(18x + {}^-4x) + {}^-9t + (23xt + 5xt)$
Combine like terms using addition
    rules for signed numbers. $(14x) + {}^-9t + (28xt)$
Adding a negative term is the same as
    subtracting a positive term. $14x - {}^+9t + 28xt$
         $\underline{14x - 9t + 28xt}$

74. Change subtraction to addition and the sign
    of the terms that follow. $4\{2a(a + 3) + 6(4 + {}^-a)\} + 5a^2$
Simplify the term inside the outer
    parentheses first. $[2a(a + 3) + 6(4 + {}^-a)]$
Use the distributive property of
    multiplication on the first term. $[2a(a + 3) = 2a \cdot a + 2a \cdot 3]$
Use the rules for multiplying signed terms. $[2a \cdot a + 2a \cdot 3 = 2a^2 + 6a]$
Use the distributive property of
    multiplication on the second term. $[6(4 + {}^-a) = 6 \cdot 4 + 6 \cdot {}^-a]$
Use the rules for multiplying signed terms. $[6 \cdot 4 + 6 \cdot {}^-a = 24 + {}^-6a]$
Substitute the results into the expression. $[(2a^2 + 6a) + (24 + {}^-6a)]$
Remove the parentheses. $[2a^2 + 6a + 24 + {}^-6a]$
Use the commutative property of addition. $[2a^2 + 6a + {}^-6a + 24]$
Use the associative property for addition. $[2a^2 + (6a + {}^-6a) + 24]$
Combine like terms using addition rules
    for signed numbers. $[2a^2 + (0) + 24]$
Use the identity property of addition. $[2a^2 + 24]$
Substitute the results into the expression. $4\{2a^2 + 24\} + 5a^2$
Use the distributive property of
    multiplication on the first term. $[4 \cdot 2a^2 + 4 \cdot 24]$
         $[8a^2 + 96]$
Substitute into the expression. $(8a^2 + 96) + 5a^2$
Remove the parentheses. $8a^2 + 96 + 5a^2$
Use the commutative property of addition. $8a^2 + 5a^2 + 96$
Use the associative property for addition. $(8a^2 + 5a^2) + 96$
Add like terms. $\underline{13a^2 + 96}$

75. Change subtraction to addition and the sign of the terms that follow.

$8(2a + {}^-b + {}^-3c) + 3(2a + {}^-b) + {}^-4(6 + {}^-b)$

Use the distributive property of multiplication on the first term.

$[8(2a + {}^-b + {}^-3c) = 8 \cdot 2a + 8 \cdot {}^-b + 8 \cdot {}^-3c]$

Use the rules for multiplying signed terms.

$[8 \cdot 2a + 8 \cdot {}^-b + 8 \cdot {}^-3c = 16a + {}^-8b + {}^-24c]$

Use the distributive property of multiplication on the second term.

$[3(2a + {}^-b) = 3 \cdot 2a + 3 \cdot {}^-b]$

Use the rules for multiplying signed terms.

$[3 \cdot 2a + 3 \cdot {}^-b = 6a + {}^-3b]$

Use the distributive property of multiplication on the third term.

$[{}^-4(6 + {}^-b) = {}^-4 \cdot 6 + {}^-4 \cdot {}^-b]$

Use the rules for multiplying signed terms.

$[{}^-4 \cdot 6 + {}^-4 \cdot {}^-b = {}^-24 + {}^+4b]$

Substitute the results into the expression.

$(16a + {}^-8b + {}^-24c) + (6a + {}^-3b) + ({}^-24 + {}^+4b)$

Remove the parentheses.

$16a + {}^-8b + {}^-24c + 6a + {}^-3b + {}^-24 + {}^+4b$

Use the commutative property of addition to move like terms together.

$16a + 6a + {}^-8b + {}^-3b + {}^+4b + {}^-24c + {}^-24$

Use the associative property for addition.

$(16a + 6a) + ({}^-8b + {}^-3b + {}^+4b) + {}^-24c + {}^-24$

Combine like terms using addition rules for signed numbers.

$(22a) + ({}^-7b) + {}^-24c + {}^-24$

Adding a negative term is the same as subtracting a positive term.

$\underline{22a - 7b - 24c - 24}$

Solving Basic Equations

Solving equations is not very different from working with numerical or algebraic expressions. An equation is a mathematical statement where two expressions are set equal to each other. Using logic and mathematical operations, you can manipulate the equation to find a solution. Simply put, that is what you have done when you have the variable on one side of the equal sign and a number on the other. The answer explanations will show and identify all the steps you will need to solve basic equations. There will be different solutions to similar problems to show a variety of methods for solving equations. But they all rely on the same rules. Look over the **Tips for Solving Basic Equations** before you begin this chapter's questions.

Tips for Solving Basic Equations

- If a number is being added to or subtracted from a term on one side of an equation, you can eliminate that number by performing the inverse operation.
- The inverse of addition is subtraction. The inverse of subtraction is addition. If you add or subtract an amount from one side of the equation, you must do the same to the other side to maintain the equality.

- The inverse of multiplication is division. If a variable is being multiplied by a coefficient, you can eliminate the coefficient by dividing both sides of the equation by that coefficient, leaving you with just one of the variables. If a is a number $\neq 0$, then $ax \div a = x$.
- The inverse of division is multiplication. If a number is dividing a variable, you can multiply the term by the number, leaving you with one of the variables. If b is a number $\neq 0$, then $b(\frac{y}{b}) = y$.
- You can perform any operation to a term in an equation. Just remember that you must do it to both sides. When you have the variable isolated on one side of the equation, the value on the other side is your solution.

76. $a + 16 = 30$

77. $x - 25 = 32$

78. $y + 17 = {}^-12$

79. $b - 24 = 86$

80. $12 - c = {}^-9$

81. $s - {}^-3 = {}^-1$

82. $a + 1\frac{3}{4} = 6\frac{1}{4}$

83. $b - \frac{5}{2} = {}^-\frac{2}{3}$

84. $c - 4(\frac{1}{2} - 5) = 20$

85. $m + 2(5 - 24) = {}^-76$

86. $2a = 18$

87. $4x = {}^-20$

88. ${}^-3y = 18$

89. $27b = 9$

90. $45r = {}^-30$

91. $0.2c = 5.8$

92. $\frac{x}{9} = 16$

93. $\frac{y}{{}^-4} = {}^-12$

94. $\frac{2}{3}a = 54$

95. $\frac{8}{5}b = {}^-56$

96. Jack paid $21,000 for his new car. This was $\frac{7}{8}$ the suggested selling price of the car. What was the suggested selling price of the car?

97. After putting 324 teddy bears into packing crates, there were 54 crates filled with bears. If each crate contained the same number of bears, how many bears were in each packing crate?

98. Only 2% of turtle hatchlings will live to become breeding adults. How many turtles must have been born if the current number of breeding adults is 1,200?

99. This year a farmer planted 300 acres of corn. This was 1.5 times as many acres as he planted last year. How many acres did he plant this year?

100. A business executive received a $6,000 bonus check from her company at the end of the year. This was 5% of her annual salary. How much was her annual salary before receiving the bonus?

Answers

Numerical expressions in parentheses like this [ ] are operations performed on only part of the original expression. The operations performed within these symbols are intended to show how to evaluate the various terms that make up the entire expression.

Expressions with parentheses that look like this ( ) contain either numerical substitutions or expressions that are part of a numerical expression. Once a single number appears within these parentheses, the parentheses are no longer needed and need not be used the next time the entire expression is written.

When two pair of parentheses appear side by side like this ( )( ), it means that the expressions within are to be multiplied.

Sometimes parentheses appear within other parentheses in numerical or algebraic expressions. Regardless of what symbol is used, ( ), { }, or [ ], perform operations in the innermost parentheses first and work outward.

<u>Underlined</u> equations show the simplified result.

76. Subtract 16 from both sides of the equation.
Associate like terms. $\qquad a + (16 - 16) = (30 - 16)$
Perform the numerical operation in the
    parentheses. $\qquad a + (0) = (14)$
Zero is the identity element for addition. $\qquad \underline{a = 14}$

77. Add 25 to each side of the equation. $\qquad 25 + x - 25 = 32 + 25$
Use the commutative property for addition. $\qquad x + 25 - 25 = 32 + 25$
Associate like terms. $\qquad x + (25 - 25) = (32 + 25)$
Perform the numerical operation in the
    parentheses. $\qquad x + (0) = (57)$
Zero is the identity element for addition. $\qquad \underline{x = 57}$

78. Subtract 17 from both sides of the equation. $\qquad y + 17 - 17 = {}^-12 - 17$
Associate like terms. $\qquad y + (17 - 17) = ({}^-12 - 17)$
Change subtraction to addition and
    change the sign of the term that follows. $\qquad y + (17 + {}^-17) = ({}^-12 + {}^-17)$
Apply the rules for operating with signed
    numbers. $\qquad y + (0) = {}^-29$
Zero is the identity element for addition. $\qquad \underline{y = {}^-29}$

79. Change subtraction to addition and change
    the sign of the term that follows. $\qquad b + {}^-24 = 86$
Add $^+24$ to each side of the equation. $\qquad b + {}^-24 + {}^+24 = 86 + {}^+24$
Associate like terms. $\qquad b + ({}^-24 + 24) = (86 + 24)$
Apply the rules for operating with
    signed numbers. $\qquad b + (0) = 110$
Zero is the identity element for addition. $\qquad \underline{b = 110}$

80. Change subtraction to addition and change
the sign of the term that follows. $12 + {}^-c = {}^-9$
Add ^+c to each side of the equation. $12 + {}^-c + {}^+c = {}^-9 + {}^+c$
Associate like terms. $12 + ({}^-c + {}^+c) = {}^-9 + {}^+c$
$12 + (0) = {}^-9 + c$
$12 = {}^-9 + c$

Add $^+9$ to each side of the equation. $^+9 + 12 = {}^+9 + {}^-9 + c$
Associate like terms. $(^+9 + 12) = ({}^+9 + {}^-9) + c$
Apply the rules for operating with signed
numbers. $(21) = (0) + c$
Zero is the identity element for addition. $\underline{21 = c}$

81. Change subtraction to addition and change the
sign of the term that follows. $s + {}^+3 = {}^-1$
Add $^-3$ to each side of the equation. $s + {}^+3 + {}^-3 = {}^-1 + {}^-3$
Associate like terms. $s + ({}^+3 + {}^-3) = {}^-1 + {}^-3$
Apply the rules for operating with
signed numbers. $s + (0) = ({}^-4)$
Subtracting zero is the same as adding zero. $\underline{s = {}^-4}$

82. Add $^-1\frac{3}{4}$ to each side of the equation. $a + 1\frac{3}{4} + {}^-1\frac{3}{4} = 6\frac{1}{4} + {}^-1\frac{3}{4}$

Associate like terms. $a + (1\frac{3}{4} + {}^-1\frac{3}{4}) = 6\frac{1}{4} + {}^-1\frac{3}{4}$
Apply the rules for operating with
signed numbers. $a + (0) = 4\frac{1}{2}$
Zero is the identity element for addition. $\underline{a = 4\frac{1}{2}}$

83. Change subtraction to addition and change
the sign of the term that follows. $b + \frac{5}{2} = \frac{-2}{3}$

Subtract $\frac{-5}{2}$ from both sides of the equation. $b + \frac{-5}{2} - \frac{-5}{2} = \frac{-2}{3} - \frac{-5}{2}$

Associate like terms. $b + (\frac{-5}{2} - \frac{-5}{2}) = \frac{-2}{3} - \frac{-5}{2}$
Change subtraction to addition and change
the sign of the term that follows. $b + (\frac{-5}{2} + \frac{+5}{2}) = \frac{-2}{3} + \frac{+5}{2}$
Apply the rules for operating with signed
numbers. $b + (0) = \frac{11}{6}$
Change the improper fraction to a
mixed number. $\underline{b = 1\frac{5}{6}}$

84. Change subtraction to addition and change
   the sign of the term that follows. $\quad c + {}^-4(\frac{1}{2} + {}^-5) = 20$
   Use the distributive property of multiplication. $\quad c + ({}^-4 \cdot \frac{1}{2} + {}^-4 \cdot {}^-5) = 20$
   Perform the operation in parentheses. $\quad c + ({}^-2 + {}^+20) = 20$
   Apply the rules for operating with
     signed numbers. $\quad c + (18) = 20$
   Subtract 18 from both sides of the equation. $\quad c + 18 - 18 = 20 - 18$
   Associate like terms. $\quad c + (18 - 18) = 20 - 18$
   Perform the operation in parentheses. $\quad c + 0 = 2$
   Zero is the identity element for addition. $\quad \underline{c = 2}$

85. Use the distributive property of multiplication. $\quad m + (2 \cdot 5 - 2 \cdot 24) = {}^-76$
   The order of operations is to multiply first. $\quad m + (10 - 48) = {}^-76$
   Add $^+38$ to each side of the equation. $\quad m + {}^-38 + {}^+38 = {}^-76 + {}^+38$
   Associate like terms. $\quad m + ({}^-38 + {}^+38) = {}^-76 + {}^+38$
   Apply the rules for operating with
     signed numbers. $\quad m + (0) = {}^-38$
   $\qquad\qquad\qquad\qquad\qquad\qquad\quad \underline{m = {}^-38}$

86. Divide both sides of the equation by 2. $\qquad 2a \div 2 = 18 \div 2$
   $\qquad\qquad\qquad\qquad\qquad\qquad\qquad\qquad a = 18 \div 2$

   Apply the rules for operating with signed numbers. $\quad \underline{a = 9}$
   Another method is as follows: $\qquad\qquad\qquad \frac{2a}{2} = \frac{18}{2}$
   $\qquad\qquad\qquad\qquad\qquad\qquad\qquad\qquad \underline{a = 9}$

87. Divide both sides of the equation by 4. $\qquad 4x \div 4 = {}^-20 \div 4$
   $\qquad\qquad\qquad\qquad\qquad\qquad\qquad\qquad x = {}^-20 \div 4$

   Apply the rules for operating with signed numbers. $\quad \underline{x = {}^-5}$
   Another look for this solution method is as follows: $\quad \frac{4x}{4} = \frac{-20}{4}$
   $\qquad\qquad\qquad\qquad\qquad\qquad\qquad\qquad \underline{x = {}^-5}$

88. Divide both sides of the equation by $^-3$. $\qquad \frac{-3y}{-3} = \frac{18}{-3}$
   $\qquad\qquad\qquad\qquad\qquad\qquad\qquad\qquad y = \frac{18}{-3}$

   Apply the rules for operating with signed numbers. $\quad \underline{y = {}^-6}$

89. Divide both sides of the equation by 27. $\qquad \frac{27b}{27} = \frac{9}{27}$
   $\qquad\qquad\qquad\qquad\qquad\qquad\qquad\qquad b = \frac{9}{27}$

   Reduce fractions to their simplest form. $\qquad \underline{b = \frac{1}{3}}$

90. Divide both sides of the equation by 45. $\qquad \frac{45r}{45} = \frac{-30}{45}$
   $\qquad\qquad\qquad\qquad\qquad\qquad\qquad\qquad r = \frac{-30}{45}$

   Reduce fractions to their simplest form (common factor
     of 15). $\qquad\qquad\qquad\qquad\qquad\qquad\quad \underline{r = \frac{-2}{3}}$

91. Divide both sides of the equation by 0.2.

$$\frac{0.2c}{0.2} = \frac{5.8}{0.2}$$
$$c = \frac{5.8}{0.2}$$

Divide.

$$c = 29$$

92. Multiply both sides of the equation by 9.

$$9(\tfrac{x}{9}) = 9(16)$$
$$x = 9(16)$$

Multiply.

$$x = 144$$

93. Multiply both sides of the equation by $^-4$.

$$^-4 \cdot \tfrac{y}{^-4} = {^-4} \cdot {^-12}$$
$$y = {^-4} \cdot {^-12}$$

Signs the same? Multiply and give the result a
positive sign.

$$y = {^+48} = 48$$

94. Divide both sides of the equation by $\tfrac{2}{3}$.

$$\tfrac{2}{3}a \div \tfrac{2}{3} = 54 \div \tfrac{2}{3}$$
$$a = 54 \div \tfrac{2}{3}$$

Dividing by a fraction is the same as multiplying
by its reciprocal.

$$a = 54 \cdot \tfrac{3}{2}$$
$$a = 81$$

95. Divide both sides of the equation by $\tfrac{8}{5}$.

$$\tfrac{8}{5}b \div \tfrac{8}{5} = {^-56} \div \tfrac{8}{5}$$
$$b = {^-56} \div \tfrac{8}{5}$$

Dividing by a fraction is the same as multiplying
by its reciprocal.
There are several ways to multiply fractions and
whole numbers. Here's one.

$$b = {^-56} \cdot \tfrac{5}{8}$$
$$b = \tfrac{^-56}{1} \cdot \tfrac{5}{8}$$
$$b = \tfrac{^-280}{8}$$
$$b = {^-35}$$

96. Let x = the suggested selling price of the car. The
first and second sentences tell you that $\tfrac{7}{8}$ of the
suggested price = \$21,000. So your equation is:

$$\tfrac{7}{8}x = \$21{,}000$$

Divide both sides of the equation by $\tfrac{7}{8}$.

$$\tfrac{7}{8}x \div \tfrac{7}{8} = 21{,}000 \div \tfrac{7}{8}$$
$$x = 21{,}000 \div \tfrac{7}{8}$$

Dividing by a fraction is the same as multiplying
by its reciprocal.

$$x = 21{,}000 \cdot \tfrac{8}{7}$$
$$x = \$24{,}000$$

97. Let b = the number of bears in each packing crate.
The first sentence tells you that the number of
packing crates times the number of bears in each
is equal to the total number of bears. Your
equation is: $\qquad$ $54b = 324$
Divide both sides of the equation by 54. $\qquad$ $54b \div 54 = 324 \div 54$
$\qquad$ $b = 324 \div 54$
Divide. $\qquad$ $\underline{b = 6}$

98. Let t = the number of turtle hatchlings born.
The first sentence tells you that only 2%
survive to adulthood. Two percent of the
turtles born is 1,200. Your equation will be: $(2\%)t = 1,200$
The numerical equivalent of 2% is 0.02,
so the equation becomes $\qquad$ $0.02t = 1,200.$
Divide both sides of the equation by 0.02. $\qquad$ $0.02t \div 0.02 = 1,200 \div 0.02$
$\qquad$ $t = 1,200 \div 0.02$
Divide. $\qquad$ $\underline{t = 60,000}$

99. Let c = the number of acres he planted last year.
1.5 times c is 300. $\qquad$ $1.5c = 300$
Divide both sides of the equation by 1.5. $\qquad$ $1.5\,c \div 1.5 = 300 \div 1.5$
$\qquad$ $c = 300 \div 1.5$
Divide. $\qquad$ $\underline{c = 200}$

100. Let d = her annual salary. Five percent of her
salary equals her yearly bonus. Your
equation will be: $\qquad$ $(5\%)d = \$6,000$
The numerical equivalent of 5% is
0.05, so the equation becomes $\qquad$ $0.05d = 6,000.$
Divide both sides of the equation by 0.05. $\qquad$ $0.05d \div 0.05 = 6,000 \div 0.05$
$\qquad$ $d = 6,000 \div 0.05$
Divide. $\qquad$ $\underline{d = \$120,000}$

Solving Multi-Step Equations

Solving multi-step equations simply combines the work you have done in the previous chapters. The solution techniques for the two types of basic equations you worked on in Chapter 4 are both utilized in the equations in this chapter.

Tips for Solving Multi-Step Equations

- There are at least two ways to show multiplication. You may be used to seeing multiplication shown with an × like this: $5 \times 3 = 15$. In equations, this becomes confusing. In algebra, the convention is to show multiplication with either a · like this: $5 \cdot 3 = 15$, or with parentheses like this: $5(3) = 15$. Both conventions will be used in the answers, so you should get used to either one.
- Similarly, division can be shown using the standard division symbol ÷, as in $10 \div 2 = 5$. Or it can be shown using a fraction bar like this: $10 \div 2 = \frac{10}{2} = 5$. Use and get used to both.
- Check your answers before looking at the answer solutions. Just substitute the value you find for the variable and work

each side of the equation as if it were a numerical expression. If the
quantities you find are equal, your solution is correct.

- Dividing by a fraction is the same as multiplying by its reciprocal. For
  example, $9 \div \frac{2}{3} = 9(\frac{3}{2})$.
- To write an equation for a word problem, let the unknown quantity be
  equal to the variable. Then write the equation based on the
  information stated in the problem.

Find the solutions to the following equations.

101. $4x + 3 = 11$

102. $13x + 21 = 60$

103. $3x - 9 = 15$

104. $5x - 6 = {}^-26$

105. $\frac{x}{3} + 4 = 10$

106. $\frac{x}{7} - 5 = 1$

107. $36 = 3a - 9$

108. $4 = 4a + 20$

109. $10a + 5 = 7$

110. $0.3a + 0.25 = 1$

111. $\frac{2}{3}m + 8 = 20$

112. $9 = \frac{3}{4}m - 3$

113. $41 - 2m = 61$

114. $4m - 14 = 50$

115. $\frac{2m}{5} + 16 = 24$

116. $7m - 6 = {}^-2.5$

117. $10s - 6 = 0$

118. $\frac{s}{4} + 2.7 = 3$

119. $8s - 5 = 35$

120. ${}^-55 = 25 - s$

Solve the following word problems by letting a variable equal the unknown quantity, making an equation from the information given, and then solving the equation.

121. A farmer is raising a hog that weighed 20 lbs. when he bought it. He expects it to gain 12 pounds per month. He will sell it when it weighs 200 lbs. How many months will it be before he will sell the animal?

122. Mary earns $1.50 less than twice Bill's hourly wage. Mary earns $12.50 per hour. What is Bill's hourly wage?

123. At year's end, a share of stock in Axon Corporation was worth $37. This was $8 less than three times its value at the beginning of the year. What was the price of a share of Axon stock at the beginning of the year?

124. Jennifer earned $4,000 more than 1.5 times her former salary by changing jobs. She earned $64,000 at her new job. What was her salary at her previous employment?

125. Twenty-five more girls than $\frac{2}{3}$ the number of boys participate in interscholastic sports at a local high school. If the number of girls participating is 105, how many boys participate?

Answers

Numerical expressions in parentheses like this [ ] are operations performed on only part of the original expression. The operations performed within these symbols are intended to show how to evaluate the various terms that make up the entire expression.

Expressions with parentheses that look like this ( ) contain either numerical substitutions or expressions that are part of a numerical expression. Once a single number appears within these parentheses, the parentheses are no longer needed and need not be used the next time the entire expression is written.

When two pair of parentheses appear side by side like this ( )( ), it means that the expressions within are to be multiplied.

Sometimes parentheses appear within other parentheses in numerical or algebraic expressions. Regardless of what symbol is used, ( ), { }, or [ ], perform operations in the innermost parentheses first and work outward.

Underlined equations show the simplified result.

101. Subtract 3 from both sides of the equation. $\quad 4x + 3 - 3 = 11 - 3$
Associate like terms. $\quad 4x + (3 - 3) = (11 - 3)$
Perform numerical operations. $\quad 4x + (0) = (8)$
Zero is the identity element for addition. $\quad 4x = 8$
Divide both sides of the equation by 4. $\quad 4x \div 4 = 8 \div 4$
$\underline{x = 2}$

102. Subtract 21 from both sides of the equation. $\quad 13x + 21 - 21 = 60 - 21$
Associate like terms. $\quad 13x + (21 - 21) = (60 - 21)$
Perform numerical operations. $\quad 13x + (0) = (39)$
Zero is the identity element for addition. $\quad 13x = 39$
Divide both sides of the equation by 13. $\quad 13x \div 13 = 39 \div 13$
$\underline{x = 3}$

103. Add 9 to each side of the equation. $\quad 3x - 9 + 9 = 15 + 9$
Change subtraction to addition and change
  the sign of the term that follows. $\quad 3x + {}^-9 + 9 = 15 + 9$
Associate like terms. $\quad 3x + ({}^-9 + 9) = 15 + 9$
Perform numerical operations. $\quad 3x + (0) = 24$
Zero is the identity element for addition. $\quad 3x = 24$
Divide both sides of the equation by 3. $\quad 3x \div 3 = 24 \div 3$
$\underline{x = 8}$

104. Add 6 to each side of the equation. $\quad 5x - 6 + 6 = {}^-26 + 6$
Change subtraction to addition and change
  the sign of the term that follows. $\quad 5x + {}^-6 + 6 = {}^-26 + 6$
Associate like terms. $\quad 5x + ({}^-6 + 6) = {}^-26 + 6$
Perform numerical operations. $\quad 5x + (0) = {}^-20$
Zero is the identity element for addition. $\quad 5x = {}^-20$
Divide both sides of the equation by 5. $\quad 5x \div 5 = {}^-20 \div 5$
$\underline{x = {}^-4}$

105. Subtract 4 from both sides of the equation.

$\frac{x}{3} + 4 - 4 = 10 - 4$

Associate like terms.

$\frac{x}{3} + (4 - 4) = 10 - 4$

Perform numerical operations.

$\frac{x}{3} + (0) = 6$

Zero is the identity element for addition.

$\frac{x}{3} = 6$

Multiply both sides of the equation by 3.

$3(\frac{x}{3}) = 3(6)$

$\underline{x = 18}$

106. Add 5 to each side of the equation.

$\frac{x}{7} - 5 + 5 = 1 + 5$

Change subtraction to addition and change the sign of the term that follows.

$\frac{x}{7} + {}^-5 + 5 = 1 + 5$

Associate like terms.

$\frac{x}{7} + ({}^-5 + 5) = 1 + 5$

Perform numerical operations.

$\frac{x}{7} + (0) = 6$

Zero is the identity element for addition.

$\frac{x}{7} = 6$

Multiply both sides of the equation by 7.

$7(\frac{x}{7}) = 7(6)$

$\underline{x = 42}$

107. Add 9 to each side of the equation.

$36 + 9 = 3a - 9 + 9$

Change subtraction to addition and change the sign of the term that follows.

$36 + 9 = 3a + ({}^-9 + 9)$

Associate like terms.

$36 + 9 = 3a + ({}^-9 + 9)$

Perform numerical operations.

$45 = 3a + (0)$

Zero is the identity element for addition.

$45 = 3a$

Divide both sides of the equation by 3.

$45 \div 3 = 3a \div 3$

$\underline{15 = a}$

108. Subtract 20 from both sides of the equation.

$4 - 20 = 4a + 20 - 20$

Associate like terms.

$4 - 20 = 4a + (20 - 20)$

Perform numerical operations.

${}^-16 = 4a + (0)$

Zero is the identity element for addition.

${}^-16 = 4a$

Divide both sides of the equation by 4.

$\frac{{}^-16}{4} = \frac{4a}{4}$

$\underline{{}^-4 = a}$

109. Subtract 5 from both sides of the equation.

$10a + 5 - 5 = 7 - 5$

Associate like terms.

$10a + (5 - 5) = 7 - 5$

Perform numerical operations.

$10a + (0) = 2$

Zero is the identity element for addition.

$10a = 2$

Divide both sides of the equation by 10.

$\frac{10a}{10} = \frac{2}{10}$

$\underline{a = 0.2 \text{ or } \frac{1}{5}}$

110. Subtract 0.25 from both sides of the equation.

Associate like terms.

Perform numerical operations.

Zero is the identity element for addition.

Divide both sides of the equation by 0.3.

Simplify the result.

$0.3a + 0.25 - 0.25 = 1 - 0.25$

$0.3a + (0.25 - 0.25) = 1 - 0.25$

$0.3a + (0) = 0.75$

$0.3a = 0.75$

$\frac{0.3a}{0.3} = \frac{0.75}{0.3}$

$\underline{a = 2.5}$

111. Subtract 8 from both sides of the equation.

Associate like terms.

Perform numerical operations.

Zero is the identity element for addition.
Multiply both sides of the equation by the reciprocal of $\frac{2}{3}$.

$\frac{2}{3}m + 8 - 8 = 20 - 8$

$\frac{2}{3}m + (8 - 8) = 20 - 8$

$\frac{2}{3}m + (0) = 12$

$\frac{2}{3}m = 12$

$\frac{3}{2}(\frac{2}{3}m) = \frac{3}{2}(12)$

$\underline{m = 18}$

112. Add 3 to both sides of the equation.
Change subtraction to addition and change the sign of the term that follows.

Associate like terms.

Perform numerical operations.

Zero is the identity element for addition.

Multiply both sides of the equation by the reciprocal of $\frac{3}{4}$.

$9 + 3 - \frac{3}{4}m - 3 + 3$

$9 + 3 - \frac{3}{4}m + {}^-3 + 3$

$9 + 3 = \frac{3}{4}m + ({}^-3 + 3)$

$12 = \frac{3}{4}m + (0)$

$12 = \frac{3}{4}m$

$\frac{4}{3}(12) = \frac{4}{3}(\frac{3}{4}m)$

$\underline{16 = m}$

113. Subtract 41 from both sides of the equation.
Associate like terms.
Perform numerical operations.
Zero is the identity element for addition.
You can change the subtraction to addition and the sign of the term following to its opposite, which in this case is ^-2m.

Divide both sides of the equation by $^-2$.
Use the rules for operating with signed numbers.

$41 - 41 - 2m = 61 - 41$

$(41 - 41) - 2m = 61 - 41$

$(0) - 2m = 20$

$^-2m = 20$

$^-2m = 20$

$\frac{^-2m}{^-2} = \frac{20}{^-2}$

$\underline{m = {}^-10}$

114. Add 14 to each side of the equation.
Change subtraction to addition and change the sign of the term that follows.
Associate like terms.

$4m - 14 + 14 = 50 + 14$

$4m + {}^-14 + 14 = 50 + 14$

$4m + ({}^-14 + 14) = 50 + 14$

Perform numerical operations. $\quad\quad\quad$ $4m + (0) = 64$

Zero is the identity element for addition. $\quad$ $4m = 64$

Divide both sides of the equation by 4. $\quad\quad$ $\frac{4m}{4} = \frac{64}{4}$

$\underline{m = 16}$

115. This equation presents a slightly different look.
The variable in the numerator has a coefficient.
There are two methods for solving.

Subtract 16 from both sides of the equation. $\quad$ $\frac{2m}{5} + 16 - 16 = 24 - 16$

Associate like terms. $\quad\quad\quad\quad\quad\quad\quad\quad\quad$ $\frac{2m}{5} + (16 - 16) = 24 - 16$

Perform numerical operations. $\quad\quad\quad\quad\quad$ $\frac{2m}{5} + (0) = 8$

Zero is the identity element for addition. $\quad$ $\frac{2m}{5} = 8$

Multiply both sides of the equation by 5. $\quad$ $5\left(\frac{2m}{5}\right) = 5(8)$
Use rules for multiplying whole numbers
and fractions. $\quad\quad\quad\quad\quad\quad\quad\quad\quad\quad$ $\frac{5}{1}\left(\frac{2m}{5}\right) = 40$

$\frac{5 \cdot 2m}{1 \cdot 5} = 40$

$\frac{10m}{5} = 40$

$2m = 40$

Divide both sides by 2. $\quad\quad\quad\quad\quad\quad\quad$ $\frac{2m}{2} = \frac{40}{2}$

$m = 20$

Or you can recognize that $\quad\quad\quad\quad\quad$ $\frac{2m}{5} = \left(\frac{2}{5}\right)m.$
Then you would multiply by the reciprocal
of the coefficient. $\quad\quad\quad\quad\quad\quad\quad\quad$ $\frac{5}{2}\left(\frac{2}{5}\right)m = \left(\frac{5}{2}\right)8$

$\underline{m = 20}$

116. Add 6 to each side of the equation. $\quad\quad\quad$ $7m - 6 + 6 = {}^-2.5 + 6$
Change subtraction to addition and change
the sign of the term that follows. $\quad\quad\quad$ $7m + {}^-6 + 6 = {}^-2.5 + 6$
Associate like terms. $\quad\quad\quad\quad\quad\quad\quad$ $7m + ({}^-6 + 6) = {}^-2.5 + 6$
Perform numerical operations. $\quad\quad\quad\quad\quad$ $7m + (0) = 3.5$

Divide both sides of the equation by 7. $\quad\quad$ $\frac{7m}{7} = \frac{3.5}{7}$

$\underline{m = 0.5}$

117. Add 6 to each side of the equation. $\quad\quad\quad$ $10s - 6 + 6 = 0 + 6$
Change subtraction to addition and change
the sign of the term that follows. $\quad\quad\quad$ $10s + {}^-6 + 6 = 0 + 6$
Associate like terms. $\quad\quad\quad\quad\quad\quad\quad$ $10s + ({}^-6 + 6) = 0 + 6$
Perform numerical operations. $\quad\quad\quad\quad\quad$ $10s + (0) = 6$

Divide both sides of the equation by 10. $\quad$ $\frac{10s}{10} = \frac{6}{10}$

Express the answer in the simplest form. $\quad$ $\underline{s = \frac{3}{5} = 0.6}$

118. Subtract 2.7 from both sides of the equation. $\frac{s}{4} + 2.7 - 2.7 = 3 - 2.7$

Associate like terms. $\frac{s}{4} + (2.7 - 2.7) = 3 - 2.7$

Perform numerical operations. $\frac{s}{4} + (0) = 0.3$

Multiply both sides of the equation by 4. $4(\frac{s}{4}) = 4(0.3)$

$s = 1.2$

119. Add 5 to each side of the equation. $8s - 5 + 5 = 35 + 5$
Change subtraction to addition and
    change the sign of the term that follows. $8s + {}^-5 + 5 = 35 + 5$
Associate like terms. $8s + ({}^-5 + 5) = 35 + 5$
Perform numerical operations. $8s + (0) = 40$
Divide both sides of the equation by 8. $\frac{8s}{8} = \frac{40}{8}$
Express the answer in simplest form. $s = 5$

120. Subtract 25 from both sides of the equation. ${}^-55 - 25 = 25 - 25 - s$
Change subtraction to addition and change
    the sign of the term that follows. ${}^-55 + {}^-25 = 25 + {}^-25 + {}^-s$
Associate like terms. $({}^-55 + {}^-25) = (25 + {}^-25) + {}^-s$
Perform numerical operations. ${}^-80 = (0) + {}^-s$
Zero is the identity element for addition. ${}^-80 = {}^-s$
You are to solve for s, but the term remaining
    is ${}^-s$. If you multiply both sides by ${}^-1$, you
    will be left with a ${}^+s$ or just s. ${}^-1({}^-80) = {}^-1({}^-s)$
Use the rules for operating with signed
    numbers. $80 = s$

121. Let x = the number of months. The number
    of months (x), times 12 (pounds per month),
    plus the starting weight (20), will be equal to
    200 pounds. An equation that represents
    these words would be $12x + 20 = 200.$
Subtract 20 from both sides of the equation. $12x + 20 - 20 = 200 - 20$
Associate like terms. $12x + (20 - 20) = 200 - 20$
Perform numerical operations. $12x + (0) = 180$
Divide both sides of the equation by 12. $\frac{12x}{12} = \frac{180}{12}$
$x = 15$

The farmer would have to wait 15 months before selling his hog.

122. Let x = Bill's hourly wage. Then $2x$ less
    $1.50 is equal to Mary's hourly wage.
    The equation representing the last
    statement would be $2x - 1.50 = 12.50.$
Add 1.50 to both sides of the equation. $2x - 1.50 + 1.50 = 12.50 + 1.50$

Perform numerical operations. $2x = 14.00$

Divide both sides of the equation by 2. $\frac{2x}{2} = \frac{14.00}{2}$

$x = 7.00$

Bill's hourly wage is $7.00 per hour.

123. Let x = the share price at the beginning of the year. The statements tell us that if we multiply the share price at the beginning of the year by 3 and then subtract $8, it will equal $37. An equation that represents this amount is $3x - 8 = 37.$

Add 8 to both sides of the equation. $3x - 8 + 8 = 37 + 8$

Perform numerical operations. $3x = 45$

Divide both sides of the equation by 3. $\frac{3x}{3} = \frac{45}{3}$

$x = 15$

One share of Axon cost $15 at the beginning of the year.

124. Let x = her previous salary. The statements tell us that $64,000 is equal to 1.5 times x plus $4,000. An algebraic equation to represent this statement is $64,000 = 1.5x + 4,000.$

Subtract 4,000 from both sides of the equation. $64,000 - 4,000 = 1.5x + 4,000 - 4,000$

Perform numerical operations. $60,000 = 1.5x$

Divide both sides of the equation by 1.5. $\frac{60,000}{1.5} = \frac{1.5x}{1.5}$

$40,000 = x$

Jennifer's former salary was $40,000 per year.

125. Let x = the number of boys who participate in interscholastic sports. The question tells us that $\frac{2}{3}$ the number of boys plus 25 is equal to the number of girls who participate. An equation that represents this statement is

$\frac{2}{3}x + 25 = 105.$

Subtract 25 from both sides of the equation. $\frac{2}{3}x + 25 - 25 = 105 - 25$

Perform numerical operations. $\frac{2}{3}x = 80$

Multiply by the reciprocal of $\frac{2}{3}$. $\frac{3}{2}(\frac{2}{3}x) = \frac{3}{2}(80)$

$x = 120$

The number of boys who participate is 120.

Solving Equations with Variables on Both Sides of an Equation

If you have been solving the problems in this book with some success, you will move easily into this chapter. Work through the questions carefully, and refer to the answer explanations as you try and solve the equations by yourself. Then check your answers with the solutions provided. If your sequence of steps is not identical to the solution shown, but you are getting the correct answers, that's all right. There is often more than one way to find a solution. And it demonstrates your mastery of the processes involved in doing algebra.

Tips for Solving Equations with Variables on Both Sides of the Equation

Use the distributive property of multiplication to expand and separate terms. Notice that what follows are variations on the basic distributive property.

$$a(b - c) = ab - ac$$
$$^-1(b + c) = ^-b - c$$
$$^-1(b - c) = ^-b + c \text{ or}$$
$$^-(b - c) = ^-b + c$$

The object is to isolate the variable on one side of the equation. When the variable stands alone on one side of the equation, you have found the solution. There are two instances that sometimes occur when solving equations. In the instance where you have eliminated the variable altogether from the equation and end up with two values that do not equal each other—such as $5 = 7$, which we know is not true—there is said to be no solution for the equation. Stated another way, the solution is the null set—that is, a set containing no elements. In another instance, you find that the solution seems to be the variable, or some number, is equal to itself. In that instance, any value can make the equation true; therefore there are an infinite number of solutions.

As you begin to practice solving the following equations, remember that you can add, subtract, multiply, and divide variables on both sides of an equation just as you did with numerical values.

Find the solutions for the following equations.

126. $10x + 9 = 2x - 7$

127. $3x - 23 = 54 - 4x$

128. $5x + 3 + 6x = 10x + 9 - x$

129. $10x + 27 - 5x - 46 = 32 + 3x - 19$

130. $20x - 11 - 3x = 9x + 43$

131. $0.4 + 3x - 0.25 = 1.15 - 2x$

132. $2x + 17 - 1.2x = 10 - 0.2x + 11$

133. $2 + 5x - 0.3 = 4x + 2$

134. $1.3 + 5x - 0.1 = ^-1.2 - 3x$

135. $3x + 12 - 0.8x = 3.4 - 0.8x - 9.4$

136. $7(x + 2) + 1 = 3(x + 14) - 4x$

137. $3(5x + 4) = 5x - 28$

138. $13 - 8(x - 2) = 7(x + 4) + 46$

139. $13x + 3(3 - x) = ^-3(4 + 3x) - 2x$

140. $2(2x + 19) - 9x = 9(13 - x) + 21$

141. $12x - 4(x - 1) = 2(x - 2) + 16$

142. $2x + 1\frac{4}{5}x = 1 + 3x$

143. $\frac{5}{2}(x - 2) + 3x = 3(x + 2) - 10$

144. $6(\frac{1}{2}x + \frac{1}{2}) = 3(x + 1)$

145. $0.7(0.2x - 1) = 0.3(3 - 0.2x)$

146. $10(x + 2) + 7(1 - x) = 3(x + 9)$

147. $4(9 - x) = 2x - 6(x + 6)$

148. $3(3x + 4) - 7 = 13(x + 1)$

149. $7(x - 10) + 110 = 4(x - 25) + 7x$

150. $0.8(x + 20) - 4.5 = 0.7(5 + x) - 0.9x$

Answers

Numerical expressions in parentheses like this [ ] are operations performed on only part of the original expression. The operations performed within these symbols are intended to show how to evaluate the various terms that make up the entire expression.

Expressions with parentheses that look like this ( ) contain either numerical substitutions or expressions that are part of a numerical expression. Once a single number appears within these parentheses, the parentheses are no longer needed and need not be used the next time the entire expression is written.

When two pair of parentheses appear side by side like this ( )( ), it means that the expressions within are to be multiplied.

Sometimes parentheses appear within other parentheses in numerical or algebraic expressions. Regardless of what symbol is used, ( ), { }, or [ ], perform operations in the innermost parentheses first and work outward.

Underlined equations show the simplified result.

126.
Subtract 9 from both sides of the equation.	$10x + 9 - 9 = 2x - 7 - 9$
Simplify.	$10x + (0) = 2x - 16$
Identity property of 0 for addition.	$10x = 2x - 16$
Subtract $2x$ from both sides of the equation.	$10x - 2x = 2x - 2x - 16$
Simplify.	$8x = {}^-16$
Divide both sides of the equation by 8.	$\frac{8x}{8} = \frac{{}^-16}{8}$
Simplify.	$1x = {}^-2$
Solution.	$\underline{x = {}^-2}$
Let's check the answer. Substitute $^-2$ for x in the original equation.	$10({}^-2) + 9 = 2({}^-2) - 7$
Simplify.	${}^-20 + 9 = {}^-4 - 7$
	${}^-11 = {}^-11$

The result is a true statement, so this answer is a correct solution.

127.
Add 23 to both sides of the equation.	$3x - 23 + 23 = 54 + 23 - 4x$
Simplify by combining like terms.	$3x + 0 = 77 - 4x$
Identity property of 0 for addition.	$3x = 77 - 4x$
Now add $4x$ to both sides.	$3x + 4x = 77 - 4x + 4x$
Simplify.	$7x = 77$
Divide both sides of the equation by 7.	$\frac{7x}{7} = \frac{77}{7}$
Simplify.	$\underline{x = 11}$

128. Use the commutative property of addition with like terms.

$5x + 6x + 3 = 10x - x + 9$

Combine like terms on each side of the equation.

$11x + 3 = 9x + 9$

Subtract 3 from both sides.

$11x + 3 - 3 = 9x + 9 - 3$

Simplify.

$11x = 9x + 6$

Now subtract $9x$ from both sides of the equation.

$11x - 9x = 9x - 9x + 6$

Simplify.

$2x = 6$

Divide both sides by 2.

$\frac{2x}{2} = \frac{6}{2}$

Simplify.

$\underline{x = 3}$

129. Use the commutative property of addition with like terms.

$10x - 5x + 27 - 46 = 3x + 32 - 19$

Combine like terms on each side of the equation.

$5x - 19 = 3x + 13$

Add 19 to both sides of the equation.

$5x + 19 - 19 = 3x + 19 + 13$

Combine like terms on each side of the equation.

$5x = 3x + 32$

Subtract $3x$ from both sides of the equation to isolate the variable on one side of the equation.

$5x - 3x = 3x - 3x + 32$

Simplify.

$2x = 32$

Divide both sides of the equation by 2.

$\frac{2x}{2} = \frac{32}{2}$

Simplify.

$\underline{x = 16}$

Let's check this answer.

Substitute 16 for x in the original equation.

$10(16) + 27 - 5(16) - 46 = 32 + 3(16) - 19$

Simplify by multiplying factors.

$(160) + 27 - (80) - 46 = 32 + (48) - 19$

Parentheses are not needed. Add and subtract from left to right.

$187 - 80 - 46 = 80\ ^-19$

$107 - 46 = 61$

$61 = 61$

The previous statement is true; therefore, the solution is correct.

130. Use the commutative property to move
  like terms. $20x - 3x - 11 = 9x + 43$

Combine like terms on each side of
  the equation. $17x - 11 = 9x + 43$

Add 11 to both sides of the equation. $17x + 11 - 11 = 9x + 43 + 11$

Simplify. $17x = 9x + 54$

Subtract $9x$ from both sides of the
  equation. $17x - 9x = 9x - 9x + 54$

Simplify. $8x = 54$

Divide both sides of the equation by 8. $\frac{8x}{8} = \frac{54}{8}$

Simplify the expression. $x = 6.75$

131. Use the commutative property to move
  like terms. $3x + 0.4 - 0.25 = 1.15 - 2x$

Combine like terms on each side of
  the equation. $3x + 0.15 = 1.15 - 2x$

Subtract 0.15 from both sides of
  the equation. $3x + 0.15 - 0.15 = 1.15 - 0.15 - 2x$

Combine like terms on each side
  of the equation. $3x + (0) = 1 - 2x$

Identity property of addition. $3x = 1 - 2x$

Add $2x$ to both sides of the
  equation. $3x + 2x = 1 - 2x + 2x$

Simplify. $5x = 1$

Divide both sides of the equation
  by 5. $\frac{5x}{5} = \frac{1}{5}$

Simplify the expression. $x = \frac{1}{5}$

132. Use the commutative property with
  like terms. $2x - 1.2x + 17 = 10 + 11 - 0.2x$

Combine like terms on each side of
  the equation. $0.8x + 17 = 21 - 0.2x$

Subtract 17 from both sides of
  the equation. $0.8x + 17 - 17 = 21 - 17 - 0.2x$

Combine like terms on each side of
  the equation. $0.8x = 4 - 0.2x$

Add $0.2x$ to both sides of the equation. $0.8x + 0.2x = 4 - 0.2x + 0.2x$

Combine like terms on each side of
  the equation. $1x = 4$

Identity property of multiplication. $x = 4$

133. Use the commutative property with like terms.

$5x + 2 - 0.3 = 4x + 2$

Combine like terms and simplify the expression.

$5x + 1.7 = 4x + 2$

Subtract 1.7 from both sides of the equation.

$5x + 1.7 - 1.7 = 4x + 2 - 1.7$

Combine like terms and simplify the expression.

$5x = 4x + 0.3$

Subtract $4x$ from both sides of the equation. $5x - 4x = 4x - 4x + 0.3$

Combine like terms on each side of the equation.

$\underline{x = 0.3}$

Let's try this a slightly different way. Instead of adding 1.7, try subtracting 2 from both sides of the equation.

$5x + 1.7 - 2 = 4x + 2 - 2$

Combine like terms on each side of the equation.

$5x - 0.3 = 4x$

Now subtract $5x$ from both sides of the equation.

$5x - 5x - 0.3 = 4x - 5x$

Combine like terms on each side of the equation.

$^-0.3 = {}^-x$

Now divide both sides by the coefficient of the variable x which is $^-1$.

$\frac{^-0.3}{^-1} = \frac{^-x}{^-1}$

Dividing like signs results in a positive. Simplify.

$\underline{0.3 = x}$

The answer will be the same. As long as you do proper math, you can manipulate an equation many ways and still get the correct solution.

134. Use the commutative property with like terms.

$3x + 0.4 - 0.25 = 1.15 - 2x$

Associate like terms on each side of the equation.

$3x + (0.4 - 0.25) = 1.15 - 2x$

Simplify the expression. $3x + (0.15) = 1.15 - 2x$

Remove the parentheses. $3x + 0.15 = 1.15 - 2x$

Add $2x$ to both sides of the equation. $3x + 2x + 0.15 = 1.15 + 2x - 2x$

Associate like terms. $(3x + 2x) + 0.15 = 1.15 + (2x - 2x)$

Simplify the expression. $5x + 0.15 = 1.15$

Subtract 0.15 from both sides of the equation.

$5x + 0.15 - 0.15 = 1.15 - 0.15$

Combine like terms on each side of the equation.

$5x + 0 = 1$

Identity property of addition. $5x = 1$

Divide both sides of the equation by 5.

$\frac{5x}{5} = \frac{1}{5}$

Simplify the expression. $\underline{x = 0.2}$

135. Use the commutative property with
 like terms. $3x - 0.8x + 12 = 3.4 - 9.4 - 0.8x$
 Associate like terms on each side
  of the equation. $(3x - 0.8x) + 12 = (3.4 - 9.4) - 0.8x$
 Simplify the expression. $2.2x + 12 = {}^-6 - 0.8x$
 Subtract 12 from both sides of
  the equation. $2.2x + 12 - 12 = {}^-6 - 12 - 0.8x$
 Associate like terms on each side
  of the equation. $2.2x + (12 - 12) = ({}^-6 - 12) - 0.8x$
 Simplify the expression. $2.2x + (0) = ({}^-18) - 0.8x$
 Identity property of addition. $2.2x = {}^-18 - 0.8x$
 Add $0.8x$ to both sides of the
  equation. $2.2x + 0.8x = {}^-18 + 0.8x - 0.8x$
 Combine like terms on each side
  of the equation. $3x = {}^-18$
 Divide both sides of the equation
  by 3. $\frac{3x}{3} = \frac{{}^-18}{3}$
 Simplify the expression. $\underline{x = {}^-6}$

136. Use the distributive property of
 multiplication. $7(x) + 7(2) + 1 = 3(x) + 3(14) - 4x$
 Simplify the expression. $7x + 14 + 1 = 3x + 42 - 4x$
 Use the commutative property with
  like terms. $7x + 14 + 1 = 3x - 4x + 42$
 Combine like terms on each side
  of the equation. $7x + 15 = {}^-1x + 42$
 Subtract 15 from both sides of
  the equation. $7x + 15 - 15 = {}^-1x + 42 - 15$
 Combine like terms on each side of
  the equation. $7x = {}^-1x + 27$
 Add x to both sides of the equation. $7x + x = x + {}^-1x + 27$
 Combine like terms on each side of
  the equation. $8x = 27$
 Divide both sides of the equation
  by 8. $\frac{8x}{8} = \frac{27}{8}$
 Simplify the expression. $\underline{x = 3\frac{3}{8}}$

137. Use the distributive property of multiplication.

$3(5x) + 3(4) = 5x - 28$

Simplify the expression.

$15x + 12 = 5x - 28$

Subtract 12 from both sides of the equation.

$15x + 12 - 12 = 5x - 28 - 12$

Combine like terms on each side of the equation.

$15x = 5x - 40$

Subtract $5x$ from both sides of the equation.

$15x - 5x = 5x - 5x - 40$

Simplify the expression.

$10x = {}^-40$

Divide both sides of the equation by 10.

$\frac{10x}{10} = \frac{{}^-40}{10}$

Simplify the expression.

$\underline{x = {}^-4}$

138. Use the distributive property of multiplication.

$13 - 8(x) - 8({}^-2) = 7(x) + 7(4) + 46$

Simplify the expression.

$13 - 8x + 16 = 7x + 28 + 46$

Use the commutative property with like terms.

$13 + 16 - 8x = 7x + 28 + 46$

Combine like terms on each side of the equation.

$29 - 8x = 7x + 74$

Add $8x$ to both sides of the equation.

$29 + 8x - 8x = 8x + 7x + 74$

Combine like terms on each side of the equation.

$29 = 15x + 74$

Subtract 74 from both sides of the equation.

$29 - 74 = 15x + 74 - 74$

Combine like terms on each side of the equation.

${}^-45 = 15x$

Divide both sides of the equation by 15.

$\frac{{}^-45}{15} = \frac{15x}{15}$

Simplify the expression.

$-3 = x$

139. Use the distributive property of multiplication.

$13x + 3(3) - 3(x) = {}^-3(4) - 3(3x) - 2x$

Simplify the expression.

$13x + 9 - 3x = {}^-12 - 9x - 2x$

Use the commutative property with like terms.

$9 + 13x - 3x = {}^-12 - 9x - 2x$

Combine like terms on each side of the equation.

$9 + 10x = {}^-12 - 11x$

Add $11x$ to both sides of the equation.

$9 + 10x + 11x = {}^-12 - 11x + 11x$

Combine like terms on each side of the equation.

$9 + 21x = {}^-12$

Subtract 9 from both sides of the equation.

$9 - 9 + 21x = {}^-12 - 9$

Combine like terms on each side
of the equation.

$21x = {}^-21$

Divide both sides of the equation
by 21.

$\frac{21x}{21} = \frac{-21}{21}$

Simplify the expression.

$x = {}^-1$

140. Use the distributive property of
multiplication.

$2(2x) + 2(19) - 9x = 9(13) - 9(x) + 21$

Simplify the expression.

$4x + 38 - 9x = 117 - 9x + 21$

Use the commutative property
with like terms.

$38 + 4x - 9x = 117 + 21 - 9x$

Combine like terms on each side
of the equation.

$38 - 5x = 138 - 9x$

Subtract 38 from both sides
of the equation.

$38 - 38 - 5x = 138 - 38 - 9x$

Combine like terms on each side
of the equation.

$^-5x = 100 - 9x$

Add 9x to both sides of the
equation.

$^-5x + 9x = 100 - 9x + 9x$

Combine like terms on each
side of the equation.

$4x = 100$

Divide both sides of the
equation by 4.

$\frac{4x}{4} = \frac{100}{4}$

Simplify the expression.

$x = 25$

Now let's check the answer by
substituting the solution into
the original equation.

$2(2(25) + 19) - 9(25) = 9(13 - (25)) + 21$

Simplify the expression. Use
order of operations.

$2(50 + 19) - 225 = 9(^-12) + 21$
$2(69) - 225 = {}^-108 + 21$
$138 - 225 = {}^-87$
$^-87 = {}^-87$

The solution is correct.

141. Use the distributive property of
    multiplication. $12x - 4(x) - 4(^-1) = 2(x) + 2(^-2) + 16$
Simplify the expression. $12x - 4x + 4 = 2x - 4 + 16$
Combine like terms on each side
    of the equation. $8x + 4 = 2x + 12$
Subtract 4 from both sides of the
    equation. $8x + 4 - 4 = 2x + 12 - 4$
Simplify the expression. $8x = 2x + 8$
Subtract $2x$ from both sides of the
    equation. $8x - 2x = 2x - 2x + 8$
Simplify the expression. $6x = 8$
Divide both sides of the equation
    by 6. $\frac{6x}{6} = \frac{8}{6}$

Simplify the expression. $x = \frac{4}{3}$
Reduce fractions to simplest
    terms. $x = 1\frac{1}{3}$
Now let's check the answer by
    substituting the solution into the
    original equation. $12(\frac{4}{3}) - 4((\frac{4}{3}) - 1) = 2((\frac{4}{3}) - 2) + 16$
Operate inside the parentheses
    first. Change whole numbers to
    fractional equivalents.

$$12(\tfrac{4}{3}) - 4(\tfrac{4}{3} - \tfrac{3}{3}) = 2(\tfrac{4}{3} - \tfrac{6}{3}) + 16$$
$$12(\tfrac{4}{3}) - 4(\tfrac{1}{3}) = 2(\tfrac{^-2}{3}) + 16$$

Multiply. $\frac{48}{3} - \frac{4}{3} = \frac{^-4}{3} + 16$
Add $\frac{4}{3}$ to both sides of the
    equation. $\frac{48}{3} + \frac{4}{3} - \frac{4}{3} = \frac{4}{3} - \frac{4}{3} + 16$
Simplify the expression. $16 = 16$
A true statement, so this solution is correct.

142. Simplify the equation by adding like terms. $3\frac{4}{5}x = 1 + 3x$

Subtract $3x$ from both sides of the equation. $3\frac{4}{5}x - 3x = 1 + 3x - 3x$
Combine like terms on each side of the
    equation. $\frac{4}{5}x = 1$
Divide both sides of the equation by $\frac{4}{5}$.
    Remember that division by a fraction is the
    same as multiplication by the reciprocal
    of the fraction. You can multiply by $\frac{5}{4}$. $\frac{5}{4}(\frac{4}{5}x) = \frac{5}{4}(1)$

Simplify the expression. $x = \frac{5}{4}$

143. Use the distributive property
    on both sides. $\frac{5}{2}(x) - \frac{5}{2}(2) + 3x = 3(x) + 3(2) - 10$

Simplify the expression. $\frac{5}{2}x - 5 + 3x = 3x + 6 - 10$

Use the commutative property with like terms.	$\frac{5}{2}x + 3x - 5 = 3x + 6 - 10$
A simple way to avoid having to operate with fractions is to multiply the equation by a factor that will eliminate the denominator. In this case, that would be a 2.	$2(\frac{5}{2}x + 3x - 5) = 2(3x + 6 - 10)$
Use the distributive property.	$2(\frac{5}{2}x) + 2(3x) - 2(5) = 2(3x) + 2(6) - 2(10)$
Simplify the expressions.	$5x + 6x - 10 = 6x + 12 - 20$
Combine like terms on each side of the equation.	$11x - 10 = 6x - 8$
Add 10 to both sides of the equation.	$11x - 10 + 10 = 6x - 8 + 10$
Simplify the expression.	$11x = 6x + 2$
Subtract $6x$ from both sides of the equation.	$11x - 6x = 6x - 6x + 2$
Combine like terms on each side of the equation.	$5x = 2$
Divide both sides of the equation by 5.	$\frac{5x}{5} = \frac{2}{5}$
Simplify the expression.	$x = \frac{2}{5}$

144.

Use the distributive property on both sides.	$6(\frac{1}{2}x) + 6(\frac{1}{2}) = 3(x) + 3(1)$
Simplify the expression.	$3x + 3 = 3x + 3$
Subtract 3 from both sides of the equation.	$3x + 3 - 3 = 3x + 3 - 3$
Simplify the expression.	$3x = 3x$
Divide both sides of the equation by 3.	$\frac{3x}{3} = \frac{3x}{3}$
Simplify the expression.	$x = x$

There are an infinite number of solutions for this equation.

145.

Use the distributive property on both sides.	$0.7(0.2x) - 0.7(1) = 0.3(3) - 0.3(0.2x)$
Simplify the expressions.	$0.14x - 0.7 = 0.9 - 0.06x$
Add $0.06x$ to both sides of the equation.	$0.14x + 0.06x - 0.7 = 0.9 - 0.6x + 0.06x$
Combine like terms on each side of the equation.	$0.2x - 0.7 = 0.9$
Add 0.7 to both sides of the equation.	$0.2x - 0.7 + 0.7 = 0.9 + 0.7$
Combine like terms on each side of the equation.	$0.2x = 1.6$
Divide both sides of the equation by 0.2.	$\frac{0.2x}{0.2} = \frac{1.6}{0.2}$
Simplify the expression.	$x = 8$

146. Use the distributive property of
    multiplication. $10(x) + 10(2) + 7(1) - 7(x) = 3(x) + 3(9)$

Simplify the expression. $10x + 20 + 7 - 7x = 3x + 27$

Use the commutative property
    with like terms. $10x - 7x + 20 + 7 = 3x + 27$

Combine like terms on each
    side of the equation. $3x + 27 = 3x + 27$

Looking familiar? Subtract 27
    from both sides. $3x + 27 - 27 = 3x + 27 - 27$

Simplify the expression. $3x = 3x$

Divide both sides of the
    equation by 3. $\underline{x = x}$

The solutions for this equation are infinite.

147. Use the distributive property of
    multiplication. $4(9) - 4(x) = 2x - 6(x) - 6(6)$

Simplify the expressions. $36 - 4x = 2x - 6x - 36$

Combine like terms. $36 - 4x = {}^-4x - 36$

Add $4x$ to both sides of the equation. $36 + 4x - 4x = 4x - 4x - 36$

Combine like terms on each side of
    the equation. $36 = {}^-36$

This is not true. <u>There is no solution for this equation.</u> Another way of
saying this is to say that the solution for this equation is the null set.

148. Use the distributive property of
    multiplication. $3(3x) + 3(4) - 7 = 13(x) + 13(1)$

Simplify the expressions. $9x + 12 - 7 = 13x + 13$

Combine like terms. $9x + 5 = 13x + 13$

Subtract $9x$ from both sides of the
    equation. $9x - 9x + 5 = 13x - 9x + 13$

Combine like terms on each side of
    the equation. $5 = 4x + 13$

Subtract 13 from both sides of the
    equation. $5 - 13 = 4x + 13 - 13$

Combine like terms on each side of
    the equation. ${}^-8 = 4x$

Divide both sides of the equation by 4. $\frac{{}^-8}{4} = \frac{4x}{4}$

Simplify the expression. $\underline{-2 = x}$

149. Use the distributive property of multiplication.

$$7(x) - 7(10) + 110 = 4(x) - 4(25) + 7x$$

Simplify the expressions.

$$7x - 70 + 110 = 4x - 100 + 7x$$

Combine like terms on each side of the equation.

$$7x + 40 = 11x - 100$$

Subtract 40 from both sides of the equation.

$$7x + 40 - 40 = 11x - 100 - 40$$

Combine like terms on each side of the equation.

$$7x = 11x - 140$$

Subtract $11x$ from both sides of the equation.

$$7x - 11x = 11x - 11x - 140$$

Combine like terms on each side of the equation.

$$^-4x = {}^-140$$

Divide both sides of the equation by $^-4$.

$$\frac{^-4x}{^-4} = \frac{^-140}{^-4}$$

Simplify the expressions.

$$\underline{x = 35}$$

150. You should look for opportunities to simplify your work. In this equation, many of the terms are in decimal form. If you multiply the equation by 10, it might make it easier for you.

$$10[0.8(x + 20) - 4.5] = 10[0.7(5 + x) - 0.9x]$$

Use the distributive property of multiplication.

$$10[0.8(x + 20)] - 10[4.5] = 10[0.7(5 + x)] - 10[0.9x]$$

Simplify the expressions.

$$8(x + 20) - 45 = 7(5 + x) - 9x$$

Use the distributive property again.

$$8(x) + 8(20) - 45 = 7(5) + 7(x) - 9x$$

Simplify the expressions.

$$8x + 160 - 45 = 35 + 7x - 9x$$

Combine like terms on each side of the equation.

$$8x + 115 = 35 - 2x$$

Subtract 115 from both sides of the equation.

$$8x + 115 - 115 = 35 - 115 - 2x$$

Combine like terms on each side of the equation.

$$8x = {}^-80 - 2x$$

Add $2x$ to both sides of the equation.

$$8x + 2x = {}^-80 - 2x + 2x$$

Combine like terms on each side of the equation.

$$10x = {}^-80$$

Divide both sides of the equation by 10.

$$\frac{10x}{10} = \frac{^-80}{10}$$

Simplify the expression.

$$\underline{x = {}^-8}$$

7

Using Formulas to Solve Equations

Chances are you have been asked to use formulas to solve problems in math, science, social studies, or technology. Algebra is a useful skill to know when faced with problems in these areas. In this chapter, you will have the chance to solve word problems that could pop up in any one of these subject areas. These word problems require you to find an unknown value in a formula. You will be using your algebra problem solving skills in every problem.

Tips for Using Formulas to Solve Equations

Given a formula with several variables, you will generally be given values for all but one. Then you will be asked to solve the equation for the missing variable. It can be helpful to list each variable with its given value. Put a question mark next to the equal sign in place of the value for the unknown variable.

Keep in mind the rules for order of operations.

Select from these formulas the appropriate one to solve the following word problems:

<u>Volume of a rectangular solid:</u> $V = lwh$ where l = length, w = width, h = height.

Distance formula: $D = rt$ where r = rate, t = time.

Simple interest: $I = prt$ where p = principal, r = interest rate, t = time in years.

Area of a trapezoid: $A = \frac{1}{2}h(b_1 + b_2)$ where h = height and b_1 and b_2 are the bases.

Fahrenheit/Celsius equivalence: $C = \frac{5}{9}(F - 32)$

Volume of a cylinder: $V = \pi r^2 h$ (let π = 3.14) where r = radius and h = height

Surface area of a cylinder: $S = 2\pi r(r + h)$ where r = radius of the base, h = height of cylinder (let π = 3.14).

151. Find the volume of a rectangular solid whose length is 12 cm, width is 9 cm, and height is 4 cm.

152. A rectangular container has a volume of 98 ft^3. If the length of the box is 7 ft, and its width is 3.5 ft, what is its height?

153. An airplane flies at an average velocity of 350 miles per hour. A flight from Miami to Aruba takes 3.5 hours. How far is it from Miami to Aruba?

154. A bicycle tour group planned to travel 68 miles between two New England towns. How long would the trip take if they averaged 17 miles per hour for the trip?

155. A hiking group wanted to travel along a chapter of the Appalachian Trail for 3 days. They planned to hike 6 hours per day and wanted to complete a trail chapter that was 45 miles long. What rate of speed would they have to average to complete the trail chapter as planned?

156. At an interest rate of 6%, how much interest would $12,000 earn over 2 years?

157. Over a three year period, the total interest paid on a $4,500 loan was $1,620. What was the interest rate?

158. In order to earn $1,000 in interest over 2 years at an annual rate of 4%, how much principal must be put into a savings account?

159. How long will it take for a $3,000 savings account to double its value at a simple interest rate of 10%?

160. What is the area of a trapezoid whose height is 8 cm and whose bases are 12 cm and 16 cm?

161. What would be the height of a trapezoidal building if at its base it measured 80 feet, its roofline measured 40 feet, and the surface area of one side was 7,200 ft^2?

162. A trapezoid with an area of 240 square inches has a height of 12 inches. What are the lengths of the bases, if the lower base is three times the length of the upper?

163. You plan to visit a tropical island where the daytime temperature can reach 45° Celsius. What would that temperature be on the Fahrenheit scale?

164. Jeff won't play golf if the temperature falls below 50° Fahrenheit. He is going to a country where the temperature is reported in Celsius. What would Jeff's low temperature limit be in that country? (Round your answer to the nearest degree.)

165. A steel drum has a base with a radius of 2 feet and a height of 4 feet. What is its volume in cubic feet?

166. Find the radius of a cylinder whose volume is 339.12 cubic centimeters and whose height is 12 centimeters.

167. The volume of a cylindrical aquarium tank is 13,565 cubic feet. If its radius is 12 feet, what is its height to the nearest foot?

168. The radius of the base of a cylinder is 20 cm. The height of the cylinder is 40 cm. What is its surface area?

169. What is the height of a cylinder whose surface area is 282.6 square inches and whose radius is 3 inches?

170. A cylinder has a surface area of 2,512 square feet. The height of the cylinder is three times the radius of the base of the cylinder. Find the radius and the height of the cylinder.

Answers

Numerical expressions in parentheses like this [ ] are operations performed on only part of the original expression. The operations performed within these symbols are intended to show how to evaluate the various terms that make up the entire expression.

    Expressions with parentheses that look like this ( ) contain either numerical substitutions or expressions that are part of a numerical expression. Once a single number appears within these parentheses, the parentheses are no longer needed and need not be used the next time the entire expression is written.

    When two pair of parentheses appear side by side like this ( )( ), it means that the expressions within are to be multiplied.

    Sometimes parentheses appear within other parentheses in numerical or algebraic expressions. Regardless of what symbol is used, ( ), { }, or [ ], perform operations in the innermost parentheses first and work outward.

    The simplified result is underlined.

151. Write the applicable formula. $V = lwh$
List the values for the variables. $V = ?$
$l = 12$ cm
$w = 9$ cm
$h = 4$ cm

Substitute the values into the formula. $V = (12)(9)(4)$
Simplify the expression. $V = 432$
Include the units. $\underline{V = 432 \text{ cm}^3}$

152. Write the appropriate formula. $V = lwh$
List the values for the variables. $V = 98$
$l = 7$
$w = 3.5$
$h = ?$

Substitute the values into the formula. $98 = (7)(3.5)h$
Simplify the expression. $98 = 24.5h$
Divide both sides of the equation by 24.5. $\frac{98}{24.5} = \frac{24.5h}{24.5}$
Simplify the expression. $4 = h$
Include the units. $\underline{h = 4 \text{ feet}}$

153. Write the applicable formula. $D = rt$
List the values for the variables. $D = ?$
$r = 350$
$t = 3.5$

Substitute the values for the variables. $D = (350)(3.5)$
Simplify the expression. $D = 1,225$
Include the units. $\underline{D = 1,225 \text{ miles}}$

154. Write the applicable formula. $D = rt$
List the values for the variables. $D = 68$
                                                  $r = 17$
                                                  $t = ?$

Substitute the values for the variables. $68 = (17)t$
Simplify the expression. $68 = 17t$

Divide both sides of the equation by 17. $\frac{68}{17} = \frac{17t}{17}$
Simplify the expression. $4 = t$
Include the units. $\underline{4 \text{ hours} = t}$

155. Write the applicable formula. $D = rt$
List the values for the variables. $D = 45$
                                                  $r = ?$

Calculate the total number of hours. $3 \text{ days} \cdot \frac{6 \text{ hrs}}{\text{day}} = 18 \text{ hrs.}$
                                                  $t = 18$

Substitute the given values into the formula. $45 = r(18)$
Simplify the expression. $45 = 18r$

Divide both sides of the equation by 18. $\frac{45}{18} = \frac{18r}{18}$
Simplify the expression. $2.5 = r$

Include the units. $\underline{2.5 \text{ miles per hour} = r}$

156. Write the applicable formula. $I = prt$
List the values for the variables. $I = ?$
                                                  $p = 12,000$
                                                  $r = 6\%$
                                                  $t = 2$

Substitute the given values into the formula. $I = (12,000)(0.06)(2)$
Simplify the expression. $I = 1,440$
Include the units. $\underline{I = \$1,440}$

157. Write the applicable formula. $I = prt$
List the values for the variables. $I = 1,620$
                                                  $p = 4,500$
                                                  $r = ?$
                                                  $t = 3$

Substitute the given values into the formula. $1,620 = (4,500)r(3)$
Simplify the expression. $1,620 = 13,500r$

Divide both sides of the equation by 13,500. $\frac{1620}{13500} = \frac{13,500r}{13,500}$
Simplify the expression. $0.12 = r$
Express as a percent. $\underline{12\% = r}$

158. Write the applicable formula. $I = prt$
List the values for the variables. $I = 1,000$
                                                  $p = ?$
                                                  $r = 4\%$
                                                  $t = 2$

Substitute the given values into the formula.	$1,000 = p(0.04)(2)$
Simplify the expression.	$1,000 = 0.08p$
Divide both sides of the equation by 0.08.	$\frac{1,000}{0.08} = \frac{0.08p}{0.08}$
Simplify the expression.	$12,500 = p$
Include the units.	$\$12,500 = p$

159. Write the applicable formula. $\quad I = prt$
To double its value, the account would have
to earn $3,000 in interest.
List the values for the variables.

$I = 3,000$

$p = 3,000$

$r = 10\%$

$t = ?$

Substitute the given values into the formula. $\quad 3,000 = (3,000)(0.10)t$
Simplify the expression. $\quad 3,000 = 300t$
Divide both sides of the equation by 300. $\quad \frac{3,000}{300} = \frac{300t}{300}$
Simplify the expression. $\quad 10 = t$
Include the units. $\quad \underline{10 \text{ years}} = t$

160. Write the applicable formula. $\quad A = \frac{1}{2}h(b_1 + b_2)$
List the values for the variables. $\quad A = ?$

$b_1 = 12$

$b_2 = 16$

$h = 8$

Substitute the given values into the formula. $\quad A = \frac{1}{2} \cdot 8 \cdot (12 + 16)$
Simplify the expression. $\quad A = \frac{1}{2} \cdot 8 \cdot 28$

$A = \frac{1}{2} \cdot 224$

$A = 112$

Include the units. $\quad \underline{A = 112 \text{ cm}^2}$

161. Write the applicable formula. $\quad A = \frac{1}{2}h(b_1 + b_2)$
List the values for the variables. $\quad A = 7,200$

$b_1 = 40$

$b_2 = 80$

$h = ?$

Substitute the given values into the formula. $\quad 7,200 = \frac{1}{2} \cdot h \cdot (40 + 80)$
Simplify the expression. $\quad 7,200 = \frac{1}{2} \cdot h \cdot 120$

$7,200 = 60h$

Divide both sides of the equation by 60. $\quad \frac{7,200}{60} = \frac{60h}{60}$
Simplify the expression. $\quad 120 = h$
Include the units. $\quad \underline{120 \text{ ft}} = h$

162. Write the applicable formula.
List the values for the variables.

$A = \frac{1}{2}h(b_1 + b_2)$
$A = 240$
$b_1 = x$
$b_2 = 3x$
$h = 12$

Substitute the given values into the formula.

$240 = \frac{1}{2} \cdot 12 \cdot (x + 3x)$

Simplify the expression.

$240 = \frac{1}{2} \cdot 12 \cdot 4x$
$240 = 6 \cdot 4x$
$240 = 24x$

Divide both sides of the equation by 24.
$\frac{240}{24} = \frac{24x}{24}$
Simplify the expression.
$10 = x$
Substitute 10 for x in the list of variables.
$\underline{b_1 = 10}$
$b_2 = 3(10)$
$b_2 = 30$

163. Write the applicable formula.
List the values for the variables.

$C = \frac{5}{9}(F - 32)$
$C = 45$
$F = ?$

Substitute the given values into the formula.
$45 = \frac{5}{9}(F - 32)$
Multiply both sides of the equation by 9.
$9(45) = 9[\frac{5}{9}(F - 32)]$
Simplify the expression.
$405 = 5(F - 32)$
$405 = 5F - 5(32)$
$405 = 5F - 160$

Add 160 to both sides of the equation.
$405 + 160 = 5F + 160 - 160$
Combine like terms on each side of the equation.
$565 = 5F$
Divide both sides of the equation by 5.
$\frac{565}{5} = \frac{5F}{5}$
Simplify the expression.
$\underline{113 = F}$

164. Write the applicable formula.
List the values for the variables.

$C = \frac{5}{9}(F - 32)$
$C = ?$
$F = 50$

Substitute the given values into the formula.

$C = \frac{5}{9}(50 - 32)$

Simplify the expression.

$C = \frac{5}{9}(18)$
$C = \frac{5}{9}(\frac{18}{1})$
$\underline{C = 10}$

165. Write the applicable formula.
List the values for the variables.

$V = \pi r^2 h$
$V = ?$
$r = 2$
$h = 4$
$\pi = 3.14$

Substitute the given values into the formula.
Simplify the expression.
Include the units.

$V = (3.14)(2)^2(4)$
$V = 50.24$
$V = 50.24 \text{ ft}^3$

166. Write the applicable formula.
List the values for the variables.

$V = \pi r^2 h$
$V = 339.12$
$r = ?$
$h = 12$
$\pi = 3.14$

Substitute the given values into the formula.
Simplify the expression.

$339.12 = (3.14)r^2(12)$
$339.12 = 37.68 r^2$

Divide both sides of the equation by 37.68.
Simplify the expression.

$\frac{339.12}{37.68} = \frac{37.68 r^2}{37.68}$
$9 = r^2$
$3 = r$

Include the units.

$3 \text{ cm} = r$

167. Write the applicable formula.
List the values for the variables.

$V = \pi r^2 h$
$V = 13,565$
$r = 12$
$h = ?$
$\pi = 3.14$

Substitute the given values into the formula.
Simplify the expression.

$13,565 = (3.14)(12^2)h$
$13,565 = 452.16 h$

Divide both sides of the equation by 452.16.
Simplify the expression.
Include the units.

$\frac{13,565}{452.16} = \frac{452.16 h}{452.16}$
$30 = h$
$30 \text{ feet} = h$

168. Write the applicable formula.
List the values for the variables.

$S = 2\pi r(r + h)$
$S = ?$
$r = 20$
$h = 40$
$\pi = 3.14$

Substitute the given values into the formula.
Simplify the expression.
Include the units.

$S = 2(3.14)(20)(20 + 40)$
$S = 7,536$
$S = 7,536 \text{ cm}^2$

169. Write the applicable formula. $S = 2\pi r(r + h)$
List the values for the variables. $S = 282.6$

$r = 3$

$h = ?$

$\pi = 3.14$

Substitute the given values into
the formula. $282.6 = 2(3.14)(3)(3 + h)$
Simplify the expression. $282.6 = 18.84(3 + h)$
Use the distributive property
of multiplication. $282.6 = 18.84(3) + 18.84(h)$
Simplify the expression. $282.6 = 56.52 + 18.84\,h$
Subtract 56.52 from both sides
of the equation. $282.6 - 56.52 = 56.52 - 56.52 + 18.84$
Simplify the expression. $226.08 = 18.84h$
Divide both sides of the
equation by 18.84. $\frac{226.08}{18.84} = \frac{8.84h}{18.84}$
Simplify the expression. $12 = h$
Include the units. $\underline{12 \text{ in} = h}$

170. Write the applicable formula. $S = 2\pi r(r + h)$
List the values for the variables. $S = 2{,}512$

$r = x$

$h = 3x$

$\pi = 3.14$

Substitute the given values into
the formula. $2{,}512 = 2(3.14)(x)(x + 3\,x)$
Simplify the expression. $2{,}512 = 6.28\,x(4\,x)$
Divide both sides of the
equation by 25.12. $\frac{2{,}512}{25.12} = \frac{25.12x^2}{25.12}$
Simplify the expression. $100 = x^2$
Solve for x. $10 = x$
Substitute the value for x into
the values list. $\underline{r = x = 10 \text{ feet}}$
$\underline{h = 3x = 3(10) = 30 \text{ feet}}$

Graphing Linear Equations

This chapter asks you to find solutions to linear equations by graphing. The solution of a linear equation is the set of ordered pairs that form a line on a coordinate graph. Every point on the line is a solution for the equation. One method for graphing the solution is to use a table with x and y values that are solutions for the particular equation. You select a value for x and solve for the y value. But in this chapter, we will focus on the slope and y-intercept method.

The slope and y-intercept method may require you to change an equation into the slope-intercept form. That is, the equation with two variables must be written in the form $y = mx + b$. Written in this form, the m value is a number that represents the slope of the solution graph and the b is a number that represents the y-intercept. The slope of a line is the ratio of the change in the y value over the change in the x value from one point on the solution graph to another. From one point to another, the slope is the rise over the run. The y-intercept is the point where the solution graph (line) crosses the y-axis. Another way of saying that is: The y-intercept is the place where the value of x is 0.

Tips for Graphing Linear Equations

- Rewrite the given equation in the form $y = mx + b$.

- Use the **b** value to determine where the line crosses the *y*-axis. That is the point (0, *b*).
- Use the value of **m** as the slope of the equation. Write the slope as a fraction. If the value of **m** is a whole number, the slope is the whole number over 1. The value of **m** is = $\frac{\text{change in } y}{\text{change in } x}$.
- If the value of **m** is negative, use a negative sign in only the numerator or the denominator, not both. For example, $-\frac{3}{4} = \frac{-3}{4} = \frac{3}{-4}$.

Graph the following equations using the slope and *y*-intercept method.

171. $y = 2x + 3$

172. $y = 5x - 2$

173. $y = {}^-2x + 6$

174. $y = \frac{3}{4}x - 1$

175. $y = \frac{5}{2}x - 3$

176. $y - 2x = 4$

177. $y + 3x = {}^-2$

178. $y - \frac{1}{2}x = 3\frac{1}{2}$

179. $2x + 5y = 30$

180. $2y + 4x = 10$

181. $x - 3y = 15$

182. $3x + 9y = {}^-27$

183. ${}^-5x - y = -\frac{7}{2}$

184. $x = 7y - 14$

185. $0 = 2x + 3y$

186. $3x + 12y = {}^-18$

187. $y - 0.4x = {}^-2$

188. $\frac{2}{3}y - \frac{1}{2}x = 0$

189. $\frac{5}{6}x - \frac{1}{3}y = 2$

190. $7x = 4y + 8$

191. $20x - 15 = 5y$

192. $6y + 13x = 12$

193. $0.1x = 0.7y + 1.4$

194. $^-34x + 85 = 17y$

195. $6y + 27x = {}^-42$

For the following problems, use the slope/y-intercept method to write an equation that would enable you to draw a graphic solution for each problem.

196. A glider has a 25:1 descent ratio when there are no updrafts to raise its altitude. That is, for every 25 feet it moves parallel to the ground, it will lose 1 foot of altitude. Write an equation to represent the glider's descent from an altitude of 200 feet.

197. An Internet service provider charges $15 plus $0.25 per hour of usage per month. Write an equation that would represent the monthly bill of a user.

198. A scooter rental agency charges $20 per day plus $0.05 per mile for the rental of a motor scooter. Write an equation to represent the cost of one day's rental.

199. A dive resort rents scuba equipment at a weekly rate of $150 per week and charges $8 per tank of compressed air used during the week of diving. Write an equation to represent a diver's cost for one week of diving at the resort.

200. A recent backyard bird count showed that one out of every six birds that visited backyard feeders was a chickadee. Write an equation to represent this ratio.

Answers

Numerical expressions in parentheses like this [ ] are operations performed on only part of the original expression. The operations performed within these symbols are intended to show how to evaluate the various terms that make up the entire expression.

Expressions with parentheses that look like this ( ) contain either numerical substitutions or expressions that are part of a numerical expression. Once a single number appears within these parentheses, the parentheses are no longer needed and need not be used the next time the entire expression is written.

When two pair of parentheses appear side by side like this ( )( ), it means that the expressions within are to be multiplied.

Sometimes parentheses appear within other parentheses in numerical or algebraic expressions. Regardless of what symbol is used, ( ), { }, or [ ], perform operations in the innermost parentheses first and work outward.

<u>Underlined</u> expressions show the original algebraic expression as an equation with the expression equal to its simplified result.

171. The equation is in the proper slope/y-intercept form.

$b = 3$

A change in y of 2 and in x of 1 gives the point

$m = 2 = \frac{2}{1} = \frac{\text{change in } y}{\text{change in } x}$

The y-intercept is at the point (0,3).

$(0 + 1, 3 + 2)$ or $(1,5)$.

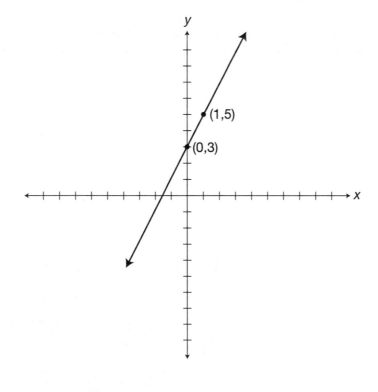

172. The equation is in the proper
slope/y-intercept form.

$m = 5 = \frac{5}{1} = \frac{\text{change in } y}{\text{change in } x}$

$b = {}^-2$.

The y-intercept is at the point $(0, {}^-2)$.

A change in y of 5 and in x of 1
gives the point

$(0 + 1, {}^-2 + 5)$ or $(1,3)$.

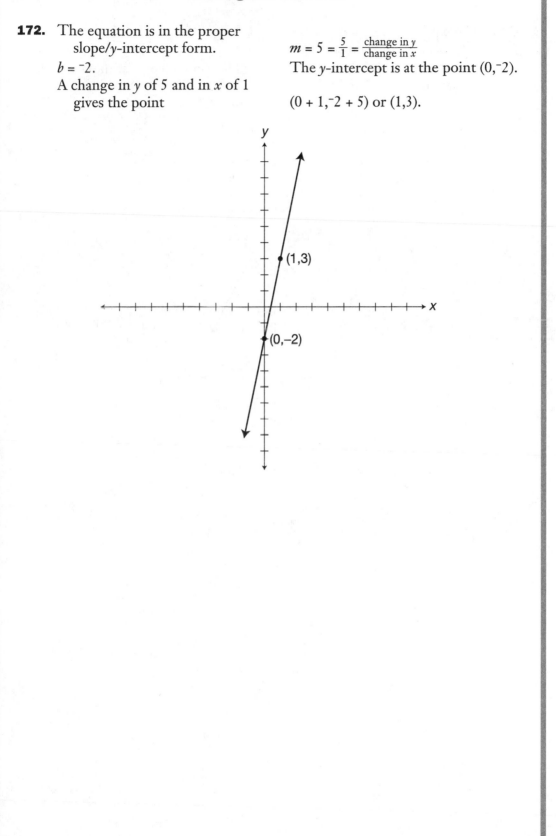

173. The equation is in the proper
slope/y-intercept form.

$m = {}^-2 = {}^-\frac{2}{1} = \frac{\text{change in } y}{\text{change in } x}$

$b = 6.$

The y-intercept is at the point (0,6).

A change in y of $^-2$ and in x of 1
gives the point

$(0 + 1, 6 - 2)$ or $(1,4)$.

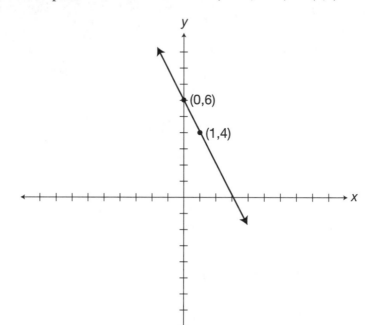

174. The equation is in the proper slope/y-intercept form.

$b = {}^-1$.

A change in y of 3 and in x of 4 gives the point

$m = \frac{3}{4} = \frac{\text{change in } y}{\text{change in } x}$

The y-intercept is at the point $(0, {}^-1)$.

$(0 + 4, {}^-1 + 3)$ or $(4,2)$.

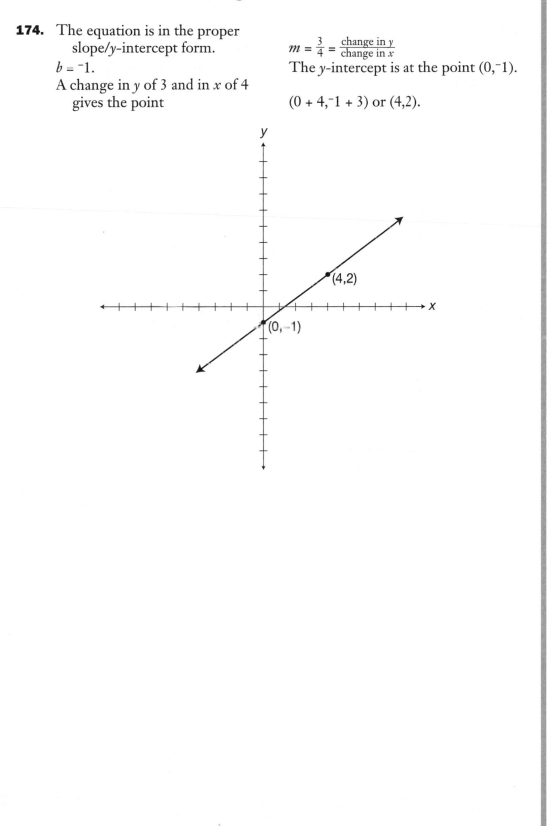

175. The equation is in the proper
slope/*y*-intercept form.

$b = {}^-3$.

A change in *y* of 5 and in *x* of 2
gives the point

$m = \frac{5}{2} = \frac{\text{change in } y}{\text{change in } x}$

The *y*-intercept is at the point $(0,{}^-3)$.

$(0 + 2, {}^-3 + 5)$ or $(2,2)$.

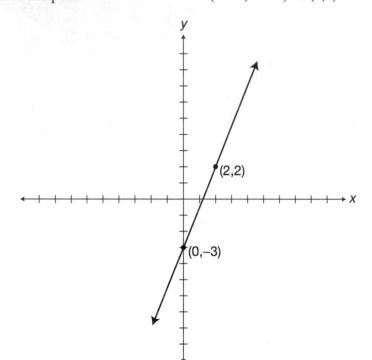

176. Put the equation in the proper form.
Add $2x$ to both sides of the
equation. $y + 2x - 2x = 2x + 4$
Simplify the equation. $y = 2x + 4$
The equation is in the proper
slope/y-intercept form. $m = 2 = \frac{2}{1} = \frac{\text{change in } y}{\text{change in } x}$
$b = 4$.   The y-intercept is at the point (0,4).
A change in y of 2 and in x of 1
gives the point $(0 + 1, 4 + 2)$ or (1,6).

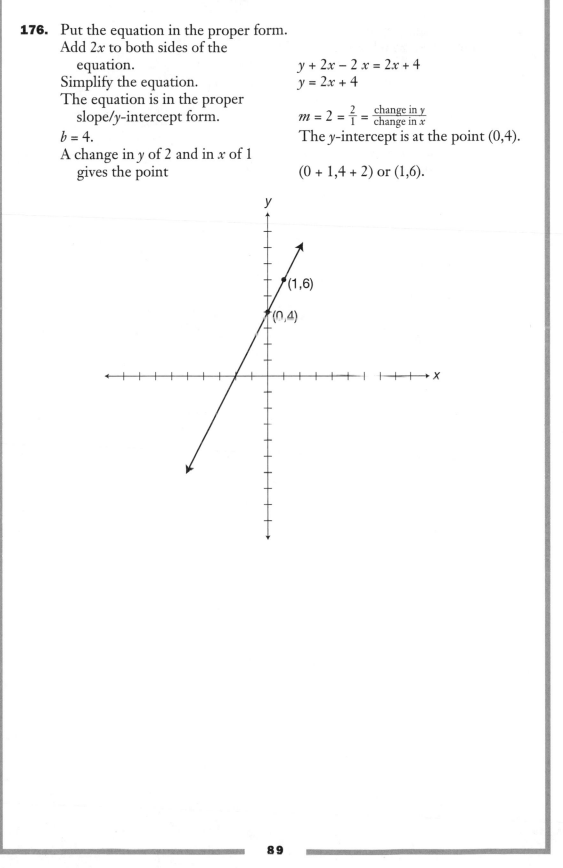

177. Put the equation in the proper form.

Subtract $3x$ from both sides of the equation.

$y + 3x - 3x = -3x - 2$

Simplify the equation.

$y = -3x - 2$

The equation is in the proper slope/y-intercept form.

$m = {}^-3 = -\frac{3}{1} = \frac{\text{change in } y}{\text{change in } x}$

$b = {}^-2$.

The y-intercept is at the point $(0, {}^-2)$.

A change in y of ${}^-3$ and in x of 1 gives the point

$(0 + 1, {}^-2 - 3)$ or $(1, {}^-5)$.

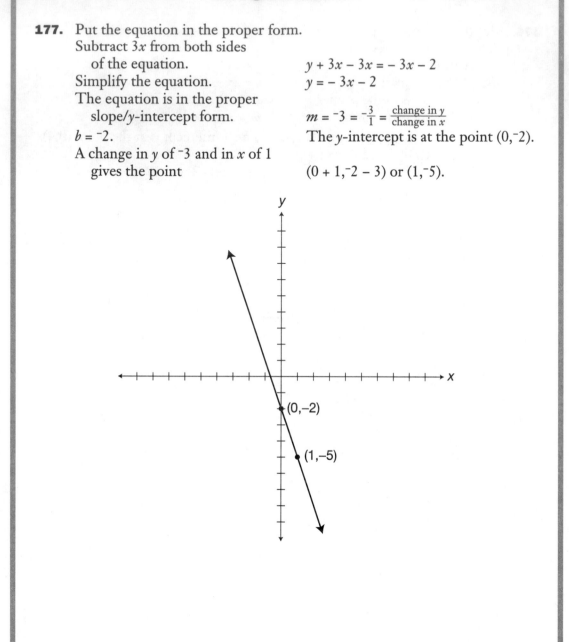

178. Put the equation in the proper form.
Add $\frac{1}{2}x$ to both sides of the
   equation. $y + \frac{1}{2}x - \frac{1}{2}x = \frac{1}{2}x + 3\frac{1}{2}$

Simplify the equation. $y = \frac{1}{2}x + 3\frac{1}{2}$
The equation is in the proper
   slope/y-intercept form. $m = \frac{1}{2} = \frac{\text{change in } y}{\text{change in } x}$
$b = 3\frac{1}{2}$.
                         The y-intercept is at the point $(0,3\frac{1}{2})$.
A change in y of 1 and in x of 2
   gives the point $(0 + 2, 3\frac{1}{2} + 1)$ or $(2, 4\frac{1}{2})$.

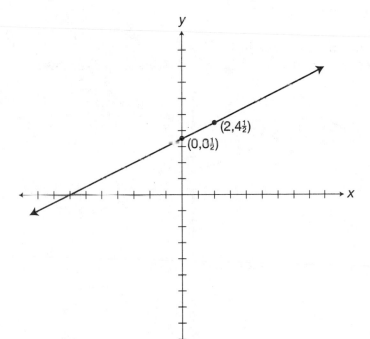

179. Put the equation in the proper form.

Subtract $2x$ from both sides of the equation.

$$2x - 2x + 5y = {}^-2x + 30$$

Simplify the equation.

$$5y = {}^-2x + 30$$

Divide both sides of the equation by 5.

$$\frac{5y}{5} = \frac{({}^-2x + 30)}{5}$$

Simplify the equation.

$$y = \frac{{}^-2x}{5} + \frac{30}{5}$$

$$y = \frac{{}^-2}{5x} + 6$$

The equation is in the proper slope/y-intercept form.

$$m = \frac{{}^-2}{5} = \frac{\text{change in } y}{\text{change in } x}$$

$b = 6$.

The y-intercept is at the point (0,6).

A change in y of $^-2$ and in x of 5 gives the point

$(0 + 5, 6 - 2)$ or $(5,4)$.

180. Put the equation in the proper form.
Subtract 4*x* from both sides of
    the equation. $2y + 4x - 4x = {}^-4x + 10$
Simplify the equation. $2y = {}^-4x + 10$
Divide both sides of the equation
    by 2. $\frac{2y}{2} = \frac{({}^-4x + 10)}{2}$

Simplify the equation. $y = \frac{{}^-4x}{2} + \frac{10}{2}$
    $y = {}^-2x + 5$

The equation is in the proper
    slope/*y*-intercept form. $m = {}^-2 = {}^-\frac{2}{1} = \frac{\text{change in } y}{\text{change in } x}$
b = 5. The *y*-intercept is at the point (0,5).
A change in *y* of ⁻2 and in *x* of 1
    gives the point (0 + 1,5 − 2) or (1,3).

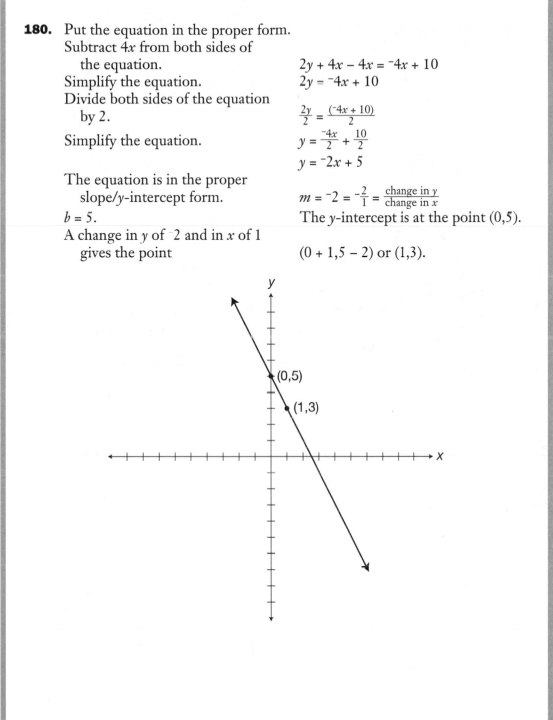

181. Put the equation in the proper form.
Add $3y$ to both sides
   of the equation. $x - 3y + 3y = 15 + 3y$
Simplify the equation. $x = 15 + 3y$
Subtract 15 from both
   sides of the equation. $x - 15 = 15 - 15 + 3y$
Simplify the equation. $x - 15 = 3y$
Divide both sides of the
   equation by 3. $\frac{(x - 15)}{3} = \frac{3y}{3}$
Simplify the equation. $\frac{x}{3} - \frac{15}{3} = y$

$$\frac{x}{3} - 5 = y$$

$\frac{x}{3} = \frac{(1)(x)}{(3)(1)} = \frac{1}{3} \cdot \frac{x}{1} = \frac{1}{3}x$ $\frac{1}{3}x - 5 = y$
The equation is equivalent
   to the proper form. $y = \frac{1}{3}x - 5$
The equation is in the proper
   slope/y-intercept form. $m = \frac{1}{3} = \frac{\text{change in } y}{\text{change in } x}$
$b = {}^-5$.   The y-intercept is at the point $(0,{}^-5)$.
A change in y of 1 and in x of 3
   gives the point $(0 + 3, {}^-5 + 1)$ or $(3, {}^-4)$.

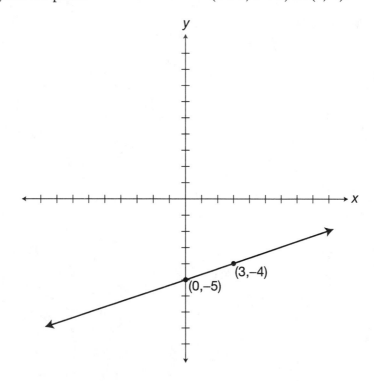

182. Put the equation in the proper form.
Divide both sides of the
equation by 3.

$$\frac{(3x + 9y)}{3} = \frac{^-27}{3}$$

Simplify the equation.

$$\frac{3x}{3} + \frac{9y}{3} = {}^-9$$
$$x + 3y = {}^-9$$

Subtract x from both sides
of the equation.

$$x - x + 3y = {}^-x - 9$$

Simplify the equation.

$$3y = {}^-x - 9$$

Divide both sides of the
equation by 3.

$$\frac{3y}{3} = \frac{(^-x - 9)}{3}$$

Simplify the equation.

$$y = \frac{^-x}{3} - \frac{9}{3}$$
$$y = \frac{^-x}{3} - \frac{^-9}{3}$$
$$y = \frac{^-1}{3x} - 3$$

The equation is in the proper
slope/y-intercept form.
$b = {}^-3$.

$$m = {}^-\frac{1}{3} = \frac{\text{change in } y}{\text{change in } x}$$

The y-intercept is at the point $(0,^-3)$.

A change in y of $^-1$ and in x of 3
gives the point

$(0 + 3,^-3 - 1)$ or $(3,^-4)$.

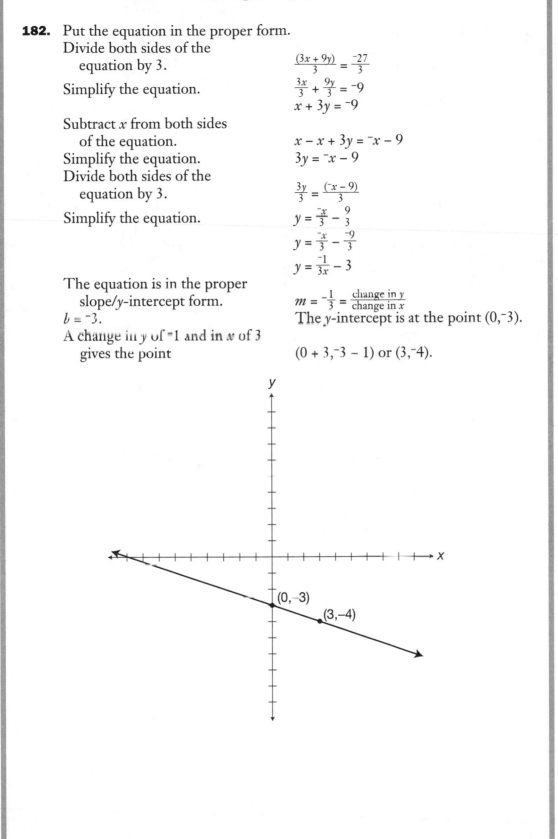

183. Put the equation in the proper form.

Add $5x$ to both sides of the equation.

$$5x - 5x - y = 5x - \frac{7}{2}$$

Simplify the equation.

$$^-y = 5x - \frac{7}{2}$$

Multiply both sides of the equation by $^-1$.

$$^-1(^-y) = ^-1(5x - \frac{7}{2})$$

Simplify the equation.

$$y = ^-5x + \frac{7}{2}$$

The equation is in the proper slope/y-intercept form.

$$m = ^-5 = ^-\frac{5}{1} = \frac{\text{change in } y}{\text{change in } x}$$

$b = \frac{7}{2} = 3\frac{1}{2}.$

The y-intercept is at the point $(0, 3\frac{1}{2})$.

A change in y of $^-5$ and in x of 1 gives the point of

$$(0 + 1, 3\frac{1}{2} - 5) \text{ or } (1, ^-1\frac{1}{2}).$$

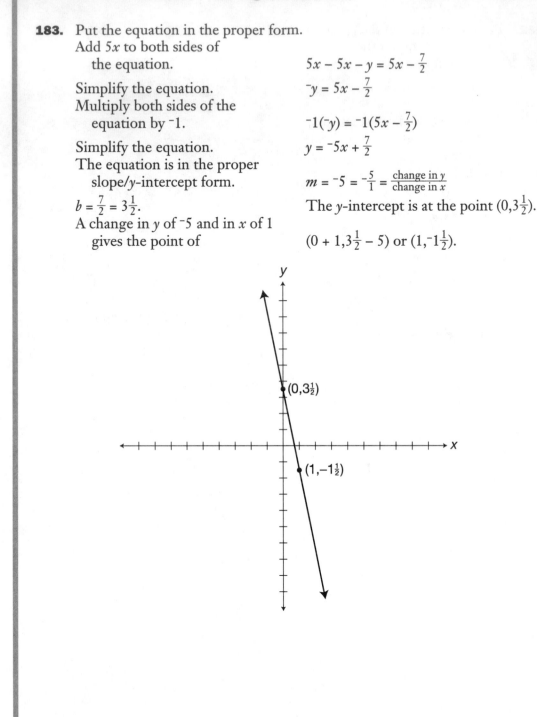

184. Put the equation in the proper form.

Add 14 to both sides of
the equation. $x + 14 = 7y + 14 - 14$

Simplify the equation. $x + 14 = 7y$

Divide both sides of the
equation by 7. $\frac{(x + 14)}{7} = \frac{7y}{7}$

Simplify the equation. $\frac{x}{7} + 2 = y$

$$\frac{1}{7}x + 2 = y$$

$$y = \frac{1}{7}x + 2$$

The equation is in the
proper slope/y-intercept form. $m = \frac{1}{7} = \frac{\text{change in } y}{\text{change in } x}$

$b = 2$.   The y-intercept is at the point (0,2).

A change in y of 1 and in x of 7
gives the point   (0 + 7,2 + 1) or (7,3).

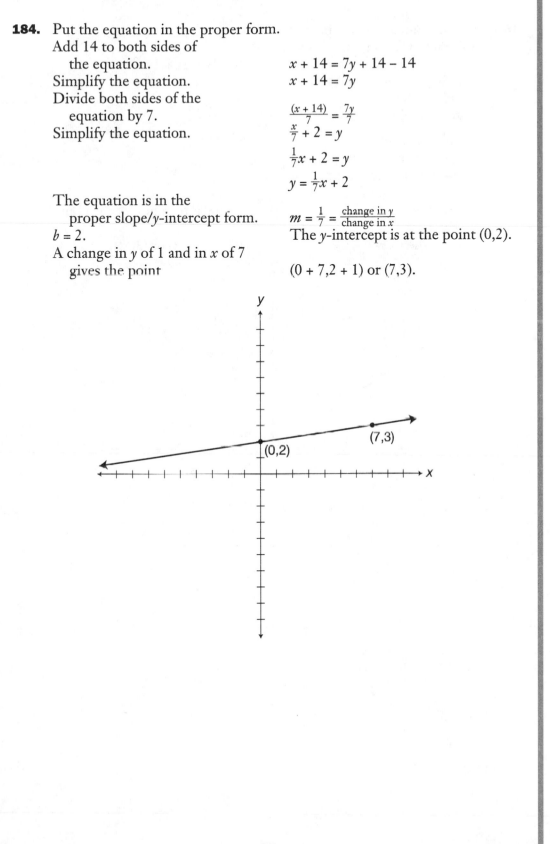

185. Put the equation in the proper form.
Subtract $3y$ from both sides
of the equation. $0 - 3y = 2x + 3y - 3y$
Simplify the equation. $^-3y = 2x$
Divide both sides of the
equation by $^-3$. $\frac{^-3y}{^-3} = \frac{2x}{^-3}$

Simplify the equation. $y = -\frac{2}{3}x$
The equation is in the proper
slope/y-intercept form. $m = -\frac{2}{3} = \frac{\text{change in } y}{\text{change in } x}$
There is no b showing in the
equation, so $b = 0$.   The y-intercept is at the point (0,0).
A change in y of $^-2$ and in x of 3
gives the point $(0 + 3, 0 - 2)$ or $(3, ^-2)$.

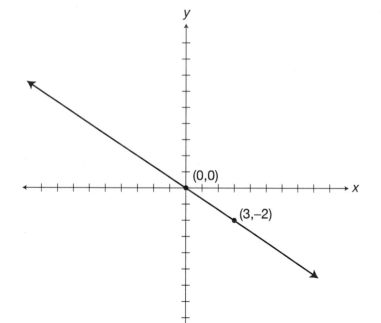

186. Put the equation in the proper form.

Divide both sides of the equation by 3.

$$\frac{(3x + 12y)}{3} = \frac{^-18}{3}$$

Simplify the equation.

$$\frac{3x}{3} + \frac{12y}{3} = {}^-6$$
$$x + 4y = {}^-6$$

Subtract x from both sides of the equation.

$$x - x + 4y = -x - 6$$

Simplify the equation.

$$4y = -x - 6$$

Divide both sides of the equation by 4.

$$\frac{4y}{4} = \frac{(^-x - 6)}{4}$$

Simplify the equation.

$$y = \frac{^-x}{4} - \frac{6}{4}$$
$$y = {}^-\tfrac{1}{4}x - 1\tfrac{1}{2}$$

The equation is in the proper slope/y-intercept form.

$$m = \frac{^-1}{4} = \frac{\text{change in } y}{\text{change in } x}$$

$b = {}^-\tfrac{3}{2}$.

The y-intercept is at the point $(0, {}^-1\tfrac{1}{2})$.

A change in y of $^-1$ and in x of 4 gives the point

$(0 + 4, {}^-1\tfrac{1}{2} - 1)$ or $(4, {}^-2\tfrac{1}{2})$.

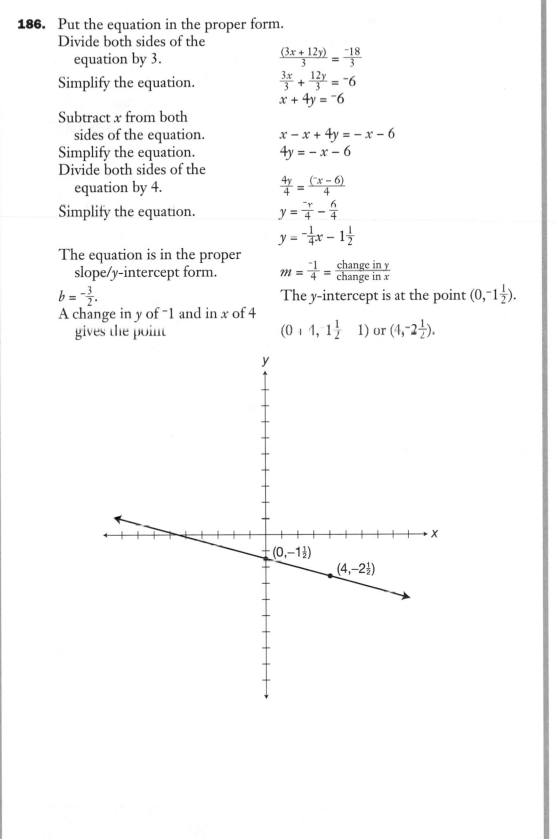

187. Put the equation in the proper form.
　Add 0.4x to both sides of the
　　equation.　　　　　　　　　$y + 0.4x - 0.4x = 0.4x - 2$
　Simplify the equation.　　　　$y = 0.4x - 2$
　The equation is in the proper
　　slope/y-intercept form.　　$m = 0.4 = \frac{4}{10} = \frac{2}{5} = \frac{\text{change in } y}{\text{change in } x}$
　$b = {}^-2$.　　　　　　　　　The y-intercept is at the point $(0,{}^-2)$.
　A change in y of 2 and in x of 5
　　gives the point　　　　　　$(0 + 5, {}^-2 + 2)$ or $(5,0)$.

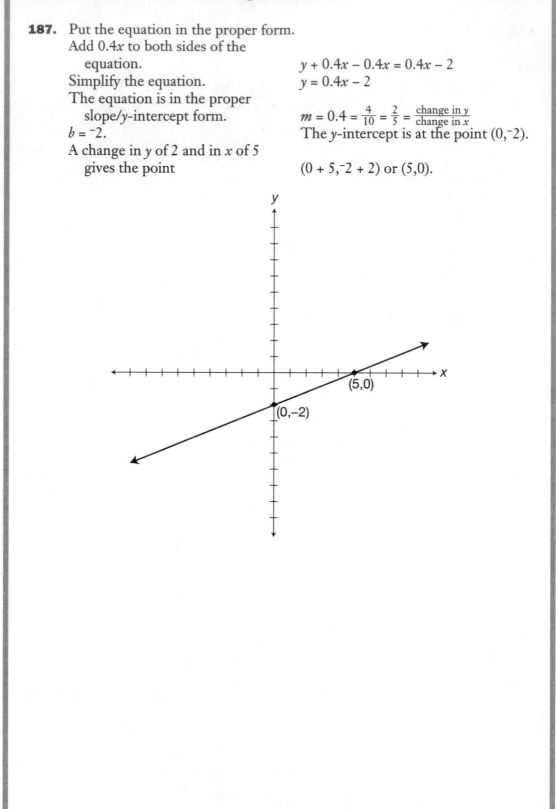

188. Put the equation in the proper form.

Add $\frac{1}{2}x$ to both sides of the
   equation.

$$\frac{2}{3}y - \frac{1}{2}x + \frac{1}{2}x = 0 + \frac{1}{2}x$$

Simplify the equation.

$$\frac{2}{3}y = \frac{1}{2}x$$

Multiply both sides of the
   equation by $\frac{3}{2}$.

$$\frac{3}{2}\left(\frac{2}{3}\right)y = \frac{3}{2}\left(\frac{1}{2}x\right)$$

Simplify the equation.

$$1y = \frac{3}{4}x$$
$$y = \frac{3}{4}x$$

The equation is in the proper
   slope/y-intercept form.
$b = 0$.

$$m = \frac{3}{4} = \frac{\text{change in } y}{\text{change in } x}$$

The y-intercept is at the point $(0,0)$.

A change in y of 3 and in x of 4
   gives the point

$(0 + 4, 0 + 3)$ or $(4,3)$.

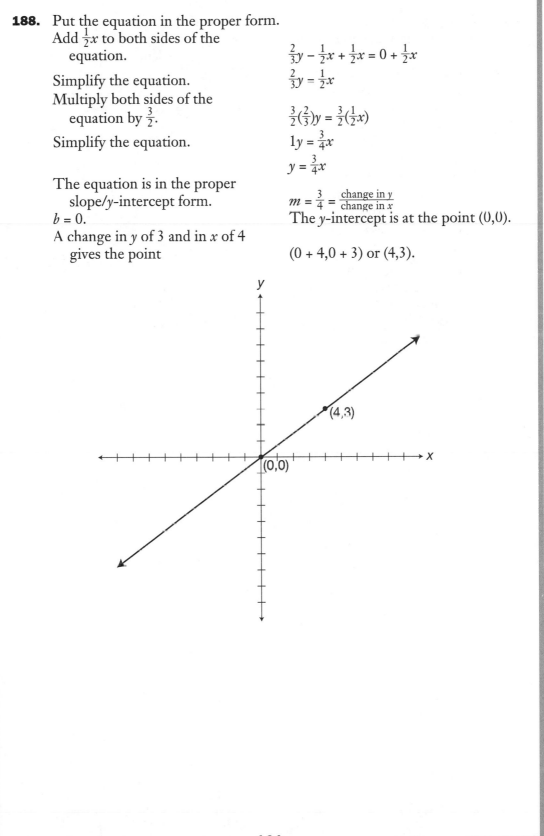

189. Simplify the equation. It would be easier to operate with an equation that doesn't have fractional coefficients. So if you multiply the whole equation by the lowest common multiple of the denominators, you will have whole numbers with coefficients.

Multiply both sides of the equation by 6.

$6(\frac{5}{6}x - \frac{1}{3}y) = 6(2)$

Use the distributive property of multiplication.

$6(\frac{5}{6}x) - 6(\frac{1}{3}y) = 6(2)$

Simplify the equation.

$5x - 2y = 12$

Subtract $5x$ from both sides of the equation.

$5x - 5x - 2y = {}^-5x + 12$

Simplify the equation.

${}^-2y = {}^-5x + 12$

Divide both sides of the equation by ${}^-2$.

$\frac{{}^-2y}{{}^-2} = \frac{{}^-5x}{{}^-2} + \frac{12}{{}^-2}$

Simplify the equation.

$y = \frac{5}{2}x - 6$

The equation is in the proper slope/y-intercept form.

$m = \frac{5}{2} = \frac{\text{change in } y}{\text{change in } x}$

$b = {}^-6$.

The y-intercept is at the point $(0, {}^-6)$.

A change in y of 5 and in x of 2 gives the point

$(0 + 2, {}^-6 + 5)$ or $(2, {}^-1)$.

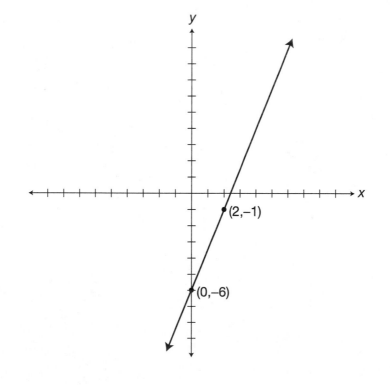

190. Put the equation in the proper form.

Subtract 8 from both sides
of the equation. $\qquad$ $7x - 8 = 4y + 8 - 8$

Simplify the equation. $\qquad$ $7x - 8 = 4y$

Exchange the terms on each
side of the equal sign. $\qquad$ $4y = 7x - 8$

Divide both sides of the
equation by 4. $\qquad$ $\frac{4y}{4} = \frac{7x}{4} - \frac{8}{4}$

Simplify the equation. $\qquad$ $y = \frac{7}{4}x - 2$

The equation is in the proper
slope/y-intercept form. $\qquad$ $m = \frac{7}{4} = \frac{\text{change in } y}{\text{change in } x}$

$b = {}^-2$. $\qquad$ The y-intercept is at the point $(0, {}^-2)$.

A change in y of 7 and in x of 4
gives the point $\qquad$ $(0 + 4, {}^-2 + 7)$ or $(4,5)$.

191. Exchange the terms on each side
of the equal sign.

$5y = 20x - 15$

Divide both sides of the
equation by 5.

$\frac{5y}{5} = \frac{20x}{5} - \frac{15}{5}$

Simplify the equation.

$y = 4x - 3$

The equation is in the proper
slope/y-intercept form.

$m = 4 = \frac{4}{1} = \frac{\text{change in } y}{\text{change in } x}$

$b = {}^-3$.

The y-intercept is at the point $(0,{}^-3)$.

A change in y of 4 and in x of 1
gives the point

$(0 + 1, {}^-3 + 4)$ or $(1,1)$.

192. Put the equation in the proper form.

Subtract $13x$ from both sides of the equation.

$6y + 13x - 13x = {}^-13x + 12$

Simplify the equation.

$6y = {}^-13x + 12$

Divide both sides of the equation by 6.

$\frac{6y}{6} = \frac{{}^-13x}{6} + \frac{12}{6}$

Simplify the equation.

$y = \frac{{}^-13}{6}x + 2$

The equation is in the proper slope/y-intercept form.

$b = 2$.

$m = \frac{{}^-13}{6} = \frac{\text{change in } y}{\text{change in } x}$

The y-intercept is at the point $(0,2)$.

A change in y of $^-13$ and in x of 6 gives the point

$(0 + 6, 2 - 13)$ or $(6, {}^-11)$.

193. Once again, if it would be easier for you to operate with whole number coefficients instead of decimals to start, you could multiply the whole equation by 10.

Multiply both sides of the equation by 10.	$10(0.1x) = 10(0.7y + 1.4)$
Simplify the expression.	$x = 7y + 14$
Subtract 14 from both sides of the equation.	$x - 14 = 7y + 14 - 14$
Simplify the equation.	$x - 14 = 7y$
If $a = b$, then $b = a$.	$7y = x - 14$
Divide both sides of the equation by 7.	$\frac{7y}{7} = \frac{x}{7} - \frac{14}{7}$
Simplify the equation.	$y = \frac{1}{7}x - 2$
The equation is in the proper slope/y-intercept form.	$m = \frac{1}{7} = \frac{\text{change in } y}{\text{change in } x}$
$b = {}^-2$.	The y-intercept is at the point $(0, {}^-2)$.
A change in y of 1 and in x of 7 gives the point	$(0 + 7, {}^-2 + 1)$ or $(7, {}^-1)$.

194. Exchange the terms on each side of the equal sign.

$$17y = {}^-34x + 85$$

Divide both sides of the equation by 17.

$$\frac{17y}{17} = \frac{{}^-34x}{17} + \frac{85}{17}$$

Simplify the equation.

$$y = {}^-2x + 5$$

The equation is in the proper slope/y-intercept form.

$$m = {}^-2 = \frac{{}^-2}{1} = \frac{\text{change in } y}{\text{change in } x}$$

$b = 5$.

The y-intercept is at the point (0,5).

A change in y of $^-2$ and in x of 1 gives the point

(0 + 1,5 − 2) or (1,3).

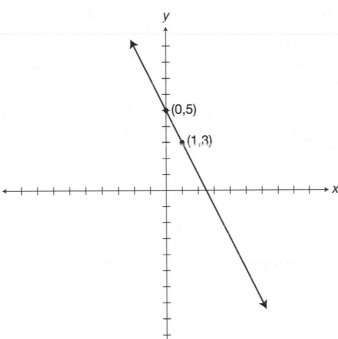

195. Put the equation in the proper form.
Add ⁻27x to both sides
   of the equation. $6y + 27x - 27x = {}^-27x - 42$
Simplify the equation. $6y = {}^-27x - 42$
Divide both sides
   of the equation by 6. $\frac{6y}{6} = \frac{{}^-27x}{6} - \frac{42}{6}$
Simplify the equation. $y = \frac{{}^-27}{6}x - 7$
Simplify the coefficient
   of x by a common factor of 3. $y = \frac{{}^-9}{2}x - 7$
The equation is in the proper
   slope/y-intercept form. $m = \frac{{}^-9}{2} = \frac{9}{{}^-2} = \frac{\text{change in } y}{\text{change in } x}$
$b = -7$.   The y-intercept is at the point $(0,{}^-7)$.
A change in y of 9 and in x of ⁻2
   gives the point $(0 - 2,{}^-7 + 9)$ or $({}^-2,2)$.

196. Let x = horizontal movement. Forward is in the positive direction.
Let y = vertical movement. Ascending is in the positive direction.
   Descending is in the negative.
The change in position of the glider is described by the slope.
The change in y is ⁻1 for every change
   in x of ⁺25.   Slope $= \frac{\text{change in } y}{\text{change in } x} = \frac{{}^-1}{25} = m$

The starting position for the purposes
of this graphic solution is at an altitude
of 200 ft. or + 200. So, $b = 200$
Using the standard form $y = mx + b$,
you substitute the given values into the
formula. $y = \frac{-1}{25}x + 200$
A graph of this equation would have a slope of
$\frac{-1}{25}$ and the y-intercept would be at (0,200)

197. Let y = the amount of a monthly bill.
Let x = the hours of Internet use for the month.
The costs for the month will equal \$15 plus the
\$.25 times the number of hours of use.
Written as an equation, this information would be
as follows: $y = 0.25x + 15$

A graph of this equation would have a slope of 0.25 or $\frac{25}{100} = \frac{1}{4}$

The y-intercept would be at   (0,15)

198. Let y = the cost of a scooter rental for one day.
Let x = the number of miles driven in one day.
The problem tells us that the cost would be equal
to the daily charges plus the 0.05 times the number
of miles driven.
Written as an equation, this would be $y = 0.05x + 20$
The graph would have a y-intercept at (0,20)
and the slope would be $\frac{5}{100} = \frac{1}{20}$

199. Let y = the total cost for equipment.
Let x = the number of tanks used during the week.
The problem tells us that the cost would be equal to
the weekly charge for gear rental plus 8 times the
number of tanks used.
A formula that would represent this information
would be: $y = 8x + 150$
The y-intercept would be at (0,150) and the
slope = 8 = $\frac{8}{1}$.

200. Let y = the number of birds that visited a backyard feeder.
Let x = the number of chickadees that visited the feeder.
An equation that represents the statement would be: $y = 6x$
The y-intercept is (0,0) and the slope = 6 = $\frac{6}{1}$.

Solving Inequalities

If you compare Chapter 9 to Chapter 6, you will find only a few differences between solving inequalities and solving equalities. The methods and procedures you use are virtually the same. Your goal is to isolate the variable on one side of the inequality, and the result will be your solution. In this chapter, there will be twenty-five inequalities so you can practice your solving skills. Look at the tips below to see what makes solving inequalities different from solving equalities.

Tips for Solving Inequalities

- Keep the inequality symbol facing the same way when you perform an addition or subtraction to both sides of the inequality. Keep the symbol facing the same way when you multiply or divide by a positive factor. But remember to change the direction of the inequality when you multiply or divide by a negative factor.
- When you have fractional coefficients or terms in an equality or inequality, multiply both sides by the least common multiple of the denominators and work with whole numbers. If the

coefficients and/or terms are decimals, multiply by multiples of ten until you have whole numbers to work with.

Solve the following inequalities.

201. $3x + 2 < 14$

202. $4x - 6 > 30$

203. $\frac{2}{5}x \le 18$

204. $4x + 26 \ge 90$

205. $8 - 6x < 50$

206. $3x - 10 \le {}^-3$

207. $2x + 0.29 > 0.79$

208. ${}^-6(x + 1) \ge 60$

209. $3(4 - 5x) < x - 116$

210. $4(x + 1) < 5(x + 2)$

211. $2(7x - 3) \ge {}^-2(5 + 3x)$

212. $16x - 1 < 4(6 - x)$

213. $\frac{-x}{0.2} \le 20$

214. $\frac{4}{3}x - 5 > x - 2$

215. $3x + 5 \ge {}^-2(x + 10)$

216. ${}^-4x + 3(x + 5) \ge 3(x + 2)$

217. $x - \frac{3}{4} < {}^-\frac{3}{4}(x + 2)$

218. $\frac{3}{2}x + 0.1 \ge 0.9 + x$

219. $x - 4\frac{1}{3} < 9 + \frac{2}{3}x$

220. ${}^-7(x + 2) < {}^-5x$

221. $\frac{5}{4}(x + 4) > \frac{1}{2}(x + 8) - 8$

222. $3(1 - 3x) \ge {}^-3\,(x + 27)$

223. ${}^-5[9 + (x - 4)] \ge 2(13 - x)$

224. $11(1 - x) \ge 3(3 - x) - 1$

225. $3(x - 16) - 2 < 9(x - 2) - 7x$

Answers

Numerical expressions in parentheses like this [ ] are operations performed on only part of the original expression. The operations performed within these symbols are intended to show how to evaluate the various terms that make up the entire expression.

Expressions with parentheses that look like this ( ) contain either numerical substitutions or expressions that are part of a numerical expression. Once a single number appears within these parentheses, the parentheses are no longer needed and need not be used the next time the entire expression is written.

When two pair of parentheses appear side by side like this ( )( ), it means that the expressions within are to be multiplied.

Sometimes parentheses appear within other parentheses in numerical or algebraic expressions. Regardless of what symbol is used, ( ), { }, or [ ], perform operations in the innermost parentheses first and work outward.

Underlined inequalities show the simplified result.

201. Subtract 2 from both sides of the inequality. $3x + 2 - 2 < 14 - 2$
Simplify the inequality. $3x < 12$
Divide both sides of the inequality by 3. $\frac{3x}{3} < \frac{12}{3}$
Simplify. $\underline{x < 4}$

202. Add 6 to both sides of the inequality. $4x - 6 + 6 > 30 + 6$
Simplify the inequality. $4x > 36$
Divide both sides of the inequality by 4. $\frac{4x}{4} > \frac{36}{4}$
Simplify. $\underline{x > 9}$

203. Multiply both sides of the inequality by $\frac{5}{2}$. $\frac{5}{2}(\frac{2}{5})x \leq \frac{5}{2}(18)$
Simplify. $(\frac{10}{10})x \leq \frac{5}{2}(\frac{18}{1})$
    $(1)x \leq 45$
    $\underline{x \leq 45}$

204. Subtract 26 from both sides of the inequality. $4x + 26 - 26 \geq 90 - 26$
Simplify. $4x \geq 64$
Divide both sides of the inequality by 4. $\frac{4x}{4} \geq \frac{64}{4}$
Simplify the inequality. $\underline{x \geq 16}$

205. Subtract 8 from both sides of the inequality. $8 - 8 - 6x < 50 - 8$
Simplify the inequality. $^-6x < 42$
Divide both sides of the inequality by $^-6$ and
     change the direction of the inequality sign. $\frac{^-6x}{^-6} > \frac{42}{^-6}$
Simplify. $\underline{x > {}^-7}$

206. Add 10 to both sides of the inequality.

Combine like terms on each side of the inequality.

Divide both sides of the inequality by 3.

Simplify.

$3x - 10 + 10 \leq -3 + 10$

$3x \leq 7$

$\frac{3x}{3} \leq \frac{7}{3}$

$x \leq \frac{7}{3}$

$x \leq 2\frac{1}{3}$

207. Subtract 0.29 from both sides of the inequality.

Combine like terms on each side of the inequality.

Divide both sides of the inequality by 2.

Simplify the inequality.

$2x + 0.29 - 0.29 > 0.79 - 0.29$

$2x > 0.50$

$\frac{2x}{2} > \frac{0.50}{2}$

$x > 0.25$

208. Divide both sides of the inequality by ⁻6 and change the direction of the inequality sign.

Simplify the expressions.

Subtract 1 from both sides of the inequality.

Simplify.

$\frac{^-6(x + 1)}{^-6} \leq \frac{60}{^-6}$

$x + 1 \leq {^-10}$

$x + 1 - 1 \leq {^-10} - 1$

$x \leq {^-11}$

209. Use the distributive property of multiplication.

Simplify.

Add 15x to both sides of the inequality.

Combine like terms on each side of the inequality.

Add 116 to both sides of the inequality.

Simplify the inequality.

Divide both sides of the inequality by 16.

Simplify.

$3(4) - 3(5x) < x - 116$

$12 - 15x < x - 116$

$12 - 15x + 15x < x + 15x - 116$

$12 < 16x - 116$

$12 + 116 < 16x - 116 + 116$

$128 < 16x$

$\frac{128}{16} < \frac{16x}{16}$

$8 < x$

210. Use the distributive property of
multiplication.

$4(x) + 4(1) < 5(x) + 5(2)$

Simplify.

$4x + 4 < 5x + 10$

Subtract 4 from both sides of the
inequality.

$4x + 4 - 4 < 5x + 10 - 4$

Combine like terms on each side
of the inequality.

$4x < 5x + 6$

Subtract $5x$ from both sides of
the inequality.

$4x - 5x < 5x - 5x + 6$

Simplify the inequality.

$^-x < 6$

Multiply both sides of the equation
by $^-1$ and change the direction of the
inequality sign.

$^-1(^-x) > ^-1(6)$

Simplify.

$\underline{x > \,^-6}$

211. Use the distributive property of
multiplication.

$2(7x) - 2(3) \geq \,^-2(5) - 2(3x)$

Simplify the expressions.

$14x - 6 \geq \,^-10 - 6x$

Add $6x$ to both sides of the inequality.

$14x + 6x - 6 \geq \,^-10 - 6x + 6x$

Combine like terms.

$20x - 6 \geq -10$

Add 6 to both sides of the inequality.

$20x - 6 + 6 \geq \,^-10 + 6$

Simplify.

$20x \geq \,^-4$

Divide both sides of the inequality
by 20.

$\frac{20x}{20} \geq \,^-\frac{4}{20}$

Simplify.

$x \geq \,^-\frac{4}{20}$

Reduce the fraction to lowest terms.

$\underline{x \geq \frac{^-1}{5}}$

212. Use the distributive property of
multiplication.

$16x - 1 < 4(6) - 4(x)$

Simplify.

$16x - 1 < 24 - 4x$

Add 1 to both sides of the inequality.

$16x - 1 + 1 < 1 + 24 - 4x$

Combine like terms.

$16x < 25 - 4x$

Add $4x$ to both sides of the
inequality.

$16x + 4x < 25 - 4x + 4x$

Combine like terms on each side
of the inequality.

$20x < 25$

Divide both sides of the
inequality by 20.

$\frac{20x}{20} < \frac{25}{20}$

Simplify and express the fraction
in simplest terms.

$\underline{x < 1\frac{1}{4}}$

213. Multiply both sides of the
inequality by 0.2.

$0.2(\frac{^-x}{0.2}) \leq 0.2(20)$

Simplify the expressions
on both sides.

$^-x \leq 4$

Multiply both sides of the inequality by $^-1$ and change the direction of the inequality sign.

$^-1(-x) \geq ^-1(4)$

Simplify the expressions.

$x \geq ^-4$

214. Add 5 to both sides of the inequality.

$\frac{4}{3}x - 5 + 5 > x - 2 + 5$

Simplify.

$\frac{4}{3}x > x + 3$

Subtract $1x$ from both sides of the inequality.

$\frac{4}{3}x - x > x - x + 3$

$\frac{4}{3}x - \frac{3}{3}x > x - x + 3$

Simplify the expressions.

$\frac{1}{3}x > 3$

Multiply both sides of the inequality by 3.

$3(\frac{1}{3}x) > 3(3)$

$\frac{3}{1}(\frac{1}{3}x) > 3 (3)$

Simplify the expressions.

$x > 9$

215. Use the distributive property of multiplication.

$3x + 5 \geq ^-2(x) - 2(10)$

Simplify.

$3x + 5 \geq ^-2x - 20$

Subtract 5 from both sides of the inequality.

$3x + 5 - 5 \geq ^-2x - 20 \; ^-5$

Combine like terms on each side of the inequality.

$3x \geq ^-2x - 25$

Add $2x$ to both sides of the inequality.

$3x + 2x \geq 2x - 2x - 25$

Combine like terms.

$5x \geq ^-25$

Divide both sides of the inequality by 5.

$\frac{5x}{5} \geq \frac{^-25}{5}$

Simplify.

$x \geq -5$

216. Use the distributive property of multiplication.

$^-4x + 3(x) + 3(5) \geq 3(x) + 3(2)$

Simplify.

$^-4x + 3x + 15 \geq 3x + 6$

Combine like terms.

$(^-4x + 3x) + 15 \geq 3x + 6$

Simplify.

$-x + 15 \geq 3x + 6$

Add x to both sides of the inequality.

$x - x + 15 \geq x + 3x + 6$

Combine like terms.

$15 \geq 4x + 6$

Subtract 6 from both sides of the inequality.

$15 - 6 \geq 4x + 6 - 6$

Simplify.

$9 \geq 4x$

Divide both sides of the inequality by 4.

$\frac{9}{4} \geq \frac{4x}{4}$

Simplify.

$\frac{9}{4} \geq x$

Express the fraction in its simplest form.

$2\frac{1}{4} \geq x$

217. You can simplify equations (and inequalities) with fractions by multiplying them by a common multiple of the denominators.

Multiply both sides of the inequality by 4.

$$4(x - \tfrac{3}{4}) < 4(\tfrac{-3}{4}(x + 2))$$

Use the distributive property of multiplication.

$$4(x) - 4(\tfrac{3}{4}) < 4(\tfrac{-3}{4})(x + 2)$$

Simplify the expressions.

$$4x - 3 < {}^-3(x + 2)$$

Use the distributive property of multiplication.

$$4x - 3 < {}^-3(x)\,{}^-3(2)$$

Simplify.

$$4x - 3 < {}^-3x - 6$$

Add 3 to both sides of the inequality.

$$4x - 3 + 3 < {}^-3x - 6 + 3$$

Combine like terms.

$$4x < -3x - 3$$

Add $3x$ to both sides of the equation.

$$3x + 4x < 3x - 3x - 3$$

Combine like terms.

$$7x < {}^-3$$

Divide both sides of the inequality by 7.

$$\tfrac{7x}{7} < \tfrac{-3}{7}$$

Sure, you have a fraction for an answer, but it can be easier to operate with whole numbers until the last step.

Simplify the expressions.

$$\underline{x < \tfrac{-3}{7}}$$

218. Subtract 0.1 from both sides of the inequality.

$$\tfrac{3}{2}x + 0.1 - 0.1 \geq 0.9 - 0.1 + x$$

Combine like terms on each side of the inequality.

$$\tfrac{3}{2}x \geq 0.8 + x$$

Subtract x from both sides of the inequality.

$$\tfrac{3}{2}x - x \geq 0.8 + x - x$$

Simplify.

$$\tfrac{1}{2}x \geq 0.8$$

Multiply both sides of the inequality by 2.

$$2(\tfrac{1}{2}x) \geq 2(0.8)$$

Simplify the expressions.

$$\underline{x \geq 1.6}$$

219. Change the term to an improper fraction.

$$x - \tfrac{13}{3} < 9 + \tfrac{2}{3}x$$

Multiply both sides of the inequality by 3.

$$3(x - \tfrac{13}{3}) < 3(9 + \tfrac{2}{3}x)$$

Use the distributive property of multiplication.

$$3(x) - 3(\tfrac{13}{3}) < 3(9) + 3(\tfrac{2}{3}x)$$

Simplify the terms.

$$3x - 13 < 27 + 2x$$

Add 13 to both sides of the inequality.

$$3x - 13 + 13 < 13 + 27 + 2x$$

Combine like terms and simplify.

$$3x < 40 + 2x$$

Subtract $2x$ from both sides of the inequality.

$$3x - 2x < 40 + 2x - 2x$$

Simplify.

$$\underline{x < 40}$$

220. Use the distributive property of
multiplication.

Simplify the terms.

Add 14 to both sides of the inequality.

Simplify by combining like terms.

Add $5x$ to both sides of the inequality.

Simplify the terms.

Divide both sides of the inequality by $^-2$
and change the direction of the
inequality sign.

Simplify the expressions.

$^-7(x) - 7(2) < ^-5x$

$^-7x - 14 < ^-5x$

$^-7x - 14 + 14 < ^-5x + 14$

$^-7x < ^-5x + 14$

$^-7x + 5x < 5x \; ^-5x + 14$

$^-2x < 14$

$\frac{^-2x}{^-2} > \frac{14}{^-2}$

$x > ^-7$

221. Use the distributive property of
multiplication.

Simplify the terms.

Combine like terms.
Subtract $\frac{1}{2}x$ from both sides of the
inequality.

Combine like terms.
Subtract 5 from both sides of the
inequality.

Simplify.
Multiply both sides by $\frac{4}{3}$
(the reciprocal of $\frac{3}{4}$).

Simplify the expressions.

$\frac{5}{4}(x) + \frac{5}{4}(4) > \frac{1}{2}(x) + \frac{1}{2}(8) - 8$

$\frac{5}{4}x + 5 > \frac{1}{2}x + 4 - 8$

$\frac{5}{4}x + 5 > \frac{1}{2}x - 4$

$\frac{5}{4}x \; \frac{1}{2}x \; | \; 5 > \frac{1}{2}x - \frac{1}{2}x - 4$

$\frac{3}{4}x + 5 > ^-4$

$\frac{3}{4}x + 5 - 5 > 4 - 5$

$\frac{3}{4}x > 9$

$\frac{4}{3}(\frac{3}{4}x) > \frac{4}{3}(^-9)$

$x > ^-12$

222. Use the distributive property of
multiplication.

Simplify terms.

Add $9x$ to both sides.

Combine like terms.

Add 81 to both sides of the inequality.

Combine like terms.

Divide both sides of the inequality by 6.

Simplify.

$3(1) \quad 3(3x) \geq ^-3(x) - 3(27)$

$3 - 9x \geq ^-3x - 81$

$3 - 9x + 9x \geq 9x \quad 3x \quad 81$

$3 \geq 6x - 81$

$3 + 81 \geq 6x - 81 + 81$

$84 \geq 6x$

$\frac{84}{6} \geq \frac{6x}{6}$

$14 \geq x$

223. Remove the inner brackets, use the
commutative property of addition and
combine like terms.

$$^-5[9 + x - 4] \geq 2(13 - x)$$
$$^-5[x + 9 - 4] \geq 2(13 - x)$$
$$^-5[x + 5] \geq 2(13 - x)$$

Use the distributive property of
multiplication.

$$^-5[x]\ ^-5[5] \geq 2(13) - 2(x)$$

Simplify terms.

$$^-5x - 25 \geq 26 - 2x$$

Add $5x$ to both sides of the inequality.

$$5x - 5x - 25 \geq 26 - 2x + 5x$$

Combine like terms.

$$^-25 \geq 26 + 3x$$

Subtract 26 from both sides of
the inequality.

$$^-25 - 26 \geq 26 - 26 + 3x$$

Combine like terms.

$$^-51 \geq 3x$$

Divide both sides of the inequality by 3.

$$\frac{^-51}{3} \geq \frac{3x}{3}$$

Simplify terms.

$$\underline{-17 \geq x}$$

224. Use the distributive property of
multiplication.

$$11(1) - 11(x) \geq 3(3) - 3(x) - 1$$

Simplify terms.

$$11 - 11x \geq 9 - 3x - 1$$

Use the commutative property.

$$11 - 11x \geq 9 - 1 - 3x$$

Combine like terms.

$$11 - 11x \geq 8 - 3x$$

Subtract 8 from both sides of
the inequality.

$$11 - 8 - 11x \geq 8 - 8 - 3x$$

Combine like terms.

$$3 - 11x \geq\ - 3x$$

Add $11x$ to both sides.

$$3 - 11x + 11x \geq\ - 3x + 11x$$

Combine like terms.

$$3 \geq 8x$$

Divide both sides by 8.

$$\frac{3}{8} \geq \frac{8x}{8}$$

Simplify.

$$\underline{\frac{3}{8} \geq x}$$

225. Use the distributive property of
multiplication.

$$3(x) - 3(16) - 2 < 9(x) - 9(2) - 7x$$

Simplify terms.

$$3x - 48 - 2 < 9x - 18 - 7x$$

Use the commutative property
to associate like terms.

$$3x - 48 - 2 < 9x - 7x - 18$$

Simplify terms.

$$3x - 50 < 2x - 18$$

Add 50 to both sides of the
inequality.

$$3x - 50 + 50 < 2x - 18 + 50$$

Combine like terms.

$$3x < 2x + 32$$

Subtract $2x$ from both sides of
the inequality.

$$3x - 2x < 2x - 2x + 32$$

Combine like terms.

$$\underline{x < 32}$$

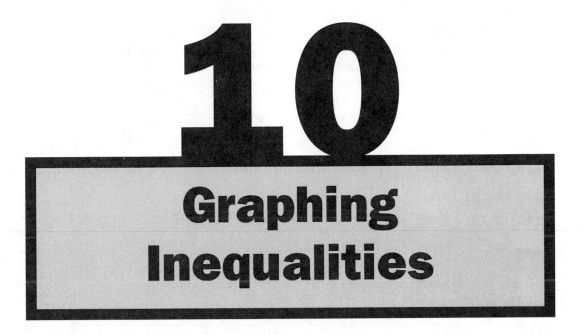

10

Graphing Inequalities

In this chapter, you will practice graphing inequalities that have one or two variables. When there is only one variable, you use a number line. When there are two variables, you use a coordinate plane.

Tips for Graphing Inequalities

When using a number line to show the solution graph for an inequality, use a solid circle on the number line as the endpoint when the inequality symbol is ≤ or ≥. When the inequality symbol is < or >, use an open circle to show the endpoint. A solid circle shows that the solution graph includes the endpoint; an open circle shows that the solution graph does not include the endpoint.

When there are two variables, use a coordinate plane to graph the solution. Use the skills you have been practicing in the previous chapters to transform the inequality into the slope/y-intercept form you used to graph equalities with two variables. Use the slope and the y-intercept of the transformed inequality to show the boundary line for your solution graph. Draw a solid line when the inequality symbol is ≤ or ≥. Draw a dotted line when the inequality symbol is < or >. To complete the graph, shade the region above the boundary line when the inequality symbol is > or ≥. Shade the region below the boundary line when the inequality symbol is < or ≤.

A simple way to check your graphic solution is to pick a point on either side of the boundary line and substitute the x and y values in your inequality. If the result is a true statement, then you have shaded the correct side of the boundary line. An easy point to use, if it is not your y-intercept, is the origin (0, 0).

Graph the following inequalities on a number line.

226. $x \geq 4$

227. $x < {}^-1$

228. $x \leq 6$

229. $x > 5$

230. $x > {}^-1$

Graph the following inequalities on a coordinate plane. (Use graph paper.)

231. $y > x + 1$

232. $y \geq -x + 2$

233. $y > 4x - 5$

234. $\frac{1}{2}x + y \leq 3$

235. $2y - 3x < 8$

236. $y + 2 \leq 3x + 5$

237. $3x - 4 > 2y$

238. $\frac{3}{4}y + 6 \geq 3x$

239. $0.5y - x + 3 > 0$

240. $x - y \leq 7$

241. $\frac{y}{3} < \frac{2}{3} - x$

242. ${}^-3y + 9x \leq -6$

243. $0.5x > 0.3\,y - 0.9$

244. $3x - y \leq 7x + y - 8$

245. $3y + 4x < 9 - x$

246. ${}^-12 \leq -3(x + y)$

247. $9y + 7 \geq 2(x + 8)$

248. $\frac{x}{3} + y \leq 3x - 5$

249. $2(y + 3) - x \geq 6(1 - x)$

250. ${}^-28y \geq 2x - 14(y + 10)$

Answers

Numerical expressions in parentheses like this [ ] are operations performed on only part of the original expression. The operations performed within these symbols are intended to show how to evaluate the various terms that make up the entire expression.

Expressions with parentheses that look like this ( ) contain either numerical substitutions or expressions that are part of a numerical expression. Once a single number appears within these parentheses, the parentheses are no longer needed and need not be used the next time the entire expression is written.

When two pair of parentheses appear side by side like this ( )( ), it means that the expressions within are to be multiplied.

Sometimes parentheses appear within other parentheses in numerical or algebraic expressions. Regardless of what symbol is used, ( ), { }, or [ ], perform operations in the innermost parentheses first and work outward.

The answers to these questions are the graphs.

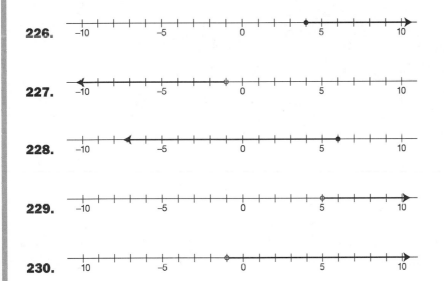

226.

227.

228.

229.

230.

231. The inequality is in the proper
    slope/y-intercept form. $m = 1 = \frac{1}{1} = \frac{\text{change in } y}{\text{change in } x}$

$b = 1$.   The y-intercept is at the point (0,1).

A change in y of 1 and in x of 1
    gives the point $(0 + 1, 1 + 1)$ or (1,2).

Draw a dotted boundary line and shade above it.

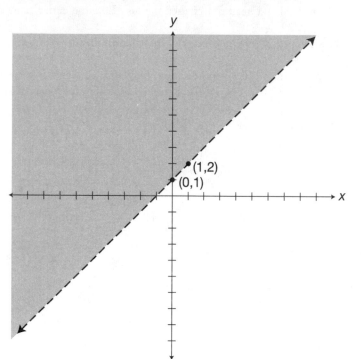

232. The inequality is in the proper slope/y-intercept form.

$m = {}^-1 = \frac{{}^-1}{1} = \frac{\text{change in } y}{\text{change in } x}$

$b = 2$.

The y-intercept is at the point $(0,2)$.

A change in y of $^-1$ and in x of 1 gives the point

$(0 + 1, 2 - 1)$ or $(1,1)$.

Draw a solid boundary line and shade above it.

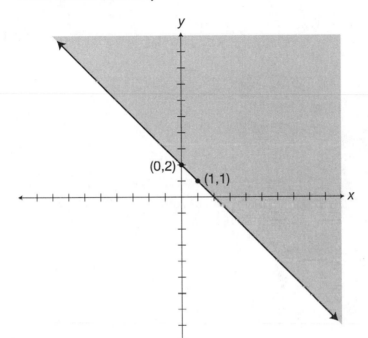

233. The inequality is in the proper
slope/y-intercept form.

$m = 4 = \frac{4}{1} = \frac{\text{change in } y}{\text{change in } x}$

$b = {}^-5$.

The y-intercept is at the point $(0, {}^-5)$.

A change in y of 4 and in x of 1
gives the point

$(0 + 1, {}^-5 + 4)$ or $(1, {}^-1)$.

Draw a dotted boundary line and shade above it.

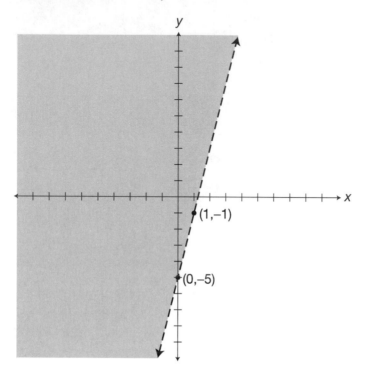

234. Subtract $\frac{1}{2}x$ from both sides
    of the inequality.

$\frac{1}{2}x - \frac{1}{2}x + y \le -\frac{1}{2}x + 3$

Combine like terms.

$y \le -\frac{1}{2}x + 3$

The inequality is in the proper
    slope/y-intercept form.

$m = \frac{^{-}1}{2} = \frac{\text{change in } y}{\text{change in } x}$

$b = 3$.

The y-intercept is at the point $(0,3)$.

A change in y of $^{-}1$ and in x of 2
    gives the point

$(0 + 2, 3 - 1)$ or $(2,2)$.

Draw a solid boundary line and shade below it.

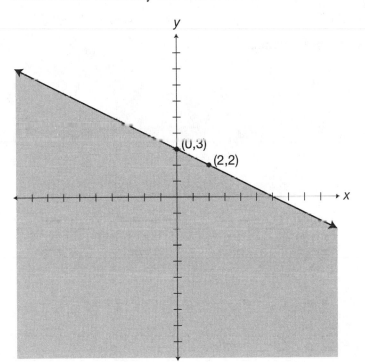

235. Add $3x$ to both sides
    of the inequality. $2y - 3x + 3x < 3x + 8$
   Combine like terms. $2y < 3x + 8$
   Divide both sides
    of the inequality by 2. $\frac{2y}{2} < \frac{3x}{2} + \frac{8}{2}$

   Simplify terms. $y < \frac{3}{2}x + 4$
   The inequality is in the proper
    slope/y-intercept form. $m = \frac{3}{2} = \frac{\text{change in } y}{\text{change in } x}$
   $b = 4.$ The y-intercept is at the point (0,4).
   A change in y of 3 and in x of 2
    gives the point   (0 + 2,4 + 3) or (2,7).

Draw a dotted boundary line and shade below it.

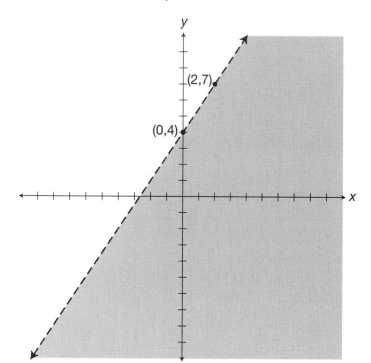

236. Subtract 2 from both
  sides of the inequality. $y + 2 - 2 \leq 3x + 5 - 2$
  Combine like terms. $y \leq 3x + 3$
  The inequality is in the proper
  slope/y-intercept form. $m = 3 = \frac{3}{1} = \frac{\text{change in } y}{\text{change in } x}$
  $b = 3$.   The y-intercept is at the point (0,3).
  A change in y of 3 and in x of 1
  gives the point   (0 + 1, 3 + 3) or (1,6).

Draw a solid boundary line and shade below it.

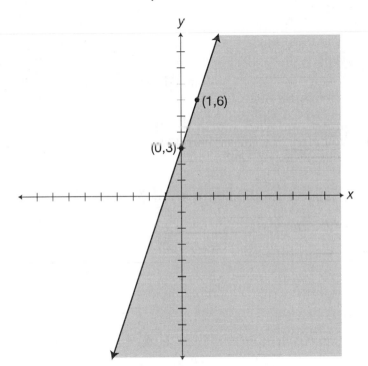

237. In an equation, if $c = d$, then $d = c$.
But for an inequality, the
direction of the inequality
symbol must change when
you change sides of the statement.
If $c > d$, then $d < c$. Rewrite the
inequality with sides exchanged
and the symbol reversed. $2y < 3x - 4$

Divide both sides

of the inequality by 2. $\frac{2y}{2} < \frac{3x}{2} - \frac{4}{2}$
Simplify terms. $y < \frac{3}{2}x - 2$
The inequality is in the proper
slope/y-intercept form. $m = \frac{3}{2} = \frac{\text{change in } y}{\text{change in } x}$

$b = {}^-2$.   The y-intercept is at the point $(0,{}^-2)$.
A change in y of 3 and in x of 2
gives the point $(0 + 2, {}^-2 + 3)$ or $(2,1)$.

Draw a dotted boundary line and shade below it.

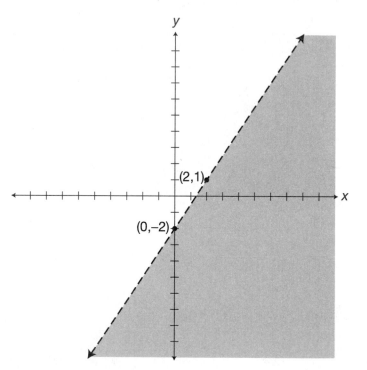

238.

Subtract 6 from both sides of the inequality.	$\frac{3}{4}y + 6 - 6 \geq 3x - 6$

Combine like terms. $\frac{3}{4}y \geq 3x - 6$

Multiply both sides of the inequality by the reciprocal $\frac{4}{3}$. $\frac{4}{3}(\frac{3}{4}y) \geq \frac{4}{3}(3x - 6)$

Use the distributive property of multiplication. $\frac{4}{3}(\frac{3}{4}y) \geq \frac{4}{3}(3x) - \frac{4}{3}(6)$

Simplify terms. $y \geq 4x - 8$

The inequality is in the proper slope/y-intercept form. $m = \frac{4}{1} = \frac{\text{change in } y}{\text{change in } x}$

$b = {}^-8.$ The y-intercept is at the point $(0, 8)$.

A change in y of 4 and in x of 1 gives the point $(0 + 1, {}^-8 + 4)$ or $(1, {}^-4)$.

Draw a solid boundary line and shade above it.

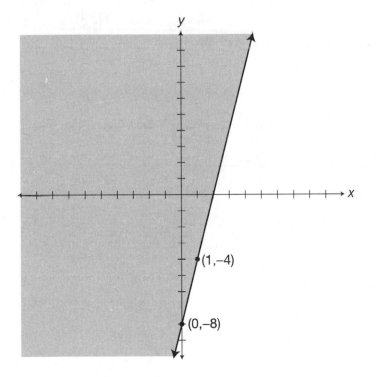

239.

Subtract 3 from both sides of the inequality.	$0.5y - x + 3 - 3 > 0 - 3$
Combine like terms on each side of the inequality.	$0.5y - x > -3$
Add $1x$ to both sides of the inequality.	$0.5y + x - x > x - 3$
Combine like terms.	$0.5y > x - 3$
Divide both sides of the inequality by 0.5.	$\frac{0.5y}{0.5} > \frac{x}{0.5} - \frac{3}{0.5}$
Simplify the expressions.	$y > \frac{x}{0.5} - \frac{3}{0.5}$
Simplify terms.	$y > 2x - 6$
The inequality is in the proper slope/y-intercept form.	$m = 2 = \frac{2}{1} = \frac{\text{change in } y}{\text{change in } x}$
$b = {}^{-}6$.	The y-intercept is at the point $(0, {}^{-}6)$.
A change in y of 2 and in x of 1 gives the point	$(0 + 1, {}^{-}6 + 2)$ or $(1, {}^{-}4)$.

Draw a dotted boundary line and shade above it.

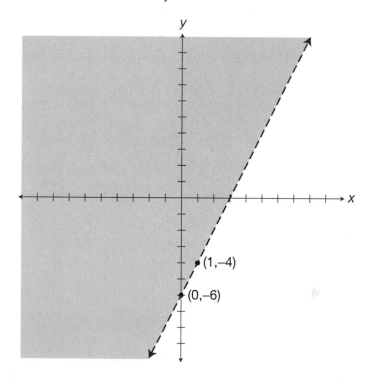

240. Subtract x from both sides of the inequality.

$x - y - x \leq 7 - x$

Use the commutative property of addition to associate like terms.

$x - x - y \leq 7 - x$

Simplify the expression.

$-y \leq 7 - x$

Multiply both sides of the inequality by $^-1$ and change the direction of the inequality symbol.

$(^-1)(^-y) \geq (^-1)(7 - x)$

Use the distributive property of multiplication.

$(^-1)(^-y) \geq (^-1)(7) - (^-1)(x)$

Simplify terms.

$y \geq {}^-7 + x$

Use the commutative property of addition.

$y \geq x - 7$

The inequality is in the proper slope/y-intercept form.

$m = 1 = \frac{1}{1} = \frac{\text{change in } y}{\text{change in } x}$

$b = {}^-7$.

The y-intercept is at the point $(0,{}^-7)$.

A change in y of 1 and in x of 1 gives the point

$(0 + 1, {}^-7 + 1)$ or $(1, {}^-6)$.

Draw a solid boundary line and shade above it.

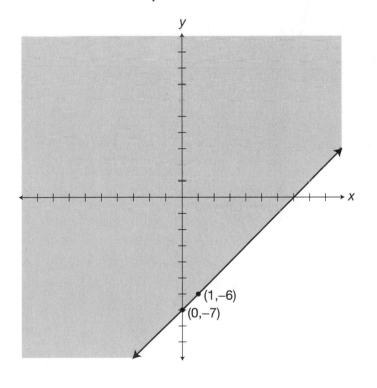

(1,–6)

(0,–7)

241. Multiply both sides of the inequality
　　by 3.　　　　　　　　　　　　　$3(\frac{y}{3}) < 3(\frac{2}{3} - x)$

Use the distributive property of
　　multiplication.　　　　　　　$3(\frac{y}{3}) < 3(\frac{2}{3}) - 3(x)$

Simplify terms.　　　　　　　$y < 2 - 3x$

Use the commutative property
　　of addition.　　　　　　　$y < {}^-3x + 2$

The inequality is in the proper
　　slope/y-intercept form.　　　$m = {}^-3 = \frac{{}^-3}{1} = \frac{\text{change in } y}{\text{change in } x}$

$b = 2.$　　　　　　　　　　The y-intercept is at the point (0,2).

A change in y of $^-3$ and in x of 1
　　gives the point　　　　　　$(0 + 1, 2 - 3)$ or $(1, {}^-1).$

Draw a dotted boundary line and shade below it.

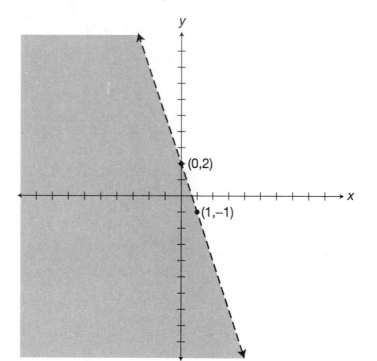

242. Subtract $9x$ from both sides
   of the inequality.

   $^-3y + 9x - 9x \leq ^-6 - 9x$

   Combine like terms.

   $^-3y \leq ^-6 - 9x$

   Divide both sides of the inequality
   by $^-3$ and change the direction
   of the inequality symbol.

   $\frac{^-3y}{^-3} \geq \frac{^-6}{^-3} - \frac{9x}{^-3}$

   Simplify the terms.

   $y \geq \frac{^-6}{^-3} - \left(\frac{9x}{^-3}\right)$

   $y \geq 2 \; ^-(^-3x)$
   $y \geq 2 + 3x$

   Use the commutative property
   of addition.

   $y \geq 3x + 2$

   The inequality is in the proper
   slope/y-intercept form.

   $m = 3 = \frac{3}{1} = \frac{\text{change in } y}{\text{change in } x}$

   $b = 2$.

   The y-intercept is at the point (0,2).

   A change in y of 3 and in x of 1
   gives the point

   $(0 + 1, 2 + 3)$ or $(1,5)$.

   Draw a solid boundary line and shade above it.

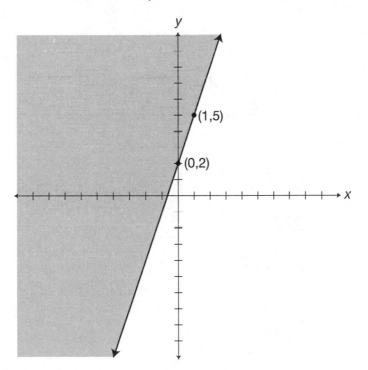

243. Subtract 0.3y from both sides of
the inequality. $\qquad$ $0.5x - 0.3y > 0.3y - 0.3y - 0.9$

Combine like terms. $\qquad$ $0.5x - 0.3y > {}^-0.9$

Subtract 0.5x from both sides
of the inequality. $\qquad$ $0.5x - 0.5x - 0.3y > {}^-0.5x - 0.9$

Combine like terms. $\qquad$ ${}^-0.3y > {}^-0.5x - 0.9$

Divide both sides of the inequality
by $^-0.3$ and change the direction
of the inequality symbol. $\qquad$ $\frac{{}^-0.3y}{{}^-0.3} < {}^-0.5x - \frac{0.9}{{}^-0.3}$

Simplify the expression. $\qquad$ $-\frac{0.3y}{{}^-0.3} < (\frac{{}^-0.5x}{{}^-0.3}) - (\frac{0.9}{{}^-0.3})$

Simplify the terms. $\qquad$ $y < \frac{5}{3}x - ({}^-3)$

Subtracting a negative number is
the same as adding a positive. $\qquad$ $y < \frac{5}{3}x + 3$

The inequality is in the proper
slope/y-intercept form. $\qquad$ $m = \frac{5}{3} = \frac{\text{change in } y}{\text{change in } x}$

$b = 3$. $\qquad$ The y-intercept is at the point (0,3).

A change in y of 3 and in x of 1
gives the point $\qquad$ $(0 + 3, 3 + 5)$ or (3,8).

Draw a dotted boundary line and shade below it.

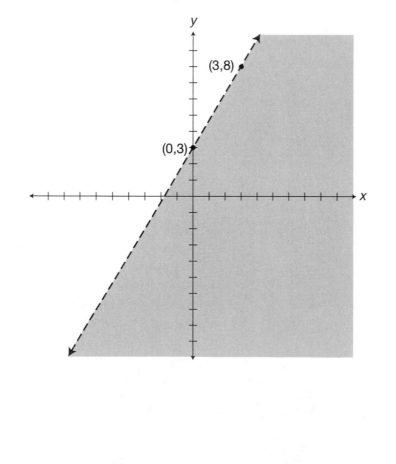

244. Subtract $3x$ from both sides
    of the inequality. $3x - 3x - y \leq 7x - 3x + y - 8$
Combine like terms. $^-y \leq 4x + y - 8$
Subtract y from both sides of the
    inequality. $^-y - y \leq 4x + y - y - 8$
Combine like terms. $^-2y \leq 4x - 8$
Divide both sides of the inequality
    by $^-2$ and change the direction
    of the inequality symbol. $\frac{^-2y}{^-2} \geq \frac{4x - 8}{^-2}$

                                 $y \geq \frac{4x}{^-2} - (\frac{8}{^-2})$
Simplify terms. $y \geq -2x - (^-4)$
Simplify. $y \geq {}^-2x + 4$
The inequality is in the proper
    slope/y-intercept form. $m = {}^-2 = \frac{^-2}{1} = \frac{\text{change in } y}{\text{change in } x}$

$b = 4$.   The y-intercept is at the point (0,4).
A change in y of $^-2$ and in x of 1
    gives the point $(0 + 1, 4 - 2)$ or $(1,2)$.

Draw a solid boundary line and shade above it.

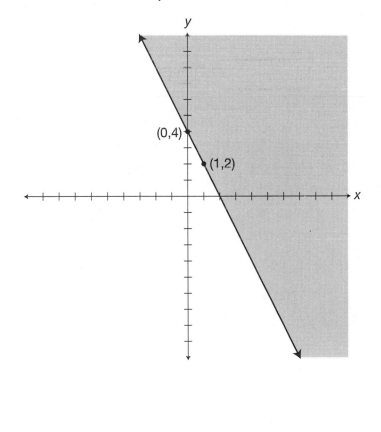

245. Subtract $4x$ from both sides of the inequality.

$$3y + 4x - 4x < 9 - x - 4x$$

Combine like terms.

$$3y < 9 - 5x$$

Divide both sides of the inequality by 3.

$$\frac{3y}{3} < \frac{9}{3} - \frac{5x}{3}$$

Simplify the expressions.

$$y < \left(\frac{9}{3}\right) - \left(\frac{5x}{3}\right)$$

Simplify the terms.

$$y < 3 - \frac{5}{3}x$$

Use the commutative property.

$$y < {}^{-}\frac{5}{3}x + 3$$

The inequality is in the proper slope/y-intercept form.

$$m = \frac{{}^{-}5}{3} = \frac{\text{change in } y}{\text{change in } x}$$

$b = 3$.

The y-intercept is at the point (0,3).

A change in y of $^{-}5$ and in x of 3 gives the point

(0 + 3,3 − 5) or (3,$^{-}$2).

Draw a dotted boundary line and shade below it.

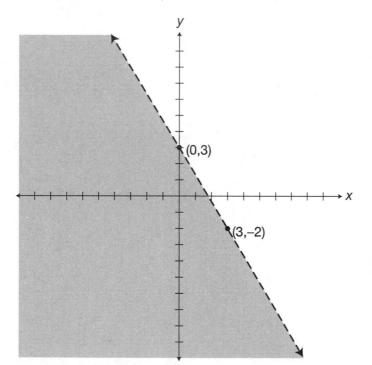

246. Use the distributive property
of multiplication. $\qquad$ $^-12 \le {}^-3x - 3y$
Add $3y$ to both sides of the
inequality. $\qquad$ $3y - 12 \le {}^-3x \; {}^-3y + 3y$
Combine like terms. $\qquad$ $3y - 12 \le {}^-3x$
Add 12 to both sides of the
inequality. $\qquad$ $3y - 12 + 12 \le {}^-3x + 12$
Combine like terms. $\qquad$ $3y \le {}^-3x + 12$
Divide both sides of the
inequality by 3. $\qquad$ $\frac{3y}{3} \le \frac{^-3x}{3} + \frac{12}{3}$
Simplify the expressions. $\qquad$ $y \le -x + 4$
The inequality is in the proper
slope/y-intercept form. $\qquad$ $m = {}^-1 = \frac{^-1}{1} = \frac{\text{change in } y}{\text{change in } x}$
$b = 4.$ $\qquad$ The y-intercept is at the point $(0,4)$.
A change in y of $^-1$ and in x of 1
gives the point $\qquad$ $(0 + 1, 4 - 1)$ or $(1,3)$.

Draw a solid boundary line and shade below it.

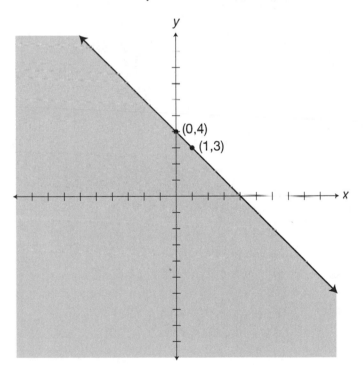

247. Use the distributive property
of multiplication. $\qquad$ $9y + 7 \geq 2x + 16$

Subtract 7 from both sides of
the inequality. $\qquad$ $9y + 7 - 7 \geq 2x + 16 - 7$

Combine like terms. $\qquad$ $9y \geq 2x + 9$

Divide both sides of the
inequality by 9. $\qquad$ $\frac{9y}{9} \geq \frac{2x}{9} + \frac{9}{9}$

Simplify the expressions. $\qquad$ $y \geq \frac{2}{9}x + 1$

The inequality is in the proper
slope/y-intercept form. $\qquad$ $m = \frac{2}{9} = \frac{\text{change in } y}{\text{change in } x}$

$b = 1$. $\qquad$ The y-intercept is at the point (0,1).

A change in y of 2 and in x of 9
gives the point $\qquad$ $(0 + 9, 1 + 2)$ or $(9,3)$.

Draw a solid boundary line and shade above it.

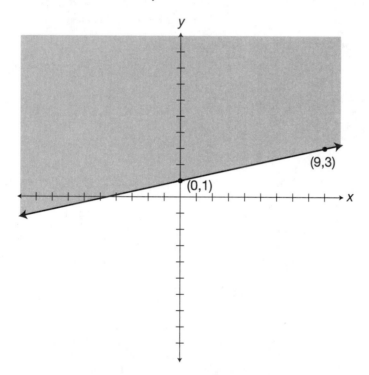

248. Multiply both sides of the inequality by 3.

$$3(\tfrac{x}{3} + y) \le 3(3x - 5)$$

Use the distributive property of multiplication.

$$3(\tfrac{x}{3}) + 3(y) \le 3(3x) - 3(5)$$

Simplify terms.

$$x + 3y \le 9x - 15$$

Subtract x from both sides of the inequality.

$$x - x + 3y \le 9x - x - 15$$

Combine like terms.

$$3y \le 8x - 15$$

Divide both sides of the inequality by 3.

$$\tfrac{3y}{3} \le \tfrac{8x}{3} - \tfrac{15}{3}$$

Simplify the expressions.

$$y \le \tfrac{8}{3}x - 5$$

The inequality is in the proper slope/y-intercept form.

$$m = \tfrac{8}{3} = \tfrac{\text{change in } y}{\text{change in } x}$$

$b = {}^-5.$

The y-intercept is at the point $(0,{}^-5)$.

A change in y of 8 and in x of 3 gives the point

$(0 + 3, {}^-5 + 8)$ or $(3,3)$.

Draw a solid boundary line and shade below it.

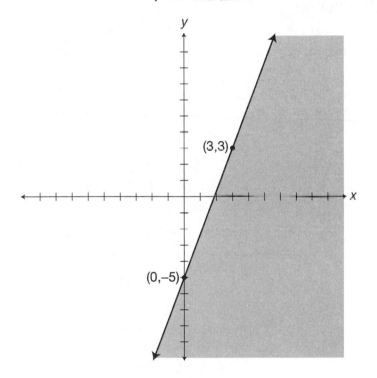

249. Use the distributive property
of multiplication.

$2(y) + 2(3) - x \geq 6(1) - 6(x)$

Simplify terms.

$2y + 6 - x \geq 6 - 6x$

Add x to both sides of the
inequality.

$2y + 6 - x + x \geq 6 - 6x + x$

Combine like terms.

$2y + 6 \geq 6 - 5x$

Subtract 6 from both sides of
the inequality.

$2y + 6 - 6 \geq 6 - 5x - 6$

Use the commutative property
with like terms.

$2y + 6 - 6 \geq 6 - 6 - 5x$

Combine like terms.

$2y \geq -5x$

Divide both sides of the inequality
by 2.

$\frac{2y}{2} \geq \frac{-5x}{2}$

Simplify terms.

$y \geq \frac{-5}{2}x$

The inequality is in the proper
slope/y-intercept form.

$m = \frac{-5}{2} = \frac{\text{change in } y}{\text{change in } x}$

$b = 0$.

The y-intercept is at the point $(0,0)$.

A change in y of $^-5$ and in x of 2
gives the point

$(0 + 2, 0 - 5)$ or $(2, ^-5)$.

Draw a solid boundary line and shade above it.

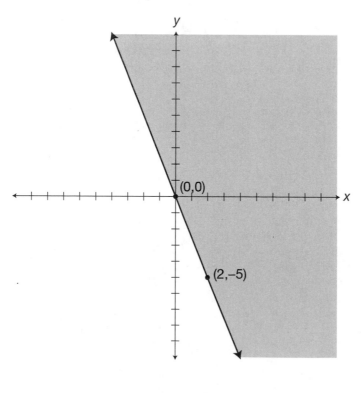

250. Use the distributive property of
multiplication.

$^-28y \geq 2x - 14(y) - 14(10)$

Simplify terms.

$^-28y \geq 2x - 14y - 140$

Add $14y$ to both sides of the
inequality.

$^-28y + 14y \geq 2x - 14y + 14y - 140$

Combine like terms on each side
of the inequality.

$^-14y \geq 2x\ ^-140$

Divide both sides of the inequality
by $^-14$ and change the direction
of the inequality symbol.

$\frac{^-14y}{^-14} \leq \frac{2x}{^-14} - \frac{140}{^-14}$

Simplify the terms.

$y \leq \frac{^-1}{7}x + 10$

The inequality is in the proper
slope/y-intercept form.

$m = \frac{^-1}{7} = \frac{\text{change in } y}{\text{change in } x}$

$b = 10.$

The y-intercept is at the point $(0,10)$.

A change in y of $^-1$ and in x of 7
gives the point

$(0 + 7, 10 - 1)$ or $(7,9)$.

Draw a solid boundary line and shade below it.

Graphing Systems of Linear Equations and Inequalities

This chapter will present fifteen systems of equalities and ten systems of inequalities as practice in finding solutions graphically. You will find complete explanations and graphs in the answer explanations.

Graphing systems of linear equations on the same coordinate plane will give you a solution that is common to both equations. There are three possibilities for a pair of equations:

- The solution will be one coordinate pair at the point of intersection.
- The solution will be all the points on the line graph because the equations coincide.
- There will be no solution if the line graphs have the same slope but different *y*-intercepts. In this case, the lines are parallel and will not intersect.

Pairs of inequalities can also have a common solution. The graphic solution will either be the common areas of the graphs of the inequalities or there will be no solution if the areas do not overlap.

Tips for Graphing Systems of Linear Equations and Inequalities

Transform each equation or inequality into the slope/y-intercept form.

For equations, graph the lines and look for the point or points of intersection. That is the solution.

For inequalities, graph the boundaries as the appropriate dotted or solid line and shade the area for each inequality depending upon the inequality symbol present. The intersection of the shaded areas will be the solution for the system.

When multiplying or dividing by a negative term, change the direction of the inequality symbol for each operation.

Find the solutions for the following systems of equations by graphing on graph paper.

251. $y = x + 2$
$y = -x + 4$

252. $2y - x = 2$
$3x + y = 8$

253. $4y = {}^-7(x + 4)$
$4y = x + 4$

254. $y - x = 5 - x$
${}^-4y = 8 - 7x$

255. $2y = 6x + 14$
$4y = x - 16$

256. $2x + y = 4$
$3(y + 9) = 7x$

257. $y = x + 9$
$4y = 16 - x$

258. $4x - 5y = 5$
$5y = 20 - x$

259. $6y = 9(x - 6)$
$3(2y + 5x) = {}^-6$

260. $15y = 6(3x + 15)$
$y = 6(1 - x)$

261. $3y = 6x + 6$
$5y = 10(x - 5)$

262. $3(2x + 3y) = 63$
$27y = 9(x - 6)$

263. $x - 20 = 5y$
$10y = 8x + 20$

264. $3x + 4y = 12$
$y = 3 - \frac{6}{8}x$

265. $16y = 10(x - 8)$
$8y - 17x = 56$

Find the solution for each of the following systems of inequalities by graphing and shading.

266. $2y - 3x \geq {}^-6$
$y \geq 5 - \frac{5}{2}x$

267. $6y < 5x - 30$
$2y < {}^-x + 4$

268. $y - x \geq 6$
$11y \geq {}^-2(x + 11)$

269. $5y \leq 8(x + 5)$
$5y \leq 12(5 - x)$

270. $2(x + 5y) > 5(x + 6)$
$4x + y < 4x + 5$

271. $3y \geq {}^-2(x + 3)$
$3y \leq 2(6 - x)$

272. $9(y - 4) < 4x$
${}^-9y < 2(x + 9)$

273. $7(y - 5) < {}^-5x$
${}^-3 < \frac{1}{4}(2x - 3y)$

274. $y > \frac{7}{4}(4 - x)$
$3(y + 5) > 7x$

275. $5x - 2(y + 10) \leq 0$
$2x + y \leq {}^-3$

Answers

Numerical expressions in parentheses like this [ ] are operations performed on only part of the original expression. The operations performed within these symbols are intended to show how to evaluate the various terms that make up the entire expression.

Expressions with parentheses that look like this ( ) contain either numerical substitutions or expressions that are part of a numerical expression. Once a single number appears within these parentheses, the parentheses are no longer needed and need not be used the next time the entire expression is written.

When two pair of parentheses appear side by side like this ( )( ), it means that the expressions within are to be multiplied.

Sometimes parentheses appear within other parentheses in numerical or algebraic expressions. Regardless of what symbol is used, ( ), { }, or [ ], perform operations in the innermost parentheses first and work outward.

Underlined ordered pair is the solution. The graph is shown.

251. Transform equations into slope/*y*-intercept form.

$y = x + 2$

The equation is in the proper slope/*y*-intercept form.

$m = 1 = \frac{1}{1} = \frac{\text{change in } y}{\text{change in } x}$

$b = 2$.

The *y*-intercept is at the point (0,2).

The slope tells you to go up 1 space and right 1 for (1,3).

* * * * * * * * * * * *

$y = {}^{-}x + 4$

The equation is in the proper slope/*y*-intercept form.

$m = {}^{-}1 = \frac{{}^{-}1}{1} = \frac{\text{change in } y}{\text{change in } x}$

$b = 4$.

The *y*-intercept is at the point (0,4).

The slope tells you to go down 1 space and right 1 for (1,3).

The solution is (1,3).

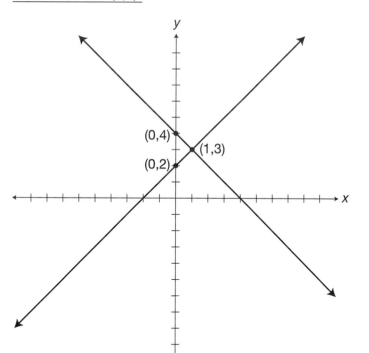

252. Transform equations into
    slope/y-intercept form. $2y - x = 2$
Add x to both sides. $2y - x + x = x + 2$
Combine like terms. $2y = x + 2$

Divide both sides by 2. $y = \frac{1}{2}x + 1$
The equation is in the proper
    slope/y-intercept form. $m = \frac{1}{2} = \frac{\text{change in } y}{\text{change in } x}$
$b = 1$.   The y-intercept is at the point (0,1).
The slope tells you to go up
    1 space and right 2 for (2,2).

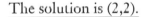

                                 $3x + y = 8$
Subtract $3x$ from both sides. $3x - 3x + y = {}^-3x + 8$
Simplify. $y = {}^-3x + 8$
The equation is in the
    proper slope/y-intercept form. $m = {}^-3 = \frac{{}^-3}{1} = \frac{\text{change in } y}{\text{change in } x}$
$b = 8$.   The y-intercept is at the point (0,8).
The slope tells you to go down
    3 spaces and right 1 for (1,5).

The solution is (2,2).

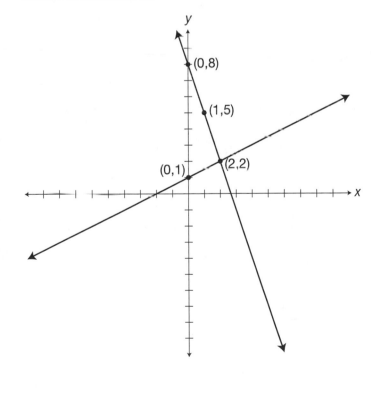

253. Transform equations into
 slope/y-intercept form.

$4y = {}^-7(x + 4)$

Use the distributive property
 of multiplication.

$4y = {}^-7x - 28$

Divide both sides by 4.
The equation is in the proper
 slope/y-intercept form.

$y = \frac{{}^-7}{4}x - 7$

$b = {}^-7$.

$m = \frac{{}^-7}{4} = \frac{\text{change in } y}{\text{change in } x}$

The slope tells you to go down
 7 spaces and right 4 for $(4, {}^-14)$.

The y-intercept is at the point $(0, {}^-7)$.

* * * * * * * * * * * *

$4y = x + 4$

Divide both sides by 4.
The equation is in the proper
 slope/y-intercept form.

$y = \frac{1}{4}x + 1$

$b = 1$.

$m = \frac{1}{4} = \frac{\text{change in } y}{\text{change in } x}$

The slope tells you to go up
 1 space and right 4 for $(4,2)$.

The y-intercept is at the point $(0,1)$.

The solution is $({}^-4,0)$.

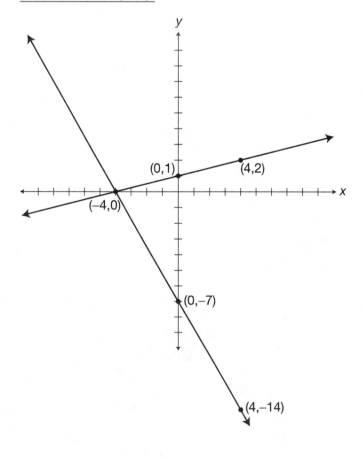

254. Transform equations into
  slope/y-intercept form. $y - x = 5 - x$

Add x to both sides. $y - x + x = 5 - x + x$

Combine like terms on each side. $y = 5$

The graph is a line parallel to
  the x-axis through $(0,5)$.

* * * * * * * * * * * *

$$^{-}4y = 8 - 7x$$

Divide both sides by $^{-}4$. $\frac{^{-}4y}{^{-}4} = \frac{8}{^{-}4} - \frac{7x}{^{-}4}$

Simplify terms. $y = {}^{-}2 + \frac{7}{4}x$

Use the commutative property. $y = \frac{7}{4}x - 2$

The equation is in the proper
  slope/y-intercept form. $m = \frac{7}{4} = \frac{\text{change in } y}{\text{change in } x}$

$b = {}^{-}2$ The y-intercept is at the point $(0,{}^{-}2)$.

The slope tells you to go up
  7 spaces and right 4 for $(4,5)$

The solution is $(4,5)$.

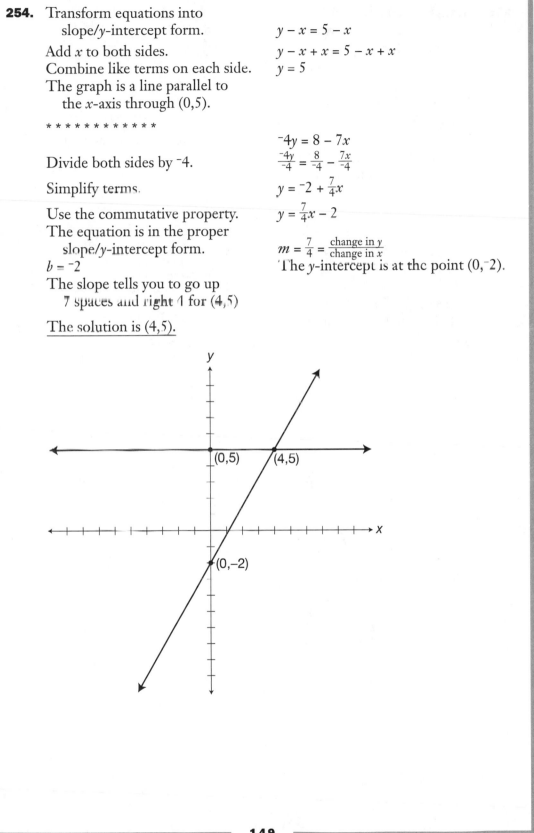

255. Transform equations into
slope/y-intercept form. $2y = 6x + 14$

Divide both sides by 2. $y = \frac{6}{2}x + 7$

The equation is in the proper
slope/y-intercept form.

Use the negatives to keep the
coordinates near the origin. $m = \frac{6}{2} = \frac{-6}{-2} = \frac{\text{change in } y}{\text{change in } x}$

$b = 7$ The y-intercept is at the point (0,7).

The slope tells you to go down
6 spaces and left 2 for (⁻2,1).

* * * * * * * * * * * *

$4y = x - 16$

Divide both sides by 4. $y = \frac{1}{4}x - 4$

The equation is in the proper
slope/y-intercept form. $m = \frac{1}{4} = \frac{\text{change in } y}{\text{change in } x}$

$b = {}^-4$ The y-intercept is at the point (0,⁻4).

The slope tells you to go up
1 space and right 4 for (4,⁻3).

The solution for the system of equations is (⁻4,⁻5).

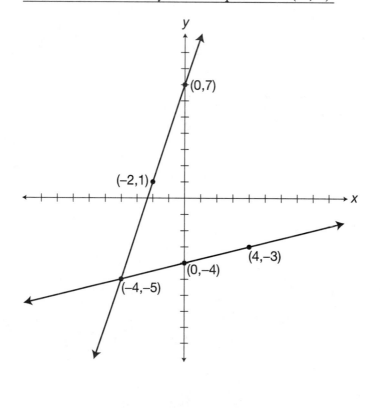

256. Transform equations into
  slope/y-intercept form. $\qquad 2x + y = 4$

Subtract $2x$ from both sides. $\qquad 2x - 2x + y = 4 - 2x$
Combine like terms on each side. $\quad y = 4 - 2x$
Use the commutative property. $\qquad y = {}^-2x + 4$
The equation is in the proper
  slope/y-intercept form. $\qquad m = {}^-2 = \frac{{}^-2}{1} = \frac{\text{change in } y}{\text{change in } x}$
$b = 4$ $\qquad$ The y-intercept is at the point (0,4).
The slope tells you to go down
  2 spaces and right 1 for (1,2).

* * * * * * * * * * * *

$\qquad\qquad\qquad\qquad\qquad 3(y + 9) = 7x$

Distributive property of
  multiplication. $\qquad\qquad 3y + 27 = 7x$
Subtract 27 from both sides. $\qquad 3y + 27 - 27 = 7x - 27$
Simplify. $\qquad\qquad\qquad 3y = 7x - 27$
Divide both sides by 3. $\qquad\qquad y = \frac{7}{3}x - 9$
The equation is in the proper
  slope/y-intercept form.
$b = {}^-9$ $\qquad\qquad m = \frac{7}{3} = \frac{\text{change in } y}{\text{change in } x}$
$\qquad\qquad\qquad$ The y-intercept is at the point (0,$^-$9).
The slope tells you to go up
  7 spaces and right 3 for (3,$^-$2).

The solution for the system of equations is (3,$^-$2).

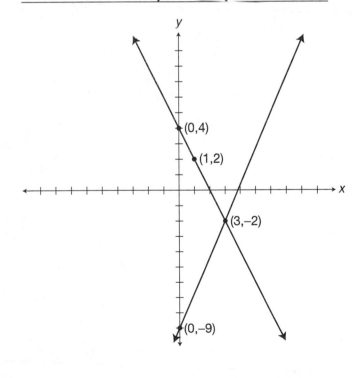

257. Transform equations into
    slope/y-intercept form. $y = x + 9$
The equation is in the proper
    slope/y-intercept form. $m = 1 = \frac{1}{1} = \frac{\text{change in } y}{\text{change in } x}$
$b = 9$ The y-intercept is at the point (0,9).
The slope tells you to go up
    1 space and right 1 for (1,10).

* * * * * * * * * * * *

                              $4y = 16 - x$
Use the commutative property. $4y = {}^-x + 16$

Divide both sides by 4. $y = {}^-\frac{1}{4}x + 4$
The equation is in the proper
    slope/y-intercept form.
$b = 4$ $m = \frac{{}^-1}{4} = \frac{\text{change in } y}{\text{change in } x}$
The slope tells you to go down   The y-intercept is at the point (0,4).
    1 space and right 4 for (4,3).

The solution for the system of equations is ($^-$4,5).

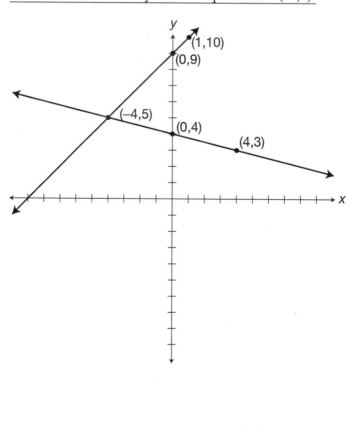

258. Transform equations into slope/y-intercept form. $4x - 5y = 5$

Subtract $4x$ from both sides. $4x - 4x - 5y = 5 - 4x$

Simplify. $^-5y = 5 - 4x$

Use the commutative property. $^-5y = ^-4x + 5$

Divide both sides by $^-5$. $y = \frac{4}{5}x - 1$

The equation is in the proper slope/y-intercept form. $m = \frac{4}{5} = \frac{\text{change in } y}{\text{change in } x}$

$b = ^-1$

The y-intercept is at the point $(0,^-1)$.

The slope tells you to go up 4 spaces and right 5 for $(5,3)$.

* * * * * * * * * * * *

$5y = 20 - x$

Divide both sides by 5. $y = 4 - \frac{1}{5}x$

Use the commutative property. $y = \frac{^-1}{5}x + 4$

The equation is in the proper slope/y-intercept form.

$m = \frac{^-1}{5} = \frac{\text{change in } y}{\text{change in } x}$

$b = 4$

The y-intercept is at the point $(0,4)$.

The slope tells you to go down 1 space and right 5 for $(5,3)$.

The solution for the system of equations is $(5,3)$.

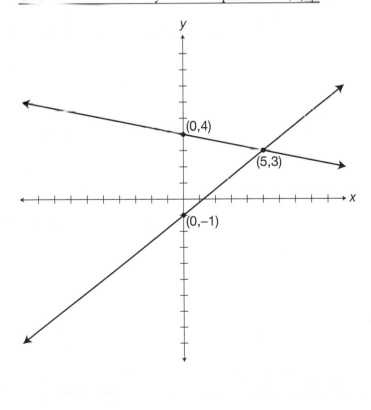

259. Transform equations into slope/y-intercept form.

$6y = 9(x - 6)$

Use the distributive property of multiplication.

$6y = 9x - 54$

Divide both sides by 6.

$y = \frac{9}{6}x - 9$

The equation is in the proper slope/y-intercept form.

$m = \frac{9}{6} = \frac{\text{change in } y}{\text{change in } x}$

$b = {}^-9$

The y-intercept is at the point $(0, {}^-9)$.

The slope tells you to go up 9 spaces and right 6 for $(6,0)$.

* * * * * * * * * * * *

$3(2y + 5x) = -6$

Use the distributive property of multiplication.

$6y + 15x = {}^-6$

Subtract $15x$ from both sides.

$6y + 15x - 15x = {}^-15x - 6$

Simplify.

$6y = {}^-15x - 6$

Divide both sides by 6.

$y = \frac{{}^-15}{6}x - 1$

The equation is in the proper slope/y-intercept form.

$m = \frac{{}^-15}{6} = \frac{{}^-5}{2} = \frac{\text{change in } y}{\text{change in } x}$

$b = {}^-1$

The y-intercept is at the point $(0, {}^-1)$.

The slope tells you to go down 5 spaces and right 2 for $(2, {}^-6)$.

The solution for the system of equations is $(2, -6)$.

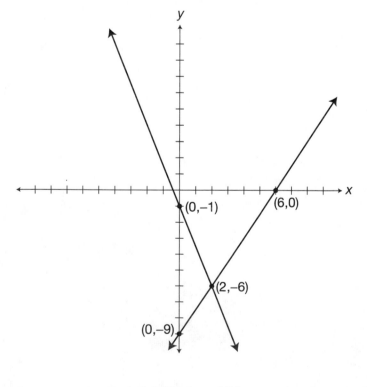

260. Transform equations into slope/y-intercept form.

$$15y = 6(3x + 15)$$

Use the distributive property of multiplication.

$$15y = 18x + 90$$

Divide both sides by 15.

$$y = \frac{18}{15}x + 6$$

The equation is in the proper slope/y-intercept form.

$$m = \frac{18}{15} = \frac{6}{5} = \frac{^-6}{^-5} = \frac{\text{change in } y}{\text{change in } x}$$

$b = 6$

The y-intercept is at the point (0,6).

The slope tells you to go down 6 spaces and left 5 for ($^-5$,0).

* * * * * * * * * * * *

$$y = 6(1 - x)$$

Use the distributive property of multiplication.

$$y = 6 - 6x$$

Use the commutative property.

$$y = {}^-6x + 6$$

The equation is in the proper slope/y-intercept form.

$$m = {}^-6 = \frac{^-6}{1} = \frac{\text{change in } y}{\text{change in } x}$$

$b = 6$

The y-intercept is at the point (0,6).

The slope tells you to go down 6 spaces and right 1 for (1,0).

The solution for the system of equations is (0,6).

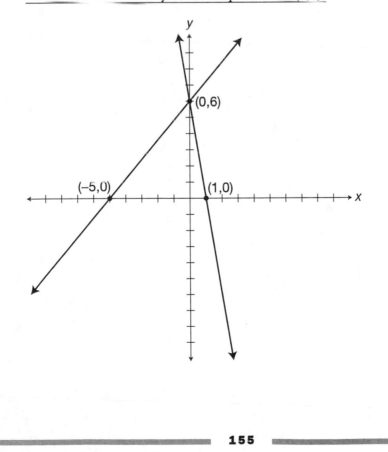

261. Transform equations into
    slope/y-intercept form. $3y = 6x + 6$
Divide both sides by 3. $y = 2x + 2$
The equation is in the proper
    slope/y-intercept form. $m = 2 = \frac{2}{1} = \frac{\text{change in } y}{\text{change in } x}$
$b = 2$ The y-intercept is at the point (0,2).
The slope tells you to go up
    2 spaces and right 1 for (1,4).

* * * * * * * * * * * *

     $5y = 10(x - 5)$
Use the distributive property. $5y = 10x - 50$
Divide both sides by 5. $y = 2x - 10$
The equation is in the proper
    slope/y-intercept form. $m = 2 = \frac{2}{1} = \frac{\text{change in } y}{\text{change in } x}$
$b = {}^-10$ The y-intercept is at the point (0,$^-$10).
The slope tells you to go up
    2 spaces and right 1 for (1,$^-$8).

The slopes are the same, so the line graphs are parallel and do not
intersect.

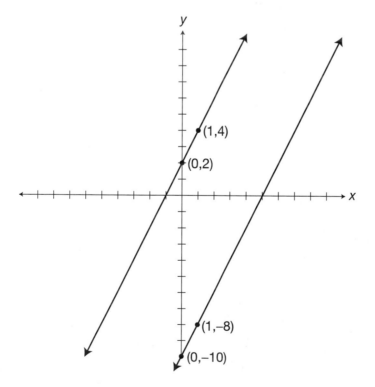

262. Transform equations into slope/y-intercept form.

$3(2x + 3y) = 63$

Use the distributive property of multiplication.

$6x + 9y = 63$

Subtract $6x$ from both sides.

$6x - 6x + 9y = 63 - 6x$

Simplify.

$9y = 63 - 6x$

Commutative property.

$9y = {}^-6x + 63$

Divide both sides by 9.

$y = \frac{{}^-6}{9}x + 7$

The equation is in the proper slope/y-intercept form.

$m = \frac{{}^-6}{9} = \frac{{}^-2}{3} = \frac{\text{change in } y}{\text{change in } x}$

$b = 7$

The y-intercept is at the point $(0,7)$.

The slope tells you to go down 2 spaces and right 3 for $(3,5)$.

* * * * * * * * * * * *

$27y = 9(x - 6)$

Use the distributive property of multiplication.

$27y = 9x - 54$

Divide both sides by 27.

$y = \frac{9}{27}x - 2$

The equation is in the proper slope/y intercept form.

$m = \frac{9}{27} = \frac{1}{3} = \frac{\text{change in } y}{\text{change in } x}$

$b = {}^-2$

The y-intercept is at the point $(0,{}^-2)$.

The slope tells you to go up 1 space and right 3 for $(3,{}^-1)$.

The solution for the system of equations is $(9,1)$.

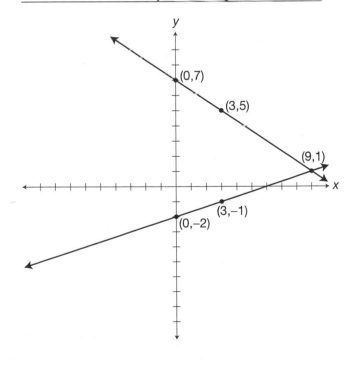

263. Transform equations into
   slope/y-intercept form. $x - 20 = 5y$

If $a = b$, then $b = a$. $5y = x - 20$

Divide both sides by 5. $y = \frac{1}{5}x - 4$

The equation is in the proper
   slope/y-intercept form. $m = \frac{1}{5} = \frac{\text{change in } y}{\text{change in } x}$

$b = {}^-4$ The y-intercept is at the point $(0, {}^-4)$.

The slope tells you to go up
   1 space and right 5 for $(5, {}^-3)$.

* * * * * * * * * * * * *

                                                        $10y = 8x + 20$

Divide both sides by 10. $y = \frac{8}{10}x + 2$

The equation is in the proper
   slope/y-intercept form. $m = \frac{8}{10} = \frac{4}{5} = \frac{\text{change in } y}{\text{change in } x}$

$b = 2$ The y-intercept is at the point $(0, 2)$.

The slope tells you to go up
   4 spaces and right 5 for $(5, 6)$.

The solution for the system of equations is $(-10, -6)$.

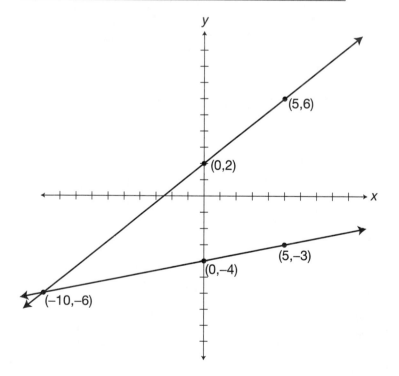

264. Transform equations into
    slope/*y*-intercept form. $3x + 4y = 12$
Subtract $3x$ from both sides. $3x - 3x + 4y = {}^-3x + 12$
Simplify. $4y = {}^-3x + 12$

Divide both sides by 4. $y = \frac{{}^-3}{4}x + 3$
The equation is in the proper
    slope/*y*-intercept form. $m = \frac{{}^-3}{4} = \frac{\text{change in } y}{\text{change in } x}$
$b = {}^+3$ The *y*-intercept is at the point (0,3).
The slope tells you to go down
    3 spaces and right 4 for (4,0).

* * * * * * * * * * * *

                               $y = 3 - \frac{6}{8}x$
Use the commutative property. $y = \frac{{}^-6}{8}x + 3$
The equation is in the proper
    slope/*y*-intercept form. $m = \frac{{}^-6}{8} = \frac{\text{change in } y}{\text{change in } x}$
$b = 3$ The *y*-intercept is at the point (0,3).
The slope tells you to go down
    6 spaces and right 8 for (8,‾3).

The solution for the system of equations is the entire line because
the graphs coincide.

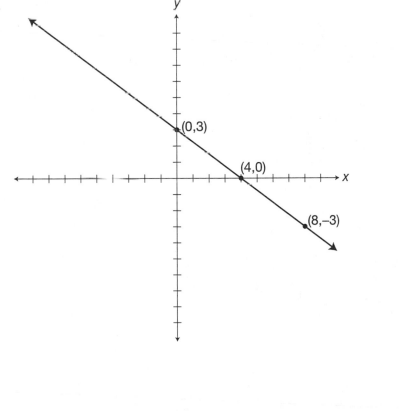

265. Transform equations into slope/y-intercept form.

$16y = 10(x - 8)$

Use the distributive property of multiplication.

$16y = 10x - 80$

Divide both sides by 16.

$y = \frac{10}{16}x - 5$

The equation is in the proper slope/y-intercept form. {Use the negatives to keep the coordinates near the origin.}

$m = \frac{10}{16} = \frac{5}{8} = \frac{^-5}{^-8} = \frac{\text{change in } y}{\text{change in } x}$

$b = ^-5$

The y-intercept is at the point (0,$^-$5).

The slope tells you to go down 5 spaces and left 8 for ($^-$8,$^-$10).

* * * * * * * * * * * *

$8y - 17x = 56$

Subtract $17x$ from both sides.

$8y - 17x + 17x = 17x + 56$

Simplify.

$8y = 17x + 56$

Divide both sides by 8.

$y = \frac{17}{8}x + 7$

The equation is in the proper slope/y-intercept form. {Use the negatives to keep the coordinates near the origin.}

$m = \frac{17}{8} = \frac{^-17}{^-8} = \frac{\text{change in } y}{\text{change in } x}$

$b = 7$

The y-intercept is at the point (0,7).

The slope tells you to go down 17 spaces and left 8 for ($^-$8,$^-$10).

The solution for the system of equations is ($^-$8,$^-$10).

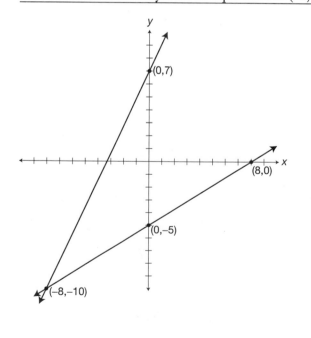

266. Transform the inequalities into slope/y-intercept form.

$2y - 3x \geq -6$

Add $3x$ to both sides.

$2y - 3x + 3x \geq {}^+3x - 6$

Simplify.

$2y \geq 3x - 6$

Divide both sides by 2.

$y \geq \frac{3}{2}x - 3$

$m = \frac{3}{2} = \frac{\text{change in } y}{\text{change in } x}$

$b = {}^-3$

The y-intercept is at the point $(0, {}^-3)$.

The slope tells you to go up 3 spaces and right 2 for (2,0).

Use a **solid** line for the border and shade **above** the line because the symbol is $\geq$.

* * * * * * * * * * * *

Use the commutative property.

$y \geq 5 - \frac{5}{2}x$

$y \geq {}^-\frac{5}{2}x + 5$

$m = \frac{{}^-5}{2} = \frac{\text{change in } y}{\text{change in } x}$

{Use the negatives to keep the coordinates near the origin.}

$b = 5$

The y-intercept is at the point (0,5)

The slope tells you to go down 5 spaces and right 2 for (2,0).

Use a **solid** line for the border and shade **above** the line because the symbol is $\geq$.

The solution for the system of inequalities is where the shaded areas overlap.

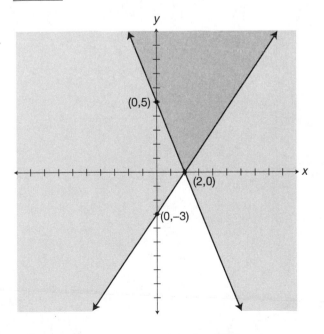

267. Transform equations into slope/y-intercept form.

Divide both sides by 6.

$b = {}^-5$
The slope tells you to go up 5 spaces and right 6 for (6,0).
Use a **dotted** line for the border and shade **below** it because the symbol is <.

* * * * * * * * * * * *

Divide both sides by 2.

$b = 2$
The slope tells you to go down 1 space and right 2 for (2,1).
Use a **dotted** line for the border and shade **below** it because the symbol is <.

$6y < 5x - 30$

$y < \frac{5}{6}x - 5$

$m = \frac{5}{6} = \frac{\text{change in } y}{\text{change in } x}$

The y-intercept is at the point (0,$^-$5).

$2y < {}^-x + 4$
$y < \frac{-1}{2}x + 2$

$m = \frac{-1}{2} = \frac{\text{change in } y}{\text{change in } x}$

The y-intercept is at the point (0,2).

The solution for the system of inequalities is the double-shaded area on the graph.

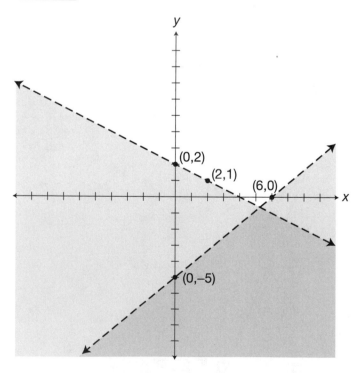

268. Transform equations into
   slope/y-intercept form. $y - x \geq 6$
   Add x to both sides. $y - x + x \geq x + 6$
   Simplify. $y \geq x + 6$
$$m = 1 = \frac{^-1}{^-1} = \frac{\text{change in } y}{\text{change in } x}$$

   $b = 6$ The y-intercept is at the point (0,6).
   The slope tells you to go down
1 space and left 1 for ($^-$1,5).
   Use a **solid** line for the border and
shade **above** it because the symbol is $\geq$.

* * * * * * * * * * * *

Use the distributive property
   of multiplication. $11y \geq ^-2(x + 11)$
Simplify. $11y \geq ^-2x - 22$

Divide both sides by 11. $y \geq \frac{-2}{11}x - 2$
$$m = \frac{^-2}{11} = \frac{\text{change in } y}{\text{change in } x}$$

   $b = ^-2$ The y-intercept is at the point (0,$^-$2)
The slope tells you to go down
   2 spaces and right 11 for (11,$^-$4).
Use a **solid** line for the border and shade
   above the line because the symbol is $\geq$.

The solution for the system of inequalities is the double-shaded area
on the graph.

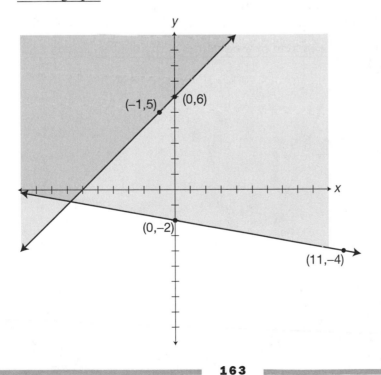

269.   Transform equations into slope/*y*-intercept form.

$3x + 4y = 12$

Use the distributive property of multiplication.

$5y \le 8x + 40$

Divide both sides by 5.

$y \le \frac{8}{5}x + 8$

$$m = \frac{8}{5} = \frac{^-8}{^-5} = \frac{\text{change in } y}{\text{change in } x}$$

{Use the negatives to keep the coordinates near the origin.}

$b = 8$

The *y*-intercept is at the point (0,8).

The slope tells you to go down 8 spaces and left 5 for (⁻5,0).

Use a **solid** line for the border and shade **below** it because the symbol is ≤.

* * * * * * * * * * * *

$5y \le 12(5 - x)$

Use the distributive property of multiplication.

$5y \le 60 - 12x$

Use the commutative property of addition.

$5y \le {^-12}x + 60$

Divide both sides by 5.

$y \le \frac{^-12}{5}x + 12$

$$m = \frac{^-12}{5} = \frac{\text{change in } y}{\text{change in } x}$$

$b = 12$

The *y*-intercept is at the point (0,12).

The slope tells you to go down 12 spaces and right 5 for (5,0).

Use a **solid** line for the border and shade **below** the line because the symbol is ≤.

The solution for the system of inequalities is the double-shaded area on the graph.

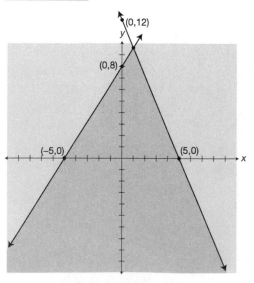

270. Transform equations into slope/y-intercept form.

$$2(x + 5y) > 5(x + 6)$$

Use the distributive property of multiplication.

$$2x + 10y > 5x + 30$$

Subtract $2x$ from both sides.

$$2x - 2x + 10y > 5x - 2x + 30$$

Simplify the inequality.

$$10y > 3x + 30$$

Divide both sides by 10.

$$y > \frac{3}{10}x + 3$$

$$m = \frac{3}{10} = \frac{\text{change in } y}{\text{change in } x}$$

$b = 3$

The y-intercept is at the point (0,3).

The slope tells you to go up 3 spaces and right 10 for (10,6).
Use a **dotted** line for the border and shade **above** it because the symbol is >.

* * * * * * * * * * * *

$$4x + y < 4x + 5$$

Subtract $4x$ from both sides.

$$4x - 4x + y < 4x - 4x + 5$$

Simplify.

$$y < 0x + 5$$

With a slope of zero, the line is parallel to the x-axis.
The y-intercept is (0,5).
Use a **dotted** line for the border and shade **below** it because the symbol is <.

The solution for the system of inequalities is the double-shaded area on the graph.

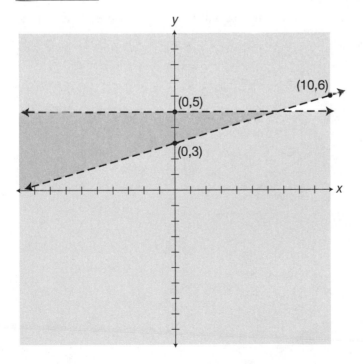

271. Transform equations into
slope/y-intercept form.

$$3y \geq {}^-2(x + 3)$$

Use the distributive property
of multiplication.

$$3\,y \geq {}^-2x - 6$$

Divide both sides by 3.

$$y \geq \tfrac{-2}{3}x - 2$$

$$m = \tfrac{-2}{3} = \tfrac{\text{change in } y}{\text{change in } x}$$

$b = {}^-2$

The y-intercept is at the point $(0,{}^-2)$.

The slope tells you to go down
2 spaces and right 3 for $(3,{}^-4)$.
Use a **solid** line for the border and
shade **above** it because the symbol is $\geq$.

* * * * * * * * * * * *

Use the distributive property
of multiplication.

$$3y \leq 12 - 2x$$

Use the commutative property.

$$3y \leq {}^-2x + 12$$

Divide both sides by 3.

$$y \leq \tfrac{-2}{3}x + 4$$

$$m = \tfrac{-2}{3} = \tfrac{\text{change in } y}{\text{change in } x}$$

{Slopes that are the same will
result in parallel lines.}

$b = 4$

The y-intercept is at the point $(0,4)$

The slope tells you to go down
2 spaces and right 3 for $(3,2)$.
Use a **solid** line for the border and shade
below the line because the symbol is $\leq$.

The solution for the system of inequalities is the double-shaded area
on the graph.

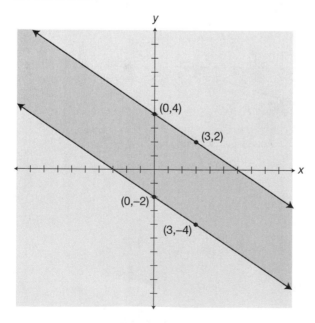

272. Transform equations into slope/y-intercept form.

$$9(y - 4) < 4x$$

Use the distributive property of multiplication.

$$9y - 36 < 4x$$

Add 36 to both sides.

$$9y - 36 + 36 < 4x + 36$$

Divide both sides by 9.

$$y < \frac{4}{9}x + 4$$

$$m = \frac{4}{9} = \frac{\text{change in } y}{\text{change in } x}$$

$b = 4$

The y-intercept is at the point (0,4).

The slope tells you to go up 4 spaces and right 9 for (9,8).

Use a **dotted** line for the border and shade **below** it because the symbol is <.

* * * * * * * * * * * *

$$^{-}9y < 2(x + 9)$$

Use the distributive property of multiplication.

$$^{-}9y < 2x + 18$$

Divide both sides by 9. Change the direction of the symbol when dividing by a negative.

$$y > \frac{^{-}2}{9}x - 2$$

$$m = \frac{^{-}2}{9} = \frac{\text{change in } y}{\text{change in } x}$$

$b = {}^{-}2$

The y-intercept is at the point (0,$^{-}$2).

The slope tells you to go down 2 spaces and right 9 for (9,$^{-}$4).

Use a **dotted** line for the border and shade **above** the line because the symbol is >.

The solution for the system of inequalities is the double-shaded area on the graph.

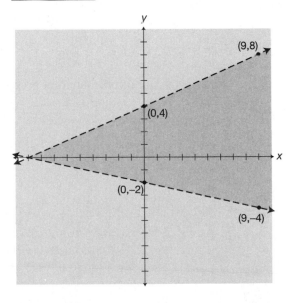

273.

Transform equations into slope/y-intercept form.	$7(y - 5) < {}^-5x$
Use the distributive property of multiplication.	$7y - 35 < {}^-5x$
Add 35 to both sides.	$7y - 35 + 35 < {}^-5x + 35$
Simplify.	$7y < {}^-5x + 35$
Divide both sides by 7.	$y < \frac{{}^-5}{7}x + 5$
	$m = \frac{{}^-5}{7} = \frac{\text{change in } y}{\text{change in } x}$

$b = 5$

The y-intercept is at the point $(0,5)$.

The slope tells you to go down
  5 spaces and right 7 for $(7,0)$.
Use a **dotted** line for the border and
  shade **below** it because the symbol is $<$.

* * * * * * * * * * * *

	${}^-3 < \frac{1}{4}(2x - 3y)$
Multiply both sides of the inequality by 4.	$4({}^-3) < 4(\frac{1}{4})(2x - 3y)$
Simplify the inequality.	${}^-12 < 1(2x - 3y)$
	${}^-12 < 2x \; {}^-3y$
Add $3y$ to both sides.	${}^-12 + 3y < 2x - 3y + 3y$
Simplify the inequality.	${}^-12 + 3y < 2x$
Add 12 to both sides.	${}^-12 + 12 + 3y < 2x + 12$
Simplify the inequality.	$3y < 2x + 12$
Divide both sides by 3.	$y < \frac{2}{3}x + 4$
	$m = \frac{2}{3} = \frac{\text{change in } y}{\text{change in } x}$

$b = 4$

The y-intercept is at the point $(0,4)$.

The slope tells you to go up
  2 spaces and right 3 for $(3,6)$.
Use a **dotted** line for the border
  and shade **below** the line because
  the symbol is $<$.

The solution for the system of inequalities is the double-shaded area
on the graph (next page).

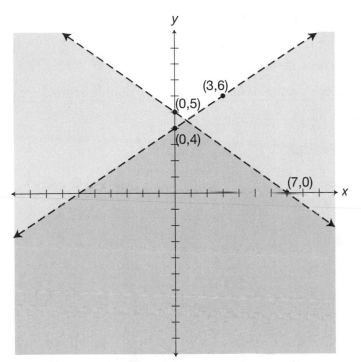

Graph for Question 273.

274. Transform equations into
slope/y-intercept form. $y > \frac{7}{4}(4 - x)$

Use the distributive property
of multiplication. $y > 7 - \frac{7}{4}x$

Use the commutative property. $y > \frac{^-7}{4}x + 7$

$m = \frac{^-7}{4} = \frac{\text{change in } y}{\text{change in } x}$

$b = 7$ The y-intercept is at the point (0,7).

The slope tells you to go down
7 spaces and right 4 for (4,0).

Use a **dotted** line for the border and
shade **above** it because the symbol is >.

* * * * * * * * * * * *

$3(y + 5) > 7x$

Use the distributive property
of multiplication. $3y + 15 > 7x$

Subtract 15 from both sides. $3y + 15 - 15 > 7x - 15$

Simplify the inequality. $3y > 7x - 15$

Divide both sides by 3. $y > \frac{7}{3}x - 5$

$m = \frac{7}{3} = \frac{\text{change in } y}{\text{change in } x}$

$b = {^-5}$ The y-intercept is at the point (0,$^-5$)

The slope tells you to go up 7 spaces
    and right 3 for (3,2).
Use a **dotted** line for the border and shade
    above the line because the symbol is >.

The solution for the system of inequalities is the double-shaded area
on the graph.

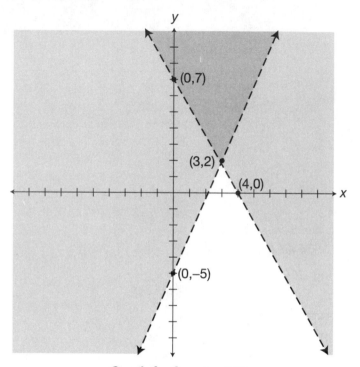

Graph for Question 274.

275. Transform equations into
    slope/*y*-intercept form. $5x - 2(y + 10) \leq 0$
Use the distributive property
    of multiplication. $5x - 2y - 20 \leq 0$
Subtract $5x$ from both sides. $5x - 5x - 2y - 20 \leq {}^-5x$
Add 20 to both sides. ${}^-2y - 20 + 20 \leq {}^-5x + 20$
Simplify the inequality. ${}^-2y \leq {}^-5x + 20$
Divide both sides by ${}^-2$. Change
    the direction of the symbol
    when dividing by a negative. $y \geq \frac{5}{2}x - 10$

$m = \frac{5}{2} = \frac{\text{change in } y}{\text{change in } x}$

$b = {}^-10$ The *y*-intercept is at the point (0,${}^-10$).
The slope tells you to go up
    5 spaces and right 2 for (2,${}^-5$).

Use a **solid** line for the border and shade
   above it because the symbol is ≥.

* * * * * * * * * * * *

	$2x + y \leq {}^-3$
Subtract $2x$ from both sides.	$2x - 2x + y \leq {}^-2x - 3$
Simplify the inequality.	$y \leq {}^-2x - 3$
	$m = \frac{^-2}{1} = \frac{\text{change in } y}{\text{change in } x}$

$b = {}^-3$ The y-intercept is at the point $(0,{}^-3)$.
The slope tells you to go down
   2 spaces and right 1 for $(1,{}^-5)$.
Use a **solid** line for the border and shade
   below the line because the symbol is ≤.

The solution for the system of inequalities is the double-shaded area
on the graph.

Graph for Question 275.

Solving Systems of Equations Algebraically

There is a faster way to solve systems of equations than graphing and finding the solution point. You can solve systems of equations using algebraic methods. The two methods you will practice here are called the **elimination method** and the **substitution method**. You will be using the skills you have practiced in the chapters on working with algebraic expressions, combining like terms, and solving equations.

In the **elimination method,** you will transform one or both of the two equations in the system so that when you add the two equations together, one of the variables will be eliminated. Then you solve the remaining equation for the remaining variable. When you find a numerical value for the remaining variable, you just substitute the found value into one of the equations and solve for the other variable.

In the **substitution method,** you will transform one of the equations so that one variable is expressed in terms of the other. Then you will eliminate the variable by substituting into the other equation and solve. When you find a numerical value for one variable, use it in one of the two equations to determine the value of the remaining variable.

One method is not better than the other. But you may find that you will begin to see which equations, because of their structure, lend themselves to one method over the other. Practice will help you decide.

Tips for Solving Systems of Equations Algebraically

When using the elimination method, first make a plan to determine which variable you will eliminate from the system. Then transform the equation or equations so that you will get the result you want.

Express your solution as a coordinate point or in the form (x, y), or as variables such as $x = 2$ and $y = 4$.

Use the elimination method to solve the following systems of equations.

276. $x + y = 4$
$2x - y = 5$

277. $3x + 4y = 17$
$^-x + 2y = 1$

278. $7x + 3y = 2$
$2x + y = 0$

279. $0.5x + 5y = 28$
$3x - y = 13$

280. $3(x + y) = 18$
$5x + y = ^-2$

281. $\frac{1}{2}x + 2y = 12$
$2x - y = 21$

282. $5x + 8y = 25$
$3x - 15 = y$

283. $6y + 3x - 30$
$2y + 6x = 0$

284. $3x = 5 - 7y$
$2y = x - 6$

285. $3x + y = 20$
$\frac{x}{3} + 10 = y$

286. $2x + 7y = 36$
$3x + 4y = 15$

287. $3x - 5y = ^-21$
$2(2y - x) = 16$

288. $\frac{1}{4}x + y = 12$
$2x - \frac{1}{3}y = 21$

Use the substitution method to solve the following systems of equations.

289. $y = 3x$
$4x + 5y = 95$

290. $x + y = 3$
$3x + 101 = 7y$

291. $5x + y = 3.6$
$y + 21x = 8.4$

292. $8x - y = 0$
$10x + y = 9$

293. $\frac{x}{3} = y + 2$
$2x - 4y = 32$

294. $y + 4x = 0$
$y - 3x = 28$

295. $5x + y = 20$
$3x = \frac{1}{2}y + 1$

296. $2x + y = 2 - 5y$
$x - y = 5$

297. $\frac{2x}{10} + \frac{y}{5} = 1$
$3x + 2y = 12$

298. $x + 5y = 10$
$x - 3 = 2y$

299. $4y + 31 = 3x$
$y + 10 = 3x$

300. $2(2 - x) = 3y - 2$
$3x + 9 = 4(5 - y)$

Answers

Numerical expressions in parentheses like this [ ] are operations performed on only part of the original expression. The operations performed within these symbols are intended to show how to evaluate the various terms that make up the entire expression.

Expressions with parentheses that look like this ( ) contain either numerical substitutions or expressions that are part of a numerical expression. Once a single number appears within these parentheses, the parentheses are no longer needed and need not be used the next time the entire expression is written.

When two pair of parentheses appear side by side like this ( )( ), it means that the expressions within are to be multiplied.

Sometimes parentheses appear within other parentheses in numerical or algebraic expressions. Regardless of what symbol is used, ( ), { }, or [ ], perform operations in the innermost parentheses first and work outward.

The underlined ordered pair is the solution. Be aware that you may have used a different method of elimination to arrive at the correct answer.

276. Add the equations.

$$x + y = 4$$
$$2x - y = 5$$
$$3x + 0 = 9$$

Additive identity. $\qquad 3x = 9$
Now solve for x.
Divide both sides by 3. $\qquad \frac{3x}{3} = \frac{9}{3}$
Simplify terms. $\qquad x = 3$
Substitute the value of x into one of the equations
    in the system and solve for y. $\qquad (3) + y = 4$
Subtract 3 from both sides. $\qquad 3 - 3 + y = 4 - 3$
Simplify. $\qquad y = 1$
The solution for the system of equations is (3,1).

277. We could add the equations together if we had
    a ^-3x in the second equation.
Multiply the second equation by 3. $\qquad 3(-x + 2y = 1)$
Simplify. $\qquad ^-3x + 6y = 3$
Add the first and transformed second equations. $\qquad 3x + 4y = 17$
$$0 + 10y = 20$$
Identity element of addition. $\qquad 10y = 20$
Divide both sides by 4. $\qquad y = 2$
Substitute the value of y into one of the equations
    in the system and solve for x. $\qquad ^-x + 2(2) = 1$
Simplify. $\qquad ^-x + 4 = 1$
Subtract 4 from both sides. $\qquad ^-x + 4 - 4 = 1 - 4$
Simplify. $\qquad ^-x = ^-3$
Multiply both sides by $^-1$. $\qquad x = 3$
The solution for the system of equations is (3,2).

278. Transform the second equation so you can
add it to the first and eliminate y.
Multiply the equation by $^-3$. $\qquad$ $^-3(2x + y = 0)$
Simplify. $\qquad$ $^-6x - 3y = 0$
Add the first equation to the transformed second.

$$\begin{array}{r} ^-6x - 3y = 0 \\ 7x + 3y = 2 \\ \hline x + 0 = 2 \\ x = 2 \end{array}$$

Substitute the value of x into one of the equations
in the system and solve for y.

$$2(2) + y = 0$$
$$4 + y = 0$$

Subtract 4 from both sides. $\qquad$ $4 - 4 + y = ^-4$
Simplify. $\qquad$ $y = ^-4$
The solution for the system of equations is $(2, ^-4)$.

279. If you multiply the second equation by 5
and add the equations together, you
can eliminate the y. $\qquad$ $5(3x - y) = 5(13)$
Distributive property of multiplication. $\qquad$ $5(3x) - 5(y) = 5(13)$
Simplify terms. $\qquad$ $15x - 5y = 65$
Add the first and second equations. $\qquad$ $\dfrac{0.5x + 5y = 28}{15.5x + 0 = 93}$

Additive identity. $\qquad$ $15.5\,x = 93$
Divide both sides by 15.5. $\qquad$ $x = 6$
Substitute the value of x into one of the equations
in the system and solve for y. $\qquad$ $3(6) - y = 13$
Simplify. $\qquad$ $18 - y = 13$
Subtract 18 from both sides. $\qquad$ $18 - 18 - y = 13 - 18$
Simplify. $\qquad$ $^-y = ^-5$
Multiply both sides by $^-1$. $\qquad$ $(^-1)(^-y) = (^-1)(^-5)$
Simplify. $\qquad$ $y = 5$
The solution for the system of equations is $(6, 5)$.

280. See what the first equation looks like after
distributing the multiplication on the left.
Use the distributive property of multiplication. $\qquad$ $3x + 3y = 18$
Multiply the second equation by $^-3$ and add
equations to eliminate y.
Use the distributive property of multiplication. $\qquad$ $^-3(5x + y) = ^-3(^-2)$
$\qquad$ $^-3(5x) - 3(y) = ^-3(^-2)$
Simplify terms. $\qquad$ $^-15x - 3y = 6$
Add the transformed first equation. $\qquad$ $\dfrac{3x + 3y = 18}{^-12x + 0 = 24}$

Additive identity. $\qquad$ $^-12x = 24$
Divide both sides by $^-12$. $\qquad$ $x = ^-2$

Substitute the value of x into one of the equations
    in the system and solve for y.

$5(^-2) + y = ^-2$
$^-10 + y = ^-2$

Add 10 to both sides.
$10 - 10 + y = 10 - 2$

Simplify.
$y = 8$

The solution for the system of equations is $(^-2,8)$.

281. Multiply the second equation by 2 and add to
    the first to eliminate y.
$2(2x - y) = 2(21)$

Use the distributive property of multiplication.
$2(2x) - 2(y) = 2(21)$

Simplify.
$4x - 2y = 42$

Add the first equation to the second.
$\frac{1}{2}x + 2y = 12$
$\overline{4\frac{1}{2}x + 0 = 54}$

Additive identity.
$4\frac{1}{2}x = 54$

Multiply the equation by 2 to simplify the fraction.
$2(4\frac{1}{2}x = 54)$

Simplify.
$9x = 108$

Divide both sides by 9.
$x = 12$

Substitute the value of x into one of the equations
    in the system and solve for y.
$2(12) - y = 21$

Subtract 24 from both sides.
$24 - 24 - y = 21 - 24$

Combine like terms on each side.
$^-y = ^-3$

Multiply the equation by 1.
$y - 3$

The solution for the system of equations is $(12,3)$.

282. Transform the second equation into a similar
    format to the first equation, then line up
    like terms.

Add 15 to both sides.
$3x - 15 + 15 = y + 15$

Simplify.
$3x = y + 15$

Subtract y from both sides.
$3x - y = y - y + 15$

Simplify.
$3x - y = 15$

Multiply the second equation by 8 and add
    the first equation to the second.
$8(3x - y) = 15$

Use the distributive property of multiplication.
$24x - 8y = 120$

Add the first equation to the second.
$5x + 8y = 25$
$\overline{29x + 0 = 145}$

Additive identity.
$29x = 145$

Divide both sides by 29.
$x = 5$

Substitute the value of x into one of the equations
    in the system and solve for y.
$3(5) - 15 = y$

Simplify.
$15 - 15 = y$
$0 = y$

The solution for the system of equations is $(5,0)$.

283. Multiply the second equation by ⁻3 and add it
    to the first equation to eliminate y.

$$⁻3(2y + 6x = 0)$$
$$⁻6y − 18x = 0$$
$$6y + 3x = 30$$
$$\overline{0 − 15x = 30}$$

Additive identity. Divide both sides by ⁻15. $x = ⁻2$

Substitute the value of x into one of the
    equations in the system and solve for y.

$$2y + 6(⁻2) = 0$$
$$2y − 12 = 0$$

Add 12 to both sides. $2y − 12 + 12 = 0 + 12$

Simplify. $2y = 12$

Divide both sides by 2. $y = 6$

The solution for the system of equations is (⁻2,6).

284. Transform the first equation into
    familiar form ($ax + by = c$). $3x = 5 − 7y$

Add $7y$ to both sides. $3x + 7y = 5 − 7y + 7y$

Simplify. $3x + 7y = 5$

Transform the second equation into
    familiar form ($ax + by = c$). $2y = x − 6$

Subtract x from both sides. $⁻x + 2y = x − x − 6$

Simplify. $⁻x + 2y = ⁻6$

Multiply equation by 3. $3(⁻x + 2y = ⁻6)$
$$3(⁻x) + 3\,(2y) = 3(⁻6)$$

Simplify terms. $⁻3x + 6y = ⁻18$

Add the transformed first equation. $\underline{3x + 7y = 5}$

$$0 + 13y = ⁻13$$

Additive identity. Divide both sides by 13. $y = ⁻1$

Substitute the value of y into one of the
    equations in the system and solve for x.

$$3x = 5 − 7(⁻1)$$
$$3x = 5 + 7$$
$$3x = 12$$

Divide both sides by 3. $x = 4$

The solution for the system of equations is (4,⁻1).

285. Transform the second equation into familiar form $(ax + by = c)$.

Multiply the equation by 3. $\qquad 3(\frac{x}{3} + 10 = y)$

Use the distributive property. $\qquad 3(\frac{x}{3}) + 3(10) = 3(y)$
Simplify terms. $\qquad x + 30 = 3y$
Subtract 30 from each side. $\qquad x + 30 - 30 = 3y - 30$
Simplify. $\qquad x = 3y - 30$
Subtract $3y$ from both sides. $\qquad x - 3y = 3y - 3y - 30$
Simplify. $\qquad x - 3y = {}^-30$
Multiply the first equation by 3 and add to the
    second equation to eliminate y. $\qquad 3(3x + y = 20)$
Use the distributive property. $\qquad 3(3x) + 3(y) = 3(20)$
Simplify terms. $\qquad 9x + 3y = 60$
Add the transformed second equation to the first. $\qquad \underline{x - 3y = {}^-30}$
$\qquad 10x + 0 = 30$

Additive identity. Divide both sides by 10. $\qquad x = 3$
Substitute the value of x into one of the equations
    in the system and solve for y. $\qquad \frac{(3)}{3} + 10 = y$
Simplify terms. $\qquad 1 + 10 = y$
$\qquad 11 = y$

The solution for the system of equations is $(3,11)$.

286. Transform the first equation by multiplying
    by 3, the second by multiplying by $^-2$, and
    eliminate the x variable by adding the
    equations together. $\qquad 3(2x + 7y = 36)$
Use the distributive property. $\qquad 3(2x) + 3(7y) = 3(36)$
Simplify terms. $\qquad 6x + 21y = 108$
Second equation. $\qquad {}^-2(3x + 4y = 15)$
Use the distributive property. $\qquad {}^-2(3x) - 2(4y) = {}^-2(15)$
Simplify terms. $\qquad {}^-6x - 8y = {}^-30$
Add the transformed first equation to the
    second equation. $\qquad \underline{6x + 21y = 108}$
$\qquad 0 + 13y = 78$

Additive identity. Divide both sides by 13. $\qquad y = 6$
Substitute the value of y into one of the
    equations in the system and solve for x. $\qquad 3x + 4(6) = 15$
Simplify terms. $\qquad 3x + 24 = 15$
Subtract 24 from both sides. $\qquad 3x + 24 - 24 = 15 - 24$
Simplify. $\qquad 3x = {}^-9$
Divide both sides by 3. $\qquad x = {}^-3$
The solution for the system of equations is $({}^-3,6)$.

287. Transform the second equation into a
similar form to the first equation.

Use the distributive property of multiplication.	$2(2y) - 2(x) = 16$
Simplify terms.	$4y - 2x = 16$
Commutative property of addition.	$^-2x + 4y = 16$

Multiply the first equation by 2 and
the second equation by 3, and add
the transformed equations to eliminate
the variable x. $\qquad$ $2(3x - 5y = {}^-21)$

Distributive property. Simplify terms.	$6x - 10y = {}^-42$
	$3(^-2x + 4y = 16)$
Distributive property. Simplify terms.	$^-6x + 12y = 48$
Add the first equation to the second.	$\underline{6x - 10y = -42}$
	$2y = 6$
Divide both sides by 2.	$y = 3$

Substitute the value of y into one of the
equations in the system and solve for x. $\quad 3x - 5(3) = {}^-21$

Simplify terms and add 15 to each side.	$3x - 15 + 15 = {}^-21 + 15$
Combine like terms on each side.	$3x = {}^-6$
Divide both sides by 3.	$x = {}^-2$

The solution for the system of equations is $(^-2,3)$.

288. Transform the second equation by multiplying it by 3.

Then, add the equations together to eliminate y.	$3(2x - \frac{1}{3}y = 21)$
Use the distributive property of multiplication.	$3(2x) - 3(\frac{1}{3}y) = 3(21)$
Simplify terms.	$6x - y = 63$
Add the first equation to the second.	$\frac{1}{4}x + y = 12$
	$\overline{6\frac{1}{4}x + 0 = 75}$
Additive identity.	$6\frac{1}{4}x = 75$
Divide both sides by $6\frac{1}{4}$.	$\dfrac{6\frac{1}{4}x}{6\frac{1}{4}} = \dfrac{75}{6\frac{1}{4}}$
Simplify.	$x = 12$

Substitute the value of x into one of the equations
in the system and solve for y. $\qquad \frac{1}{4}(12) + y = 12$

Simplify the first term and subtract from both sides.	$3 - 3 + y = 12 - 3$
Simplify.	$y = 9$

The solution for the system of equations is $(12,9)$.

289. The first equation tells you that $y = 3x$.
    Substitute $3x$ for y in the second equation
      and then solve for x. $4x + 5\,(3x) = 95$
    Simplify term and add like terms. $4x + 15x = 95$
                                                $19x = 95$
    Divide both sides by 19. $x = \frac{95}{19} = 5$
    Substitute 5 for x in one of the equations. $y = 3(5) = 15$
    The solution for the system of equations is $(5,15)$.

290. Transform the first equation so that the value of x
    is expressed in terms of y.
    Subtract y from both sides of the equation. $x + y - y = 3 - y$
    Simplify. $x = 3 - y$
    Substitute $3 - y$ for x in the second equation
      and solve for y. $3(3 - y) + 101 = 7y$
    Use the distributive property of multiplication. $9 - 3y + 101 = 7y$
    Use the commutative property of addition. $9 + 101 - 3y = 7y$
    Add like terms. Add $3y$ to both sides. $110 - 3y + 3y = 7y + 3y$
    Combine like terms. $110 = 10y$
    Divide both sides by 10. $11 = y$
    Substitute the value of y into one of the equations
      in the system and solve for x. $x + (11) = 3$
    Subtract 11 from both sides. $x + 11 - 11 = 3 - 11$
    Combine like terms on each side. $x = {}^-8$
    The solution for the system of equations is $({}^-8,11)$.

291. Transform the first equation so that y is
    expressed in terms of x. $5x + y = 3.6$
    Subtract $5x$ from both sides of the equation. $5x - 5x + y = 3.6 - 5x$
    Combine like terms on each side. $y = 3.6 - 5x$
    Substitute the value of y into the
      second equation. $(3.6 - 5x) + 21x = 8.4$
    Combine like terms. $3.6 + 16x = 8.4$
    Subtract 3.6 from both sides. $3.6 - 3.6 + 16x = 8.4 - 3.6$
    Combine like terms on each side. $16x = 4.8$
    Divide both sides by 16. $x = 0.3$
    Substitute the value of x into one of the
      equations in the system and solve for y. $5(0.3) + y = 3.6$
    Simplify terms. $1.5 + y = 3.6$
    Subtract 1.5 from both sides. $1.5 - 1.5 + y = 3.6 - 1.5$
    Combine like terms on each side. $y = 2.1$
    The solution for the system of equations is $(0.3,2.1)$.

292. Transform the first equation so that y
   is expressed in terms of x. $\qquad$ $8x - y = 0$
Add y to both sides of the equation. $\qquad$ $8x + y - y = y + 0$
Combine like terms on each side and simplify. $\qquad$ $8x = y$
Substitute the value of y into the second equation. $\qquad$ $10x + 8x = 9$
Combine like terms. $\qquad$ $18x = 9$
Divide both sides by 18. $\qquad$ $x = \frac{1}{2}$
Substitute the value of x into one of the equations
   in the system and solve for y. $\qquad$ $8(\frac{1}{2}) - y = 0$
Simplify terms. $\qquad$ $4 - y = 0$
Add y to both sides of the equation. $\qquad$ $4 - y + y = 0 + y$
Simplify. $\qquad$ $4 = y$
The solution for the system of equations is $(\frac{1}{2}, 4)$.

293. Transform the first equation so that the
   value of x is expressed in terms of y.
Multiply the equation by 3. $\qquad$ $3((\frac{x}{3}) = y + 2)$
Use the distributive property. $\qquad$ $3(\frac{x}{3}) = 3y + 6$
Simplify. $\qquad$ $x = 3y + 6$
Substitute the value of x into the second
   equation in the system and solve for y. $\qquad$ $2(3y + 6) - 4y = 32$
Use the distributive property of multiplication. $\qquad$ $6y + 12 - 4y = 32$
Use the commutative property of addition. $\qquad$ $6y - 4y + 12 = 32$
Combine like terms. Subtract 12
   from both sides. $\qquad$ $2y + 12 - 12 = 32 - 12$
Combine like terms on each side. $\qquad$ $2y = 20$
Divide both sides by 2. $\qquad$ $y = 10$
Substitute the value of y into one of the
   equations in the system and solve for x. $\qquad$ $2x - 4(10) = 32$
Simplify and add 40 to both sides. $\qquad$ $2x - 40 + 40 = 32 + 40$
Combine like terms. $\qquad$ $2x = 72$
Divide both sides by 2. $\qquad$ $x = 36$
The solution for the system of equations is $(36, 10)$.

294. Express y in terms of x in the first equation. $\qquad$ $y + 4x = 0$
Subtract $4x$ from both sides. $\qquad$ $y + 4x - 4x = 0 - 4x$
Combine like terms and simplify. $\qquad$ $y = {}^-4x$
Substitute the value of y into the second equation
   in the system and solve for x. $\qquad$ $({}^-4x) - 3x = 28$
Combine like terms. $\qquad$ ${}^-7x = 28$
Divide both sides by ${}^-7$. $\qquad$ $x = {}^-4$
Substitute the found value for x into
   one of the equations and solve for y. $\qquad$ $y + 4({}^-4) = 0$
Simplify. $\qquad$ $y - 16 = 0$
Add 16 to both sides. $\qquad$ $y = 16$
The solution for the system of equations is $({}^-4, 16)$.

295. Transform the first equation so that the value
of y is expressed in terms of x. Subtract $5x$
from both sides of the equation. $\qquad$ $5x - 5x + y = 20 - 5x$

Combine like terms. $\qquad$ $y = 20 - 5x$

Substitute the value of y into the second
equation in the system and solve for x. $\qquad$ $3x = \frac{1}{2}(20 - 5x) + 1$

Use the distributive property
of multiplication. $\qquad$ $3x = 10 - \frac{5}{2}x + 1$

Combine like terms. $\qquad$ $3x = 11 - \frac{5}{2}x$

Add $\frac{5}{2}x$ to both sides. $\qquad$ $3x + \frac{5}{2}x = 11 + \frac{5}{2}x - \frac{5}{2}x$

Combine like terms. $\qquad$ $5\frac{1}{2}x = 11$

Divide both sides by $5\frac{1}{2}$. $\qquad$ $\dfrac{5\frac{1}{2}x}{5\frac{1}{2}} = \dfrac{11}{5\frac{1}{2}}$

Simplify terms. $\qquad$ $x = 2$

Substitute the found value for x into one
of the equations and solve for y. $\qquad$ $5(2) + y = 20$

Simplify. $\qquad$ $10 + y = 20$

Subtract 10 from both sides. $\qquad$ $y = 10$

The solution for the system of equations is $(2,10)$.

296. Transform the second equation so that the
value of x is expressed in terms of y. Add y
to both sides of the equation. $\qquad$ $x - y + y = 5 + y$

Combine like terms on each side. $\qquad$ $x = 5 + y$

Substitute the value of x into the second
equation in the system and solve for y. $\qquad$ $2(5 + y) + y = 2 - 5y$

Use the distributive property
of multiplication. $\qquad$ $10 + 2y + y = 2 - 5y$

Add $5y$ to both sides of the equation. $\qquad$ $10 + 2y + y + 5y = 2 - 5y + 5y$

Combine like terms on each side. $\qquad$ $10 + 8y - 2$

Subtract 10 from both sides. $\qquad$ $10 - 10 + 8y = 2 - 10$

Combine like terms on each side. $\qquad$ $8y = {}^-8$

Divide both sides by 8. $\qquad$ $y = {}^-1$

Substitute the found value for y into one
of the equations and solve for x. $\qquad$ $x - ({}^-1) = 5$

Simplify. $\qquad$ $x + 1 = 5$

$x = 4$

The solution for the system of equations is $(4, {}^-1)$.

297. Transform the first equation by eliminating
the denominators.

Multiply both sides of the equation by 10. $\qquad$ $10(\frac{2x}{10} + \frac{y}{5}) = 10(1)$

Use the distributive property of multiplication. $\qquad$ $10(\frac{2x}{10}) + 10(\frac{y}{5}) = 10$

Simplify terms. $\qquad$ $2x + 2y = 10$

Divide both sides by 2. $\qquad$ $\frac{2x + 2y}{2} = \frac{10}{2}$

Simplify terms. $\qquad$ $x + y = 5$

Now express x in terms of y. Subtract y from
  both sides of the equation. $\qquad$ $x + y - y = 5 - y$

Simplify. $\qquad$ $x = 5 - y$

Substitute the value of x into the second equation
  and solve for y. $\qquad$ $3(5 - y) + 2y = 12$

Use the distributive property of multiplication. $\qquad$ $3(5) - 3y + 2y = 12$

Combine like terms on each side. $\qquad$ $15 - y = 12$

Add y to both sides. $\qquad$ $15 - y + y = 12 + y$

Combine like terms. $\qquad$ $15 = 12 + y$

Subtract 12 from both sides. $\qquad$ $15 - 12 = 12 - 12 + y$

Simplify. $\qquad$ $3 = y$

Substitute the value of y into one of the equations
  in the system and solve for x. $\qquad$ $3x + 2\,(3) = 12$

Simplify the term and subtract 6
  from both sides. $\qquad$ $3x + 6 - 6 = 12 - 6$

Combine like terms on each side. $\qquad$ $3x = 6$

Divide both sides by 3. $\qquad$ $x = 2$

The solution for the system of equations is (2,3).

298. Transform the second equation so that the value
  of x is expressed in terms of y. Add 3 to both sides. $\qquad$ $x - 3 + 3 = 2y + 3$

Combine like terms on each side. $\qquad$ $x = 2y + 3$

Substitute the value of x into the first equation
  in the system and solve for y. $\qquad$ $(2y + 3) + 5y = 10$

Use the commutative property of addition. $\qquad$ $2y + 5y + 3 = 10$

Combine like terms. $\qquad$ $7y + 3 = 10$

Subtract 3 from both sides. $\qquad$ $7y + 3 - 3 = 10 - 3$

Combine like terms on each side. $\qquad$ $7y = 7$

Divide both sides by 7. $\qquad$ $y = 1$

Substitute the found value for y into the first
  equation and solve for x. $\qquad$ $x + 5(1) = 10$

Subtract 5 from both sides. $\qquad$ $x + 5 - 5 = 10 - 5$

Simplify. $\qquad$ $x = 5$

The solution for the system of equations is (5,1).

299. Transform the second equation so that the
  value of y is expressed in terms of x.
  Subtract 10 from both sides of the equation. $\qquad$ $y + 10 - 10 = 3x - 10$

Combine like terms on each side. $\qquad$ $y = 3x - 10$

Substitute the value of y into the first
  equation in the system and solve for x. $\qquad$ $4(3x - 10) + 31 = 3x$

Use the distributive property of multiplication. $\qquad$ $4(3x) - 4\,(10) + 31 = 3x$

Simplify terms. $\qquad$ $12x - 40 + 31 = 3x$

Combine like terms on each side. $\qquad$ $12x - 9 = 3x$

Add 9 to both sides of the equation. $\qquad$ $12x - 9 + 9 = 3x + 9$

Combine like terms on each side.	$12x = 3x + 9$
Subtract $3x$ from both sides.	$12x - 3x = 3x - 3x + 9$
Combine like terms on each side.	$9x = 9$
Divide both sides by 9.	$x = 1$
Substitute the value of x into the second equation and solve for y.	$y + 10 = 3(1)$
Subtract 10 from both sides.	$y + 10 - 10 = 3 - 10$
Combine like terms on each side.	$y = {}^-7$

The solution for the system of equations is $(1, {}^-7)$.

300. Begin with the second equation and express x in terms of y.

Use the distributive property of multiplication.	$3x + 9 = 20 - 4y$
Subtract 9 from both sides.	$3x + 9 - 9 = 20 - 9 - 4y$
Combine like terms on each side.	$3x = 11 - 4y$
Divide both sides by 3.	$x = \frac{11 - 4y}{3}$
Substitute the value of x into the second equation and solve for y. First, use the distributive property to simplify the equation.	$4 - 2x = 3y - 2$ $4 - 2(\frac{11 - 4y}{3}) = 3y - 2$
Multiply the numerator by the factor 2.	$4 - (\frac{22 - 8y}{3}) = 3y - 2$
Multiply both sides of the equation by 3 to eliminate the denominator.	$3(4 - (\frac{22 - 8y}{3})) = 3(3y - 2)$
Use the distributive property of multiplication.	$3(4) - 3(\frac{22 - 8y}{3}) = 3(3y) - 3(2)$
Simplify each term.	$12 - (22 - 8y) = 9y - 6$
Simplify the second term and the $-$ sign.	$12 - 22 + 8y = 9y - 6$
Combine like terms.	${}^-10 + 8y = 9y - 6$
Add 6 to both sides.	$6 - 10 + 8y = 9y + 6 - 6$
Combine like terms on each side.	${}^-4 + 8y = 9y$
Subtract $8y$ from both sides.	${}^-4 + 8y - 8y = 9y - 8y$
Combine like terms on each side.	${}^-4 = y$
Substitute the value of y into the first equation in the system and solve for x.	$2(2 - x) = 3({}^-4) - 2$
Distributive property of multiplication.	$4 - 2x = {}^-12 - 2$
Subtract 4 from both sides.	$4 - 4 - 2x = {}^-12 - 2 - 4$
Simplify.	${}^-2x = {}^-18$
Divide both sides by ${}^-2$.	$x = 9$

The solution for the system of equations is $(9, {}^-4)$.

Working with Exponents

In this chapter, you will practice adding, subtracting, multiplying, and dividing expressions that contain variables with exponents. You will follow all the rules you have learned about operating with variables, but in this chapter, the variables have exponents.

Tips for Working with Exponents

Add and subtract like terms:

$$3n + 5n = 8n, \text{ or } 5x^2y - 3x^2y = 2x^2y.$$

When multiplying variables with exponents, if the variables are the same, add the exponents and write the base only once:

$$(a^4)(a^3) = a^{(4 + 3)} = a^7$$
$$(x^2y^3)(axy^5) = ax^{(2 + 1)}y^{(3 + 5)} = ax^3y^8$$

When dividing variables with exponents, if the variables are the same, you subtract the exponents:

$$\frac{n^5}{n^2} = \frac{n \cdot n \cdot n \cdot n \cdot n}{n \cdot n} = n^{5-2} = n^3$$

If the exponent of a similar term in the denominator is larger than the one in the numerator, the exponent will have a negative sign:

$$\frac{2x^3}{x^4} = 2x^{-1}$$

$$\frac{n^5}{n^8} = n^{5-8} = n^{-3}$$

A negative numerator becomes positive when the variable is moved into the denominator.

$$2x^{-1} = 2(\frac{1}{x^1}) = \frac{2}{x}$$

$$n^{-3} = \frac{1}{n^5}$$

When the result of a division leaves an exponent of zero, the term raised to the power of zero equals 1:

$$z^0 = 1$$

$$3\frac{r^2}{r^2} = 3r^0 = 3(1) = 3$$

When a variable with an exponent is raised to a power, you multiply the exponent to form the new term:

$$(b^2)^3 = b^2 \cdot b^2 \cdot b^2 = b^2 + b^2 + b^2 = b^6$$

$$(2x^2y)^2 = 2x^2y \cdot 2x^2y = 2 \cdot 2 \cdot x^2 \cdot x^2 \cdot y \cdot y = 2^2x^{2+2}y^{1+1} = 4x^4y^2$$

Remember order of operations. PEMDAS. Generally, list terms in order from highest power to lowest power.

Simplify the following expressions:

301. $3x^2 + 9x^2$

302. $5ab^4 - ab^4$

303. $9mn^3 + 8mn + 2mn^3$

304. $5c^2 + 3c - 2c^2 + 4 - 7c$

305. $3x^2 + 4ax - 8a^2 + 7x^2 - 2ax + 7a^2$

306. $(5n^2)(2n^5 - 2n^3 + 3n^7)$

307. $4xy \cdot 3xy + 7x^2y^2$

308. $(5a^2 \cdot 3ab) + 2a^3b$

309. $\frac{8xy^2}{2xy}$

310. $(4a^2)^3 + (2a^3)^2 - 11a^6$

311. $\frac{(3x)^3}{x^2 \cdot x^4}$

312. $\frac{(12s^2)(2s^4)}{3s^3}$

313. $\frac{7a^2b^5}{28ab^2}$

314. $(3xy^5)^2 - 11x^2y^2(4y^4)^2$

315. $\frac{2(3x^2y)^2(xy)^3}{3(xy)^2}$

316. $\frac{2x^2y^5}{x^5y^3}$

317. $4x^{-2}(5ax)^2$

318. $\frac{3x^{-2}}{x^5} - \frac{2x}{x^8}$

319. $(5a^2x^3y)^3$

320. $\frac{24x^3}{(2x)^2} + \frac{3x^5}{x^4} - \frac{(3ax)^2}{a^2x}$

321. $(4x^2y)^3 + \frac{(2x^2y)^4}{2x^2y}$

322. $\frac{7ax}{(a^2x)^2}$

323. $(ab^2)^3 + 2b^2 - (4a)^3b^6$

324. $\frac{(4b)^2x^{-2}}{(2ab^2x)^2}$

325. $(2xy \cdot \frac{4}{x})^2 + \frac{9y^2}{(3y)^2}$

Answers

Numerical expressions in parentheses like this [ ] are operations performed on only part of the original expression. The operations performed within these symbols are intended to show how to evaluate the various terms that make up the entire expression.

Expressions with parentheses that look like this ( ) contain either numerical substitutions or expressions that are part of a numerical expression. Once a single number appears within these parentheses, the parentheses are no longer needed and need not be used the next time the entire expression is written.

When two pair of parentheses appear side by side like this ( )( ), it means that the expressions within are to be multiplied.

Sometimes parentheses appear within other parentheses in numerical or algebraic expressions. Regardless of what symbol is used, ( ), { }, or [ ], perform operations in the innermost parentheses first and work outward.

Underlined expressions show the simplified result.

301. Add like terms.

$3x^2 + 9x^2 = 12x^2$

302. Subtract like terms.

$5ab^4 - ab^4 = 4ab^4$

303. Use the commutative property
of addition.
Combine like terms.

$9mn^3 + 2mn^3 + 8mn$
$11mn^3 + 8mn$

304. Use the commutative property
of addition.
Combine like terms.

$5c^2 - 2c^2 - 7c + 3c + 4$
$3c^2 - 4c + 4$

305. Use the commutative property
of addition.
Combine like terms.

$3x^2 + 7x^2 + 4ax - 2ax - 8a^2 + 7a^2$
$10x^2 + 2ax - a^2$

306. Use the distributive property.
Use the commutative property
of multiplication.
Add the exponents of the variables.

$(5n^2)(2n^5) - (5n^2)(2n^3) + (5n^2)(3n^7)$
$(5 \cdot 2 \cdot n^2n^5) - (5 \cdot 2 \cdot n^2n^3) + (5 \cdot 3 \cdot n^2n^7)$
$(10 \cdot n^{2+5}) - (10 \cdot n^{2+3}) + (15 \cdot n^{2+7})$
$10n^7 - 10n^5 + 15n^9$

Show expression in decreasing
exponential order.

$15n^9 + 10n^7 - 10n^5$

307. Use the commutative property
of multiplication.
When the same variables are multiplied,
add the exponents of the variables.
Combine like terms.

$(4 \cdot 3xxyy) + 7x^2y^2$

$(12x^2y^2) + 7x^2y^2$
$19x^2y^2$

308. Use the commutative property
of multiplication. $\qquad$ $(5 \cdot 3a^2ab) + 2a^3b$
When the same variables are multiplied,
add the exponents of the variables. $\qquad$ $15a^3b + 2a^3b$
Combine like terms. $\qquad$ $\underline{17a^3b}$

309. Divide numerical terms. $\qquad$ $\frac{8xy^2}{2xy} = \frac{4xy^2}{xy}$
When similar factors, or bases, are being divided,
subtract the exponent in the denominator from
the exponent in the numerator. $\qquad$ $\frac{4xy^2}{xy} = 4x^{1-1}y^{2-1}$
Simplify. $\qquad$ $\underline{4x^0y^1 = 4(1)y = 4y}$

310. Terms within parentheses are the base of
the exponent outside the parentheses. $\qquad$ $(4a^2)(4a^2)(4a^2)$
$$+ (2a^3)(2a^3) - 11a^6$$
Use the distributive property of multiplication. $(4 \cdot 4 \cdot 4)(a^2 \cdot a^2 \cdot a^2)$
$$+ (2 \cdot 2)(a^3 \cdot a^3) - 11a^6$$
When the same variables are multiplied, add
the exponents of the variables. $\qquad$ $64(a^{2+2+2}) + 4(a^{3+3}) - 11a^6$
Simplify. $\qquad$ $64a^6 + 4a^6 - 11a^6$
Combine like terms. $\qquad$ $\underline{57a^6}$
Another way of solving this problem is to
multiply the exponents of each factor
inside the parentheses by the exponent
outside of the parentheses. $\qquad$ $4^{(1)3}a^{(2)3} + 2^{(1)2}a^{(3)2} - 11a^6$
Simplify the expressions in the exponents. $4^3a^6 + 2^2a^6 - 11a^6$
Simplify terms. $\qquad$ $64a^6 + 4a^6 - 11a^6$
Combine like terms. $\qquad$ $\underline{57a^6}$

311. In the denominator, multiply the exponents of each
factor inside the parentheses by the exponent
outside of the parentheses. $\qquad$ $\frac{3^3x^3}{x^2 \cdot x^4}$
In the numerator, add the exponents of similar bases. $\frac{3^3x^3}{x^{2+4}} = \frac{27x^3}{x^6}$
When similar factors, or bases, are being divided,
you subtract the exponent in the denominator
from the exponent in the numerator. $\qquad$ $27x^{3-6} = 27x^{-3}$
A base with a negative exponent in the numerator
is equivalent to the same variable or base in the
denominator with the inverse sign for the exponent. $27x^{-3} = \frac{27x}{3}$

312. Commutative property of multiplication. $\qquad$ $\frac{12 \cdot 2s^2 \cdot s^4}{3s^3}$
When similar factors, or bases, are multiplied, add
the exponents of the variables. $\qquad$ $\frac{12 \cdot 2s^{2+4}}{3s^3}$
Simplify the exponent and coefficients. $\qquad$ $\frac{8s^6}{s^3}$

When similar factors, or bases, are being divided,
subtract the exponent in the denominator from the
exponent in the numerator.

$$8s^{6-3} = 8s^3$$

313. Divide out the common factor of 7 in the
numerator and denominator.

$$\frac{1 \cdot 7a^2b^5}{4 \cdot 7ab^2} = \frac{1a^2b^5}{4ab^2}$$

When similar factors, or bases, are being divided, subtract
the exponent in the denominator from the exponent in
the numerator.

$$\frac{1a^2b^5}{4ab^2} = \frac{1a^{2-1}b^{5-2}}{4}$$

Simplify exponents.

$$\frac{1a^1b^3}{4}$$

Separate the coefficient from the variable.
Either expression is an acceptable answer.

$$\frac{a^1b^3}{4} = \frac{1}{4}ab^3$$

314. Multiply the exponents of each factor inside
the parentheses by the exponent outside
the parentheses.

$$3^2x^2y^{10} - 11x^2y^24^2y^8$$

Use the commutative property of multiplication.

$$3^2x^2y^{10} - 11 \cdot 4^2x^2y^2y^8$$

When similar factors, or bases, are multiplied,
add the exponents of the variables.

$$3^2x^2y^{10} - 11 \cdot 16 \cdot x^2y^{10}$$

Evaluate numerical factors.

$$9x^2y^{10} - 176x^2y^{10}$$

Combine like terms.

$$-167x^2y^{10}$$

315. Multiply the exponents of each factor inside the
parentheses by the exponent outside the parentheses.

$$\frac{2(3^2x^4y^2)(x^3y^3)}{3(x^2y^2)}$$

Use the commutative property of multiplication.

$$\frac{2 \cdot 9 \cdot x^4x^3y^2y^3}{3x^2y^2}$$

When similar factors, or bases, are multiplied, add the
exponents of the variables.

$$\frac{2 \cdot 9 \cdot x^{4+3}y^{2+3}}{3x^2y^2}$$

Factor out like numerical terms in the fraction, and
simplify exponents with operations.

$$\frac{6x^7y^5}{x^2y^2}$$

When similar factors, or bases, are being divided,
subtract the exponent in the denominator from the
exponent in the numerator.

$$6x^{7-2}y^{5-2}$$

Simplify the operations in the exponents.

$$6x^5y^3$$

316. When similar factors, or bases, are being divided,
subtract the exponent in the denominator from
the exponent in the numerator.

$$\frac{2x^2y^5}{x^5y^3} = 2x^{2-5}y^{5-3}$$

Simplify the operations in the exponents.
A base with a negative exponent in the numerator
is equivalent to the same variable or base in the
denominator with the inverse sign for the exponent.

$$2x^{2-5}y^{5-3} = 2x^{-3}y^2$$

$$2x^{-3}y^2 = \frac{2y^2}{x^3}$$

317. Multiply the exponents of each factor inside the
parentheses by the exponent outside the parentheses.

$$4x^{-2}(5^2a^2x^2)$$

Use the commutative property of multiplication.

$$4 \cdot 5^2 \cdot a^2x^2x^{-2}$$

Evaluate numerical terms. $\qquad$ $100a^2x^2x^{-2}$

When similar factors, or bases, are being
   multiplied, add the exponents. $\qquad$ $100a^2x^{2-2}$

Simplify the operations in the exponents. $\qquad$ $100a^2x^0$

Any base to the power of $0 = 1$. $\qquad$ $100a^2(1)$

Identity element of multiplication. $\qquad$ $\underline{100a^2}$

318. When similar factors, or bases, are being divided,
   subtract the exponent in the denominator
   from the exponent in the numerator. $\qquad$ $3x^{-2-5} - 2x^{1-8}$

Simplify the operations in the exponents. $\qquad$ $3x^{-7} - 2x^{-7}$

Subtract like terms. $\qquad$ x^{-7}

A base with a negative exponent in the numerator
   is equivalent to the same variable or base in the
   denominator with the inverse sign for the exponent. $\qquad$ $x^{-7} = \frac{1}{x^7}$

319. Multiply the exponents of each factor inside the
   parentheses by the exponent outside the parentheses. $\qquad$ $5^3a^6x^9y^3$

Evaluate the numerical coefficient. $\qquad$ $\underline{125a^6x^9y^3}$

320. Multiply the exponents of each factor inside
   the parentheses by the exponent outside
   the parentheses. $\qquad$ $\frac{24x^3}{2^2x^2} + \frac{3x^5}{x^4} - \frac{3^2a^2x^2}{a^2x}$

Evaluate the numerical coefficients and divide
   out common numerical factors in the terms. $\qquad$ $\frac{6x^3}{x^2} + \frac{3x^5}{x^4} - \frac{9a^2x^2}{a^2x}$

When similar factors, or bases, are being divided,
   subtract the exponent in the denominator
   from the exponent in the numerator. $\qquad$ $6x^{3-2} + 3x^{5-4} - 9a^{2-2}x^{2-1}$

Simplify the operations in the exponents. $\qquad$ $6x^1 + 3x^1 - 9a^0x^1$

Any term to the power of zero equals 1. $\qquad$ $6x + 3x - 9(1)x$

Combine like terms. $\qquad$ $\underline{6x + 3x - 9x = 0x = 0}$

321. Multiply the exponents of each factor
   inside the parentheses by the exponent
   outside the parentheses. $\qquad$ $4^3x^6y^3 + \frac{2^4x^8y^4}{2x^2y}$

When similar factors, or bases, are being
   divided, subtract the exponent in the
   denominator from the exponent in the
   numerator. $\qquad$ $4^3x^6y^3 + 2^{4-1}x^{8-2}y^{4-1}$

Simplify the operations in the exponents. $\qquad$ $4^3x^6y^3 + 2^3x^6y^3$

Evaluate the numerical coefficients. $\qquad$ $64x^6y^3 + 8x^6y^3$

Add like terms. $\qquad$ $\underline{72x^6y^3}$

322. Multiply the exponents of each factor inside the parentheses by the exponent outside the parentheses. $\qquad$ $\frac{7ax}{a^4x^2}$

When similar factors, or bases, are being divided,
   subtract the exponent in the denominator from
   the exponent in the numerator. $\qquad$ $7a^{1-4}x^{1-2}$

Simplify the operations in the exponents. $\quad 7a^{-3}x^{-1}$

A base with a negative exponent in the numerator is
equivalent to the same variable or base in the denom-
inator with the inverse sign for the exponent. $\quad 7a^{-3}x^{-1} = \frac{7}{a^3 x^1} = \frac{7}{a^3 x}$

323. Multiply the exponents of each factor inside the parentheses by the exponent outside the parentheses. $\quad a^3b^6 + 2b^2 - 4^3a^3b^6$

Evaluate the numerical coefficients. $\quad a^3b^6 + 2b^2 - 64a^3b^6$

Use the commutative property of addition. $\quad 2b^2 - 64a^3b^6 + a^3b^6$

Combine like terms in the expression. $\quad 2b^2 - 63a^3b^6$

324. Multiply the exponents of each factor inside the parentheses
by the exponent outside the parentheses. $\quad \dfrac{4^2b^2x^{-2}}{2^2a^2b^4x^2}$

Evaluate the numerical coefficients. $\quad \dfrac{16b^2x^{-2}}{4a^2b^4x^2}$

Simplify the numerical factors in the numerator and the
denominator. $\quad \dfrac{4b^2x^{-2}}{a^2b^4x^2}$

When similar factors, or bases, are being divided, subtract
the exponent in the denominator from the exponent in
the numerator. $\quad \dfrac{4b^{2-4}x^{-2-2}}{a^2}$

Simplify the operations in the exponents. $\quad \dfrac{4b^{-2}x^{-4}}{a^2}$

A base with a negative exponent in the numerator is equivalent
to the same variable or base in the denominator with the
inverse sign for the exponent. $\quad \dfrac{4}{a^2b^2x^4}$

325. Multiply the exponents of each factor inside the
parentheses by the exponent outside the parentheses. $\quad (2xy)^2 \cdot \left(\frac{4}{x}\right)^2 + \frac{9y^2}{3^2y^2}$

Repeat the previous step. $\quad (2^2x^2y^2)\left(\frac{4^2}{x^2}\right) + \frac{9y^2}{3^2y^2}$

Evaluate numerical factors. $\quad (4x^2y^2)\left(\frac{16}{x^2}\right) + \frac{9y^2}{9y^2}$

The last term is equivalent to 1.
Multiply the fraction in the first term by the
factor in the first term. $\quad (4x^2y^2)\left(\frac{16}{x^2}\right) + 1$

$\quad \left(\frac{(4x^2y^2)16}{x^2}\right) + 1$

Use the commutative property of multiplication. $\quad \left(\frac{4 \cdot 16x^2y^2}{x^2}\right) + 1$

Evaluate numerical factors. $\quad \frac{64x^2y^2}{x^2} + 1$

Divide out the common factor of x^2 in the
numerator and denominator. $\quad 64y^2 + 1$

Multiplying Polynomials

This chapter will present problems for you to solve in the multiplication of polynomials. Specifically, you will practice solving problems multiplying a monomial (one term) and a polynomial, multiplying binomials (expressions with two terms), and multiplying a trinomial and a binomial.

Tips for Multiplying Polynomials

When multiplying a polynomial by a monomial, you use the distributive property of multiplication to multiply each term in the polynomial by the monomial.

$$a(b + c + d + e) = ab + ac + ad + ae$$

When multiplying a binomial by a binomial,
you use the mnemonic FOIL to remind
you of the order with which you multiply
terms in the binomials. $(a + b)(c + d)$

F is for **first**. Multiply the first terms
of each binomial. $([a] + b)([c] + d)$ gives the term ac.

O is for **outer**. Multiply the outer
terms of each binomial. $([a] + b)(c + [d])$ gives the term ad.

I is for **inner**. Multiply the inner terms
of each binomial. $(a + [b])([c] + d)$ gives the term bc.

L is for **last**. Multiply the last terms
of each binomial. $(a + [b])(c + [d])$ gives the term bd.

Then you combine the terms. $ac + ad + bc + bd$

Multiplying a trinomial by a binomial is relatively easy. You proceed similarly to the
way you would when using the distributive property of multiplication. Multiply
each term in the trinomial by the first and then the second term in the binomial.
Then add the results.

$$(a + b)(c + d + e) = (ac + ad + ae) + (bc + bd + be)$$

Multiply the following polynomials.

326. $x(3x + 4y - 8)$

327. $2a(5a^2 - 7a + 9)$

328. $4bc(3b^2c + 7b - 9c + 2bc^2 - 8)$

329. $3mn(^-4m + 6n + 7mn^2 - 3m^2n)$

330. $4x(9x^3 + \frac{3}{x^2} - x^4 + \frac{6x - 1}{x^2})$

331. $(x + 3)(x + 5)$

332. $(x - 4)(x - 9)$

333. $(2x + 1)(3x - 7)$

334. $(x + 2)(x - 3y)$

335. $(7x + 2y)(2x - 4y)$

336. $(5x + 7)(5x - 7)$

337. $(28x + 7)(\frac{x}{7} - 11)$

338. $(3x^2 + y^2)(x^2 - 2y^2)$

339. $(4 + x^2)(9 - 4x)$

340. $(2x^2 + y^2)(x^2 - y^2)$

341. $(x + 2)(3x^2 - 4x + 1)$

342. $(2x - 3)(x^3 + 3x^2 - 4x)$

343. $(4a + b)(5a^2 + 2ab - b^2)$

344. $(3y - 7)(6y^2 - 3y + 7)$

345. $(3x + 2)(2x^2 - 2x - 5)$

346. $(x + 2)(2x + 1)(x - 1)$

347. $(3a - 4)(5a + 2)(a + 3)$

348. $(2n - 3)(2n + 3)(n + 4)$

349. $(5r - 7)(3r^4 + 2r^2 + 6)$

350. $(3x^2 + 4)(x - 3)(3x^2 - 4)$

Answers

Numerical expressions in parentheses like this [ ] are operations performed on only part of the original expression. The operations performed within these symbols are intended to show how to evaluate the various terms that make up the entire expression.

Expressions with parentheses that look like this ( ) contain either numerical substitutions or expressions that are part of a numerical expression. Once a single number appears within these parentheses, the parentheses are no longer needed and need not be used the next time the entire expression is written.

When two pair of parentheses appear side by side like this ( )( ), it means that the expressions within are to be multiplied.

Sometimes parentheses appear within other parentheses in numerical or algebraic expressions. Regardless of what symbol is used, ( ), { }, or [ ], perform operations in the innermost parentheses first and work outward.

Underlined expressions show the simplified result.

326. Multiply each term in the trinomial by x.
Simplify terms.
$x(3x) + x(4y) - x(8)$
$\underline{3x^2 + 4xy - 8x}$

327. Multiply each term in the trinomial by $2a$.
Simplify terms.
$2a(5a^2) - 2a(7a) + 2a(9)$
$\underline{10a^3 - 14a^2 + 18a}$

328. Multiply each term in the polynomial by $4bc$.
$4bc(3b^2c) + 4bc(7b) - 4bc(9c) + 4bc(2bc^2) - 4bc(8)$
Simplify terms. $\underline{12b^3c^2 + 28b^2c - 36bc^2 + 8b^2c^3 - 32bc}$

329. Multiply each term in the polynomial by $3mn$.
$3mn(-4m) + 3mn(6n) + 3mn(7mn^2) - 3mn(3m^2n)$
Simplify terms. $\underline{-12m^2n + 18mn^2 + 21m^2n^3 - 9m^3n^2}$

330. Multiply each term in the polynomial by $4x$.

$$4x(9x^3) + 4x(\tfrac{3}{x^2}) - 4x(x^4) + 4x(\tfrac{6x-1}{x^2})$$

Simplify terms.

$$36x^4 + \tfrac{12x}{x^2} - 4x^5 + \tfrac{4x(6x-1)}{x^2}$$

Use the distributive property in the numerator of the 4th term.

$$36x^4 + \tfrac{12x}{x^2} - 4x^5 + \tfrac{24x^2 - 4x}{x^2}$$

When similar factors, or bases, are being divided, subtract the exponent in the denominator from the exponent in the numerator.

$$36x^4 + 12x^{1-2} - 4x^5 + 24x^{2-2} - 4x^{1-2}$$

Simplify operations in the exponents.

$$36x^4 + 12x^{-1} - 4x^5 + 24x^0 - 4x^{-1}$$

Use the associative property of addition.

$$36x^4 + 12x^{-1} - 4x^{-1} - 4x^5 + 24x^0$$

Combine like terms.

$$36x^4 + 8x^{-1} - 4x^5 + 24x^0$$

A base with a negative exponent in the numerator is equivalent to the same variable or base in the denominator with the inverse sign for the exponent.

$$36x^4 + \tfrac{8}{x} - 4x^5 + 24x^0$$

A variable to the power of zero equals 1.

$$36x^4 + \tfrac{8}{x} - 4x^5 + 24(1)$$

Simplify and put in order.

$$\underline{-4x^5 + 36x^4 + \tfrac{8}{x} + 24}$$

331. Use **FOIL** to multiply binomials.

Multiply the **first** terms in each binomial.

$$([x] + 3)([x] + 5)$$
$$x^2$$

Multiply the **outer** terms in each binomial.

$$([x] + 3)(x + [\,5\,])$$
$$+5x$$

Multiply the **inner** terms in each binomial.

$$(x + [3])([x] + 5)$$
$$+3x$$

Multiply the **last** terms in each binomial.

$$(x + [3])(x + [5])$$
$$+15$$

Add the products of FOIL together.

$$x^2 + 5x + 3x + 15$$

Combine like terms.

$$\underline{x^2 + 8x + 15}$$

332. Use **FOIL** to multiply binomials.

Multiply the **first** terms in each binomial.

$$([x] - 4)([x] - 9)$$
$$x^2$$

Multiply the **outer** terms in each binomial.

$$([x] - 4)(x - [9])$$
$$-9x$$

Multiply the **inner** terms in each binomial.

$$(x - [4])([x] - 9)$$
$$-4x$$

Multiply the **last** terms in each binomial.

$$(x - [4])(x - [9])$$
$$+36$$

Add the products of FOIL together.

$$x^2 - 9x - 4x + 36$$

Combine like terms.

$$\underline{x^2 - 13x + 36}$$

333. Use **FOIL** to multiply binomials.
Multiply the **first** terms in each binomial.

$([2x] + 1)([3x] - 7)$
$6x^2$

Multiply the **outer** terms in each binomial.

$([2x] + 1)(3x - [7])$
^-14x

Multiply the **inner** terms in each binomial.

$(2x + [1])([3x] - 7)$
^+3x

Multiply the **last** terms in each binomial.

$(2x + [1])(3x - [7])$
-7

Add the products of FOIL together.
Combine like terms.

$6x^2 - 14x + 3x - 7$
$\underline{6x^2 - 11x - 7}$

334. Use **FOIL** to multiply binomials.
Multiply the **first** terms in each binomial.

$([x] + 2)([x] - 3y)$
x^2

Multiply the **outer** terms in each binomial.

$([x] + 2)(x - [3y])$
^-3xy

Multiply the **inner** terms in each binomial.

$(x + [2])([x] - 3y)$
^+2x

Multiply the **last** terms in each binomial.

$(x + [2])(x - [3y])$
^-6y

Add the products of FOIL together.

$\underline{x^2 - 3xy + 2x - 6y}$

335. Use **FOIL** to multiply binomials.
Multiply the **first** terms in each binomial.

$([7x] + 2y)([2x] - 4y)$
$14x^2$

Multiply the **outer** terms in each binomial.

$([7x] + 2y)(2x - [4y])$
^-28xy

Multiply the **inner** terms in each binomial.

$(7x + [2y])([2x] - 4y)$
^+4xy

Multiply the **last** terms in each binomial.

$(7x + [2y])(2x - [4y])$
$^-8y^2$

Add the products of FOIL together.
Combine like terms.

$14x^2 - 28xy + 4xy - 8y^2$
$\underline{14x^2 - 24xy - 8y^2}$

336. Use **FOIL** to multiply binomials.
Multiply the **first** terms in each binomial.

$([5x] + 7)([5x] - 7)$
$25x^2$

Multiply the **outer** terms in each binomial.

$([5x] + 7)(5x - [7])$
^-35x

Multiply the **inner** terms in each binomial.

$(5x + [7])([5x] - 7)$
^+35x

Multiply the **last** terms in each binomial.

$(5x + [7] (5x - [7]))$
-49

Add the products of FOIL together.
Combine like terms.

$25x^2 - 35x + 35x - 49$
$\underline{25x^2 - 49}$

337. Use **FOIL** to multiply binomials.

Multiply the **first** terms in each binomial.
$$([28x] + 7)([\tfrac{x}{7}] - 11)$$
$$4x^2$$

Multiply the **outer** terms in each binomial.
$$([28x] + 7)(\tfrac{x}{7} - [11])$$
$$^-308x$$

Multiply the **inner** terms in each binomial.
$$(28x + [7])([\tfrac{x}{7}] - 11)$$
$$+x$$

Multiply the **last** terms in each binomial.
$$(28x + [7])(\tfrac{x}{7} - [11])$$
$$-77$$

Add the products of FOIL together.
Combine like terms.
$$4x^2 - 308x + x - 77$$
$$\underline{4x^2 - 307x - 77}$$

338. Use **FOIL** to multiply binomials.

Multiply the **first** terms in each binomial.
$$([3x^2] + y^2)([x^2] - 2y^2)$$
$$3x^4$$

Multiply the **outer** terms in each binomial.
$$([3x^2] + y^2)(x^2 - [2y^2])$$
$$^-6x^2y^2$$

Multiply the **inner** terms in each binomial.
$$(3x^2 + [y^2])([x^2] - 2y^2$$
$$^+x^2y^2$$

Multiply the **last** terms in each binomial.
$$(3x^2 + [y^2])(x^2 - [2y^2])$$
$$-2y^4$$

Add the products of FOIL together.
Combine like terms.
$$3x^4 - 6x^2y^2 + x^2y^2 - 2y^4$$
$$\underline{3x^4 - 5x^2y^2 - 2y^4}$$

339. Use **FOIL** to multiply binomials.

Multiply the **first** terms in each binomial.
$$([4] + x^2)([9] - 4x)$$
$$^+36$$

Multiply the **outer** terms in each binomial.
$$([4] + x^2)(9 - [4x])$$
$$^-16x$$

Multiply the **inner** terms in each binomial.
$$(4 + [x^2])([9] - 4x)$$
$$^+9x^2$$

Multiply the **last** terms in each binomial.
$$(4 + [x^2])(9 - [4x])$$
$$^-4x^3$$

Add the products of FOIL together.
Simplify and put them in order from the
highest power.
$$36 - 16x + 9x^2 - 4x^3$$

$$\underline{^-4x^3 + 9x^2 - 16x + 36}$$

340. Use **FOIL** to multiply binomials.

Multiply the **first** terms in each binomial.
$$([2x^2] + y^2)([x^2] - y^2)$$
$$2x^4$$

Multiply the **outer** terms in each binomial.
$$([2x^2] + y^2)(x^2 - [y^2])$$
$$^-2x^2y^2$$

Multiply the **inner** terms in each binomial.
$$(2x^2 + [y^2])([x^2] - y^2)$$
$$^+x^2y^2$$

Multiply the **last** terms in each binomial.
$$(2x^2 + [y^2])(x^2 - [y^2])$$
$$^-y^4$$

Add the products of FOIL together.
Combine like terms.
$$2x^4 - 2x^2y^2 + x^2y^2 - y^4$$
$$\underline{2x^4 - x^2y^2 - y^4}$$

341. Multiply the trinomial by the first term in the binomial, x.

$[x(3x^2 - 4x + 1)]$
$[x(3x^2) - x(4x) + x(1)]$

Simplify terms. $[3x^3 - 4x^2 + x]$

Multiply the trinomial by the second term in the binomial, 2.

$[2(3x^2 - 4x + 1)]$
$[2(3x^2) - 2(4x) + 2(1)]$

Simplify terms. $[6x^2 - 8x + 2]$

Add the results of multiplying by the terms in the binomial together. $[3x^3 - 4x^2 + x] + [6x^2 - 8x + 2]$

Use the commutative property of addition. $3x^3 - 4x^2 + 6x^2 + x - 8x + 2$

Combine like terms. $\underline{3x^3 + 2x^2 - 7x + 2}$

342. Multiply the trinomial by the first term in the binomial, $2x$.

$[2x(x^3 + 3x^2 - 4x)]$

Use the distributive property of multiplication.

$[2x(x^3) + 2x(3x^2) - 2x(4x)]$

Simplify terms. $[2x^4 + 6x^3 - 8x^2]$

Multiply the trinomial by the second term in the binomial, $^-3$.

$[^-3(x^3 + 3x^2 - 4x)]$

Use the distributive property of multiplication.

$[^-3(x^3) - 3(3x^2) - 3(^-4x)]$

Simplify terms. $[^-3x^3 - 9x^2 + 12x]$

Add the results of multiplying by the terms in the binomial together. $[2x^4 + 6x^3 - 8x^2] + [^-3x^3 - 9x^2 + 12x)]$

Use the commutative property of addition.

$2x^4 + 6x^3 - 3x^3 + 8x^2 - 9x^2 + 12x$

Combine like terms. $\underline{2x^4 + 3x^3 - 17x^2 + 12x}$

343. Multiply the trinomial by the first term in the binomial, $4a$.

$[4a(5a^2 + 2ab - b^2)]$

Use the distributive property of multiplication.

$[4a(5a^2) + 4a(2ab) - 4a(b^2)]$

Simplify terms. $[20a^3 + 8a^2b - 4ab^2]$

Multiply the trinomial by the second term in the binomial, b. $[b(5a^2 + 2ab - b^2)]$

Use the distributive property of multiplication.

$[b(5a^2) + b(2ab) - b(b^2)]$

Simplify terms. $[5a^2b + 2ab^2 - b^3]$

Add the results of multiplying by the terms in the binomial together.

$[20a^3 + 8a^2b - 4ab^2] + [5a^2b + 2ab^2 - b^3)]$

Use the commutative property of addition.

$20a^3 + 8a^2b + 5a^2b - 4ab^2 + 2ab^2 - b^3$

Combine like terms. $\underline{20a^3 + 13a^2b - 2ab^2 - b^3}$

344. Multiply the trinomial by the first
term in the binomial, $3y$. $[3y(6y^2 - 3y + 7)]$
Use the distributive property of
multiplication. $[3y(6y^2) - 3y(3y) + 3y(7)]$
Simplify terms. $[18y^3 - 9y^2 + 21y]$
Multiply the trinomial by the
second term in the binomial, $^-7$. $[^-7(6y^2 - 3y + 7)]$
Use the distributive property of
multiplication. $[^-7(6y^2) - 7(^-3y) - 7(7)]$
Simplify terms. $[^-42y^2 + 21y - 49]$
Add the results of multiplying
by the terms in the binomial
together. $[18y^3 - 9y^2 + 21y] + [^-42y^2 + 21y - 49]$
Use the commutative property
of addition. $18y^3 - 9y^2 - 42y^2 + 21y + 21y - 49$
Combine like terms. $\underline{18y^3 - 51y^2 + 42y - 49}$

345.. Multiply the trinomial by the first term
in the binomial, $3x$. $[3x(2x^2 - 2x - 5)]$
Use the distributive property
of multiplication. $[3x(2x^2) - 3x(2x) - 3x(5)]$
Simplify terms. $[6x^3 - 6x^2 - 15x]$
Multiply the trinomial by the second
term in the binomial, 2. $[2(2x^2 - 2x - 5)]$
Use the distributive property
of multiplication. $[2(2x^2) - 2(2x) - 2(5)]$
Simplify terms. $[4x^2 - 4x - 10]$
Add the results of multiplying by the
terms in the binomial together. $[6x^3 - 6x^2 - 15x] + [4x^2 - 4x - 10]$
Use the commutative property
of addition. $6x^3 + 4x^2 - 6x^2 - 15x - 4x - 10$
Combine like terms. $\underline{6x^3 - 2x^2 - 19x - 10}$

346. Multiply the first two parenthetical terms
in the expression using **FOIL**.
Multiply the **first** terms in each binomial. $([x] + 2)([2x] + 1)$
$2x^2$

Multiply the **outer** terms in each
binomial. $([x] + 2)(2x + [1])$
^+x

Multiply the **inner** terms in each
binomial. $(x + [2])([2x] + 1)$
^+4x

Multiply the **last** terms in each binomial. $(x + [2])(2x + [1])$
$^+2$

Add the products of FOIL together. $2x^2 + x + 4x + 2$
Combine like terms. $2x^2 + 5x + 2$

Multiply the resulting trinomial by the
last binomial in the original
expression. $(x - 1)(2x^2 + 5x + 2)$

Multiply the trinomial by the first term
in the binomial, x. $[x(2x^2 + 5x + 2)]$

Use the distributive property
of multiplication. $[x(2x^2) + x(5x) + x(2)]$

Simplify terms. $[2x^3 + 5x^2 + 2x]$

Multiply the trinomial by the second
term in the binomial, $^-1$. $[^-1(2x^2 + 5x + 2)]$

Use the distributive property
of multiplication. $[^-2x^2 - 5x - 2]$

Add the results of multiplying by the
terms in the binomial together. $[2x^3 + 5x^2 + 2x] + [^-2x^2 - 5x - 2]$

Use the commutative property
of addition. $2x^3 + 5x^2 - 2x^2 + 2x - 5x - 2$

Combine like terms. $\underline{2x^3 + 3x^2 - 3x - 2}$

347. Multiply the first two parenthetical terms
in the expression using **FOIL**.

Multiply the **first** terms in each
binomial. $([3a] - 4)([5a] + 2)$
$\qquad 15a^2$

Multiply the **outer** terms in each
binomial. $([3a] - 4)(5a + [2])$
$\qquad {}^+6a$

Multiply the **inner** terms in each
binomial. $(3a - [4])([5a] + 2)$
$\qquad {}^-20a$

Multiply the **last** terms in each
binomial. $(3a - [4])(5a + [2])$
$\qquad {}^-8$

Add the products of FOIL together. $15a^2 + 6a - 20a - 8$

Combine like terms. $15a^2 - 14a - 8$

Multiply the resulting trinomial by
the last binomial in the original
expression. $(a + 3)(15a^2 - 14a - 8)$

Multiply the trinomial by the first
term in the binomial, a. $[a(15a^2 - 14a - 8)]$

Use the distributive property of
multiplication. $[a(15a^2) - a(14a) - a(8)]$

Simplify terms. $[15a^3 - 14a^2 - 8a]$

Multiply the trinomial by the
second term in the binomial, 3. $[3(15a^2) - 3(14a) - 3(8)]$

Use the distributive property of
multiplication. $[45a^2 - 42a - 24]$

Add the results of multiplying by the
    terms in the binomial together. $[15a^3 - 14a^2 - 8a] + [45a^2 - 42a - 24]$
Use the commutative property
    of addition. $15a^3 - 14a^2 + 45a^2 - 8a - 42a - 24$
Combine like terms. $\underline{15a^3 + 31a^2 - 50a - 24}$

348.   Multiply the first two parenthetical terms
    in the expression using **FOIL**.

Multiply the **first** terms in each binomial. $([2n] - 3)([2n] + 3)$
                                                 $4n^2$

Multiply the **outer** terms in each binomial. $([2n] - 3)(2n + [3])$
                                                 $^{+}6n$

Multiply the **inner** terms in each binomial. $(2n - [3])([2n] + 3)$
                                                 $^{-}6n$

Multiply the **last** terms in each binomial. $(2n - [3])(2n + [3])$
                                                 $^{-}9$

Add the products of FOIL together. $4n^2 + 6n - 6n - 9$
Combine like terms. $4n^2 - 9$
Now we again have two binomials. Use FOIL
    to find the solution. $(n + 4)(4n^2 - 9)$
Multiply the **first** terms in each binomial. $([n] + 4)([4n^2] - 9)$
                                                 $4n^3$

Multiply the **outer** terms in each binomial. $([n] + 4)(4n^2 - [9])$
                                                 $^{-}9n$

Multiply the **inner** terms in each binomial. $(n + [4])([4n^2] - 9)$
                                                 $^{+}16n^2$

Multiply the **last** terms in each binomial. $(n + [4])(4n^2 - [9])$
                                                 $^{-}36$

Add the products of FOIL together. $4n^3 - 9n + 16n^2 - 36$
Order terms from the highest to lowest power. $\underline{4n^3 + 16n^2 - 9n - 36}$

349.   Multiply the trinomial by the
    first term in the binomial, $5r$. $[5r(3r^4 + 2r^2 + 6)]$
Use the distributive property of
    multiplication. $[5r(3r^4) + 5r(2r^2) + 5r(6)]$
Simplify terms. $[15r^5 + 10r^3 + 30r]$
Multiply the trinomial by the sec-
    ond term in the binomial, $^{-}7$. $[^{-}7(3r^4 + 2r^2 + 6)]$
Use the distributive property of
    multiplication. $[^{-}7(3r^4) - 7(2r^2) - 7(6)]$
Simplify terms. $[^{-}21r^4 - 14r^2 - 42]$
Add the results of multiplying
    by the terms in the binomial
    together. $[15r^5 + 10r^3 + 30r] + [^{-}21r^4 - 14r^2 - 42]$
Use the commutative property
    of addition. $\underline{15r^5 - 21r^4 + 10r^3 - 14r^2 + 30r - 42}$

350. Multiply the first two parenthetical terms
in the expression using **FOIL**.

Multiply the **first** terms in each binomial. $([3x^2] + 4)([x] - 3)$
$$3x^3$$

Multiply the **outer** terms in each binomial. $([3x^2] + 4)(x - [3])$
$$^-9x^2$$

Multiply the **inner** terms in each binomial. $(3x^2 + [4])([x] - 3)$
$$^+4x$$

Multiply the **last** terms in each binomial. $(3x^2 + [4])(x - [3])$
$$^-12$$

Add the products of FOIL together. $(3x^3 - 9x^2 + 4x - 12)$

Multiply the resulting trinomial by the last
binomial in the original expression. $(3x^2 - 4)(3x^3 - 9x^2 + 4x - 12)$

Multiply the trinomial by the first term
in the binomial, $3x^2$. $[3x^2(3x^3 - 9x^2 + 4x - 12)]$

Use the distributive property
of multiplication. $[3x^2 (3x^3) - 3x^2(9x^2)$
$$+ 3x^2(4x) - 3x^2(12)]$$

Simplify terms. $[9x^5 - 27x^4 + 12x^3 - 36x^2]$

Multiply the trinomial by the second
term in the binomial, 3. $[^-4(3x^3 - 9x^2 + 4x - 12)]$

Use the distributive property
of multiplication. $[^-12x^3 + 36x^2 - 16x + 48]$

Add the results of multiplying by the
terms in the binomial together. $[9x^5 - 27x^4 + 12x^3 - 36x^2]$
$$+ [^-12x^3 + 36x^2 - 16x + 48]$$

Use the commutative property of addition. $9x^5 - 27x^4 + 12x^3 - 12x^3 -$
$$36x^2 + 36x^2 - 16x + 48$$

Combine like terms. $\underline{9x^5 - 27x^4 - 16x + 48}$

Factoring Polynomials

This chapter will present algebraic expressions for you to factor. You can use three different techniques to factor polynomials. In the first technique, you look for common factors in the terms of the polynomial. In the second, you will factor polynomials that are the difference of two perfect squares. The third technique, called the trinomial factor method, will allow you to factor algebraic expressions that have three terms. The trinomial expressions in this chapter will be in the form of $x^2 \pm ax \pm b$, where a and b are whole numbers. The problems will be presented in random order to give you practice at recognizing which method or combination of methods will be required to factor the polynomial. Complete explanations of the solutions will follow.

Tips for Factoring Polynomials

Factoring using the greatest common factor: Look for a factor common to every term in the polynomial. Put that factor outside a set of parentheses and the polynomial inside with the factor removed from each term, e.g. $2x^2 + 8 = 2(x^2 + 4)$

Factoring using the difference of two perfect squares: Polynomials in the form $x^2 - y^2$ can be factored into two terms: $(x + y)(x - y)$.

Factoring using the trinomial method: This method requires you to factor the first and third terms and put the factors into the following factored form: $([\ ] \pm [\ ])([\ ] \pm [\ ])$. The factors of the first term go in the first position in the parentheses and the factors of the third term go in the second position in each factor, e.g. $x^2 + 2x + 1 = (x + 1)(x + 1)$.

Factor the following polynomials.

351. $6a + 15$

352. $3a^2x + 9ax$

353. $x^2 - 16$

354. $4a^2 - 25$

355. $7n^2 - 21n$

356. $7x^4y^2 - 35x^2y^2 + 14x^2y^4$

357. $x^2 + 3x + 2$

358. $9r^2 - 36$

359. $x^2 - 2x - 8$

360. $x^2 + 5x + 6$

361. $x^2 + x - 6$

362. $b^2 - 100$

363. $x^2 + 7x + 12$

364. $x^2 - 3x - 18$

365. $b^2 - 9b + 8$

366. $b^2 - 4b - 21$

367. $a^2 + 11a - 12$

368. $x^2 + 10x + 25$

369. $36y^4 - z^2$

370. $x^2 + 20x + 99$

371. $c^2 - 12c + 32$

372. $b^2 - 12b + 11$

373. $m^2 - 11m + 18$

374. $v^4 - 13v^2 - 48$

375. $x^2 - 20x + 36$

Answers

Numerical expressions in parentheses like this [ ] are operations performed on only part of the original expression. The operations performed within these symbols are intended to show how to evaluate the various terms that make up the entire expression.

Expressions with parentheses that look like this ( ) contain either numerical substitutions or expressions that are part of a numerical expression. Once a single number appears within these parentheses, the parentheses are no longer needed and need not be used the next time the entire expression is written.

When two pair of parentheses appear side by side like this ( )( ), it means that the expressions within are to be multiplied.

Sometimes parentheses appear within other parentheses in numerical or algebraic expressions. Regardless of what symbol is used, ( ), { }, or [ ], perform operations in the innermost parentheses first and work outward.

<u>Underlined</u> expressions show the original algebraic expression as an equation with the expression equal to its simplified result.

351. The terms have a common factor of 3. Factor 3 out of each term and write the expression in factored form.

$$\underline{6a + 15 = 3(2a + 5)}$$

352. The terms have a common factor of $3ax$. Factor $3ax$ out of each term and write the expression in factored form.

$$\underline{3a^2x + 9ax = 3ax(a + 3)}$$

353. Both terms in the polynomial are perfect squares. Use the form for factoring the difference of two perfect squares and put the roots of each factor in the proper place.

$$\underline{x^2 - 16 = (x + 4)(x - 4)}$$

Check using FOIL.

$$\underline{(x + 4)(x - 4) = x^2 - 4x + 4x - 16 = x^2 - 16}$$

354. Both terms in the polynomial are perfect squares. $4a^2 = (2a)^2$, and $25 = 5^2$. Use the form for factoring the difference of two perfect squares and put the roots of each factor in the proper place.

$$\underline{4a^2 - 25 = (2a + 5)(2a - 5)}$$

Check using FOIL.

$$\underline{(2a + 5)(2a - 5) = 4a^2 - 10a + 10a - 25 = 4a^2 - 25}$$

355. The terms have a common factor of $7n$. Factor $7n$ out of each term and write the expression in factored form.

$$\underline{7n^2 - 21n = 7n(n - 3)}$$

356. The terms have a common factor of $7x^2y^2$. Factor $7x^2y^2$ out of each term in the expression and write it in factored form.

$$\underline{7x^2y^2(x^2 - 5 + 2y^2)}$$

357. This expression can be factored using the trinomial
method. The factors of x^2 are x and x, and the
factors of 2 are 1 and 2. Place the factors
into the trinomial factor form
and check using FOIL. $\quad (x + 2)(x + 1) = x^2 + x + 2x + 2 = x^2 + 3x + 2$
The factors are correct.

358. Both terms in the polynomial are perfect squares.
$9r^2 = (3r)^2$ and $36 = 6^2$. Use the form for
factoring the difference of two perfect
squares and put the roots of each factor
in the proper place. $\quad 9r^2 - 36 = (3r + 6)(3r - 6)$

359. This expression can be factored using the
trinomial method. The factors of x^2 are
x and x, and the factors of 8 are (1)(8) and
(2)(4). You want the result of the O and I of
the FOIL method for multiplying factors to
add up to ^-2x. Only terms with opposite signs
will result in a negative numerical term, which
is what you need, since the third term is $^-8$.
Place the factors (2)(4) into the trinomial
factor form and check using
FOIL. $\quad (x + 4)(x - 2) = x^2 - 2x + 4x - 8 = x^2 + 2x - 8$
Almost correct! Change the position of the factors
of the numerical term and check
using FOIL. $\quad (x + 2)(x - 4) = x^2 - 4x + 2x - 8 = x^2 - 2x - 8$
The factors of the trinomial are now correct.

360. This expression can be factored using the
trinomial method. The factors of x^2 are
x and x, and the factors of 6 are (1)(6) and
(2)(3). Since the numerical term of the polynomial is positive, the signs in the factor form
for trinomials will be the same because only
two like signs multiplied together will result
in a positive. Now consider the second term
in the trinomial. In order to add up to 5x, the
result of multiplying the Inner and Outer
terms of the trinomial factors will have to be
positive. Try using two positive signs and the
factors 2 and 3, which add up
to 5. Check using FOIL. $\quad (x + 2)(x + 3) = x^2 + 2x + 3x + 6 = x^2 + 5x + 6$

361. This expression can be factored using the
trinomial method. The factors of x^2 are
x and x, and the factors of 6 are (1)(6) and
(2)(3). You want the result of the O and I of
the FOIL method for multiplying factors
to add up to ^+1x. Only terms with opposite
signs will result in a negative numerical
term that you need with the third term
being a $^-6$. Place the factors (2)(3) into
the trinomial factor form and check
using FOIL. $\qquad (x + 3)(x - 2) = x^2 - 2x + 3x - 6 = x^2 + x - 6$
The factors of the trinomial are now correct.

362. Both terms in the polynomial are perfect squares.
$b^2 = (b)^2$ and $100 = 10^2$. Use the form for
factoring the difference of two perfect squares
and put the roots of each factor in the
proper place. $\qquad\qquad\qquad\qquad b^2 - 100 = (b + 10)(b - 10)$
Check using FOIL. $\quad (b + 10)(b - 10) = b^2 - 10b + 10b - 100 = b^2 - 100$

363. This expression can be factored using the
trinomial method. The factors of x^2 are
x and x, and the factors of 12 are (1)(12) or
(2)(6) or (3)(4). You want the result of the
O and I of the FOIL method for multiplying
factors to add up to ^+7x. The factors (3)(4)
would give terms that add up to 7. Since
all signs are positive, use positive signs
in the factored form
for the trinomial. $\qquad (x + 3)(x + 4) = x^2 + 3x + 4x + 12 = x^2 + 7x + 12$
The result is correct. This is not just luck. You
can use logical guesses to find the correct
combination of factors and signs.

364. This expression can be factored using the
trinomial method. The factors of x^2 are
x and x, and the factors of 18 are (1)(18) or
(2)(9) or (3)(6). Only the product of a positive
and a negative numerical term will result in
$^-18$. The sum of the results of multiplying
the Outer and Inner terms of the trinomial
factors needs to add up to a ^-3x. So use
(3)(6) in the trinomial factors form and check
using FOIL. $\qquad (x + 3)\,(x - 6) = x^2 - 6x + 3x - 18 = x^2 - 3x - 18$

365. This expression can be factored using the
trinomial method. The factors of b^2 are b
and b, and the factors of 8 are (1)(8) or
(2)(4). You want the result of the O and I
of the FOIL method for multiplying factors
to add up to ^-9b. The signs within the parentheses of the factorization of the trinomial
must be the same to result in a positive
numerical term in the trinomial. The middle
term has a negative sign, so let's try two
negative signs. How can you get 9 from
adding the two of the factors of 8? Right!
Use the (1)(8).
Check the answer
using FOIL. $\underline{(b - 1)(b - 8) = b^2 - 8b - 1b + 8 = b^2 - 9b + 8}$

366. This expression can be factored using the
trinomial method. The factors of b^2 are
b and b, and the factors of 21 are (1)(21) or
(3)(7). You want the result of the O and I
products of the FOIL method for multiplying
factors to add up to ^-4b. Only the product
of a positive and a negative numerical term
will result in $^-21$. So let's use (3) and (7)
in the trinomial factors form because the
difference between 3 and 7 is 4.
Check using FOIL. $\underline{(b + 3)(b - 7) = b^2 - 7b + 3b - 21 = b^2 - 4b - 21}$

367. This expression can be factored using the
trinomial method. The factors of a^2 are
a and a, and the factors of 12 are (1)(12) or
(2)(6) or (3)(4). You want the result of the
O and I of the FOIL method for multiplying
factors to add up to ^+11a. Only the product
of a positive and a negative numerical term
will result in $^-12$. Since the signs in the factors
must be one positive and one negative, use the
factors 12 and 1 in the trinomial factors form.
Use FOIL to check
the answer. $\underline{(a + 12)(a - 1) = a^2 - 1a + 12a - 12 = a^2 + 11a - 12}$

368. This expression can be factored using the
trinomial method. The factors of x^2 are
x and x, and the factors of 25 are (1)(25)
or (5)(5). To get a positive 25 after multiplying
the factors of the trinomial expression, the
signs in the two factors must both be positive
or both be negative. The sum of the results
of multiplying the Outer and Inner terms of
the trinomial factors needs to add up to a
^+10x. So let's use (5)(5) in the trinomial
factors form and
check using FOIL. $(x + 5)(x + 5) = x^2 + 5x + 5x + 25 = x^2 + 10x + 25$

369. Both terms in the polynomial are perfect
squares. $36y^2 = (6y^2)^2$ and $z^2 = (z)^2$.
Use the form for factoring the difference of
two perfect squares and put the roots of
each factor in the proper place. $(6y^2 + z)(6y^2 - z)$
Check using FOIL. $(6y^2 + z)(6y^2 - z) = 36y^4 - 6y^2z + 6y^2z - z^2 = 36y^4 - z^2$

370. This expression can be factored using the
trinomial method. The factors of x^2 are
x and x, and the factors of 99 are (1)(99)
or (3)(33) or (9)(11). To get a positive 99
after multiplying the factors of the trinomial
expression, the signs in the two factors must
both be positive or both are negative. The
sum of the results of multiplying the Outer
and Inner terms of the trinomial factors
needs to add up to a ^+20x. So let's use
(9)(11) in the trinomial factors form
because 9 + 11 = 20.
Check using FOIL. $(x + 9)(x + 11) = x^2 + 9x + 11x + 99 = x^2 + 20x + 99$

371. This expression can be factored using the
trinomial method. The factors of x^2 are
x and x, and the factors of 32 are (1)(32) or
(2)(16) or (4)(8). The sign of the numerical
term is positive, so the signs in the factors
of our trinomial factorization must be the
same. The sign of the first-degree term
(the variable to the power of 1) is negative.
This leads one to believe that the signs in
the trinomial factors will both be negative.
The only factors of 32 that add up to 12
are 4 and 8.
Check using FOIL. $(c - 4)(c - 8) = c^2 - 8c - 4c + 32 = c^2 - 12c + 32$

372. The factors of h^2 are h and h, and the factors of 11 are (1)(11). The sign of the numerical term is positive, so the signs in the factors of our trinomial factorization must be the same. The sign of the first-degree term (the variable to the power of 1) is negative. So use negative signs in the trinomial factors. Check your answer. $\underline{(h - 1)(h - 11) = h^2 - 11h - 1h + 11 = h^2 - 12h + 11}$

373. This expression can be factored using the trinomial method. The factors of m^2 are m and m, and the factors of 18 are (1)(18) or (2)(9) or (3)(6). The sign of the numerical term is positive, so the signs in the factors of our trinomial factorization must be the same. The sum of the results of multiplying the Outer and Inner terms of the trinomial factors needs to add up to ^-11m. The only factors of 18 that can be added or subtracted in any way to equal 11 are 2 and 9. Use them and two subtraction signs in the trinomial factor terms. Check your answer using FOIL. $\underline{(m - 2)(m - 9) = m^2 - 9m - 2m + 18 = m^2 - 11m + 18}$

374. This expression can be factored using the trinomial method. The factors of v^4 are $(v^2)(v^2)$, and the factors of 48 are (1)(48) or (2)(24) or (3)(16) or (4)(12) or (6)(8). Only the product of a positive and a negative numerical term will result in $^-48$. The only factors of 48 that can be added or subtracted in any way to equal 13 are 3 and 16. Use 3 and 16 and a positive and negative sign in the terms of the trinomial factors. Check your answer using FOIL. $\underline{(v^2 + 3)(v^2 - 16) = v^4 - 16v^2 + 3v^2 - 48 = v^4 - 13v - 48}$
You may notice that one of the two factors of the trinomial expression can itself be factored. The second term is the difference of two perfect squares. Factor $(v^2 - 16)$ using the form for factoring the difference of two perfect squares. $\underline{(v + 4)(v - 4) = v^2 - 4v + 4v - 16 = v^2 - 16}$
This now makes the complete factorization of $\underline{v^4 - 13v^2 - 48 = (v^2 + 3)(v + 4)(v - 4)}$

375. The factors of x^2 are x and x, and the factors of 36 are (1)(36) or (2)(18) or (4)(9) or (6)(6). The sign of the numerical term is positive, so the signs in the factors of our trinomial factorization must be the same. The sign of the first-degree term (the variable to the power of 1) is negative. This leads one to believe that the signs in the trinomial factors will both be negative. The only factors of 36 that add up to 20 are 2 and 18. Use them and two negative signs in the trinomial factor form. Check your answer using FOIL.

$$(x - 2)(x - 18) = x^2 - 18x - 2x + 36 = x^2 - 20x + 36$$

Using Factoring

This chapter will present polynomial expressions for you to factor. In the previous chapter, all the coefficients of the second-degree terms were 1. In this chapter, the coefficients of the second-degree terms will often be whole numbers greater than 1. This will complicate the process of factoring by adding more possibilities to check. In some cases you will find that you can factor using more than one of the three methods of factoring polynomials on the given expression.

Always look to factor algebraic expressions using the greatest common factor method first. Then analyze the remaining expression to determine if other factoring methods can be used. The three methods for factoring polynomial expressions are:

1. Greatest common factor method.
2. Difference of two perfect squares method.
3. Trinomial method.

When presented with a polynomial with a coefficient greater than 1 for the second-degree term, use the trinomial factor form $(ax \pm (\ ))(bx \pm (\ ))$ where $a \cdot b$ = the coefficient of the second-degree term. List the factors of the numerical term of the trinomial and consider the choices of factors and signs that will result in the correct trinomial factorization.

After choosing terms to try in the trinomial factors form, use FOIL to check your guesses for the trinomial factors. You will want to do a partial check by first completing the O and the I part of FOIL to determine if you have the first-degree term right.

Tips for Using Factoring

When factoring a trinomial expression, first determine the signs that will be used in the two factors.

Next, list the possible factors of the second-degree term.

Then list the factors of the numerical term.

Finally, place the factors into the trinomial factor form in all possible ways and use FOIL to check for the correct factorization.

Be systematic in your attempts to be sure you try all possible choices. You will become better at factoring as you learn to look for the combinations of factors that will give you the required results for the first-degree term.

Factor the following expressions.

376. $2x^2 + 7x + 6$

377. $3x^2 + 13x + 12$

378. $5x^2 - 14x - 3$

379. $9x^2 + 9x + 2$

380. $9x^2 + 34x - 8$

381. $3x^2 - 3x - 18$

382. $4a^2 - 16a - 9$

383. $6a^2 - 13a - 15$

384. $6a^2 - 5a - 6$

385. $16y^2 - 36$

386. $6x^2 + 15x - 36$

387. $4bc^2 + 22bc - 42b$

388. $2a^6 + a^3 - 21$

389. $6a^2x - 39ax - 72x$

390. $8x^2 - 6x - 9$

391. $5c^2 - 4c - 1$

392. $9x^3 - 4x$

393. $8r^2 + 46r + 63$

394. $4x^4 - 37x^2 + 9$

395. $12d^2 + 7d - 12$

396. $4xy^3 + 6xy^2 - 10xy$

397. $4ax^2 - 38ax - 66a$

398. $3c^2 + 19c - 40$

399. $2a^2 + 17a - 84$

400. $4x^4 + 2x^2 - 30$

Answers

Numerical expressions in parentheses like this [ ] are operations performed on only part of the original expression. The operations performed within these symbols are intended to show how to evaluate the various terms that make up the entire expression.

Expressions with parentheses that look like this ( ) contain either numerical substitutions or expressions that are part of a numerical expression. Once a single number appears within these parentheses, the parentheses are no longer needed and need not be used the next time the entire expression is written.

When two pair of parentheses appear side by side like this ( )( ), it means that the expressions within are to be multiplied.

Sometimes parentheses appear within other parentheses in numerical or algebraic expressions. Regardless of what symbol is used, ( ), { }, or [ ], perform operations in the innermost parentheses first and work outward.

<u>Underlined</u> expressions show the original algebraic expression as an equation with the expression equal to its simplified result.

376. Both signs in the trinomial are positive, so use positive signs in the trinomial factor form.

$(ax + (\ ))(bx + (\ ))$

The factors of the second-degree term are $2x^2 = (2x)(x)$.

The numerical term $6 = (1)(6) = (2)(3)$.

You want to get $7x$ from adding the result of the Outer and Inner multiplications when using FOIL. You could make the following guesses for the factors of the original expression.

$(2x + (1))(x + (6))$
$(2x + (6))(x + (1))$
$(2x + (2))(x + (3))$
$(2x + (3))(x + (2))$

Now just consider the results of the Outer and Inner products of the terms for each guess. The one that results in a first-degree term of $7x$ is the factorization you want to fully check.

$(2x + (1))(x + (6))$ will result in Outer product plus Inner product:
$2x(6) + (1)x = 12x + x = 13x$.

$(2x + (6))(x + (1))$ will result in Outer product plus Inner product:
$2x(1) + (6)x = 2x + 6x = 8x$.

$(2x + (2))(x + (3))$ will result in Outer product plus Inner product:
$2x(3) + (2)x = 6x + 2x = 8x$.

$(2x + (3))(x + (2))$ will result in Outer product plus Inner product:
$2x(2) + (3)x = 4x + 3x = 7x$.

Place the factors in the trinomial factor form so that the product of the outer terms $(2x)(2) = 4x$ and the product of the inner terms $(3)(x) = 3x$. That way, $4x + 3x = 7x$, the middle term of the trinomial.

$(2x + (3))(x + (2))$

Check using FOIL.

First—$^-(2x)(x) = 2x^2$

Outer—$^-(2x)(2) = 4x$
Inner—$^-(3)(x) = 3x$
Last—$^-(3)(2) = 6$
Add the products of multiplication
using FOIL.
The factors check out.

$$2x^2 + 4x + 3x + 6 = 2x^2 + 7x + 6$$
$$\underline{(2x + 3)(x + 2) = 2x^2 + 7x + 6}$$

377. Both signs in the trinomial are positive, so use positive signs in the
trinomial factor form.
$(ax + (\ ))(bx + (\ ))$
The factors of the second-degree term are $3x^2 = (3x)(x)$.
The factors of the numerical term $12 = (1)(12) = (2)(6) = (3)(4)$.
You want to get $13x$ from adding the result of the Outer and Inner
multiplications when using FOIL. Place the factors in the trinomial
factor form so that the product of the outer terms $(3x)(3) = 9x$ and the
product of the inner terms $(4)(x) = 4x$. Then $9x + 4x = 13x$, the middle
term of the trinomial.
$(3x + 4)(x + 3)$
Check using FOIL.
First—$^-(3x)(x) = 3x^2$
Outer—$^-(3x)(3) = 9x$
Inner—$^-(4)(x) = 4x$
Last—$^-(4)(3) = 12$
Add the products of multiplication using FOIL
$$3x^2 + 9x + 4x + 12 = 3x^2 + 13x + 12$$
The factors check out.
$$\underline{(3x + 4)(x + 3) = 3x^2 + 13x + 12}$$

378. Both signs in the trinomial are negative. To get a negative sign for the
numerical term, the signs in the factors must be + and -.
$(ax + (\ ))(bx - (\ ))$
The factors of the second-degree term are $5x^2 = (5x)(x)$.
The factors of the numerical term $3 = (1)(3)$.
When you multiply the Outer and Inner terms of the trinomial factors,
the results must add up to be ^-14x. Multiplying, $5x(^-3) = ^-15x$, and
$1x(^+1) = ^+1x$. Adding $(^-15x) + (^+1x) = ^-14x$. Place those terms into the
trinomial factor form.
$(5x + (1))(x - (3))$
Check using FOIL.
First—$^-(5x)(x) = 5x^2$
Outer—$^-(5x)(^-3) = ^-15x$
Inner—$^-(1)(x) = x$
Last—$^-(1)(^-3) = ^-3$
Add the products of multiplication using FOIL.
$$5x^2 - 15x + 1x - 3 = 5x^2 - 14x - 3$$
The factors check out.
$$\underline{(5x + 1)(x - 3) = 5x^2 - 14x - 3}$$

379. Both signs in the trinomial are positive, so use positive signs in the trinomial factor form. $(ax + (\ ))(bx + (\ ))$

The factors of the second-degree term $9x^2 = (9x)(x)$ or $9x^2 = (3x)(3x)$.

The factors of the numerical term $2 = (1)(2)$.

To get $9x$ from adding the result of the Outer and Inner multiplications when using FOIL, place the factors in the trinomial factor form so that the product of the outer terms $(3x)(1) = 3x$ and the product of the inner terms $(2)(3x) = 6x$. Then $3x + 6x = 9x$, the middle term of the trinomial. $\qquad\qquad$ $(3x + 2)(3x + 1)$

Check using FOIL.

First—⁻$(3x)(3x) = 9x^2$

Outer—⁻$(3x)(1) = 3x$

Inner—⁻$(2)(3x) = 6x$

Last—⁻$(2)(1) = 1$

The factors check out. $\qquad$ $\underline{(3x + 2)(3x + 1) = 9x^2 + 3x + 6x + 2 = 9x^2 + 9x + 2}$

380. The sign of the numerical term is negative. So the signs in the trinomial factor form will have to be + and ⁻. That is the only way to get a negative sign by multiplying the Last terms when checking with FOIL. $(ax + (\ ))(bx - (\ ))$

The factors of the second-degree term are $9x^2 = (9x)(x)$ or $9x^2 = (3x)(3x)$.

The factors of the numerical term $8 = (1)(8)$ or $(2)(4)$. Let's try putting in factors in the trinomial factor form and see what we get. $\quad (9x + 1)(x - 8)$

Using FOIL to check, we get $9x^2 - 72x + 1x - 8 = 9x^2 - 71x - 8$.

No, that doesn't work. You are looking for a positive x term in the middle of the expression. Changing position of the signs would help but not with these factors because the term would be ⁺$71x$. Try different factors of 8. $\qquad\qquad\qquad\qquad\qquad$ $(9x - 2)(x + 4)$

Check using FOIL. $\qquad\qquad$ $\underline{9x^2 + 36x - 2x - 8 = 9x^2 + 34x - 8}$

There it is! And on only the second try. Be persistent and learn from your mistakes.

381. The three terms have a common factor of 3. You can factor out 3 and represent the trinomial as $3(x^2 - x - 6)$. Now factor the trinomial in the parentheses, and don't forget to include the factor 3 when you are done.

The sign of the numerical term is negative. So the signs in the trinomial factor form will have to be + and ⁻, because that is the only way to get a negative sign when multiplying the Last terms when checking with FOIL. $\qquad\qquad$ $(ax + (\ ))(bx - (\ ))$

The factors of the second-degree term are $3x^2 = (3x)(x)$.

The sign of the second term is negative. That tells you that the result of adding the products of the Outer and Inner terms of the trinomial factors must result in a negative sum for the x term. The factors of the numerical term 6 are $(1)(6)$ or $(2)(3)$. Put the + with the 2 and the – with the 3. $\qquad\qquad\qquad\qquad\qquad$ $(x + 2)(x - 3)$

Check using FOIL.

First—$(x)(x) = x^2$
Outer—$(x)(^-3) = ^-3x$
Inner—$(2)(x) = 2x$
Last—$(2)(^-3) = ^-6$
The factors check out. $(x + 2)(x - 3) = x^2 - 3x + 2x - 6 = x^2 - x - 6$
Include the common factor of 3 so that
   $3(x + 2)(x - 3) = 3 (x^2 - x - 6) = 3x^2 - 3x - 18.$

382. Both signs in the trinomial expression are negative. To get a negative sign
   for the numerical term, the signs within the trinomial factors must be
   + and −. $(ax + ( ))(bx - ( ))$
The factors of the second-degree term $4a^2 = (4a)(a)$ or $4a^2 = (2a)(2a)$.
The factors of the numerical term 9 are $(1)(9)$ or $(3)(3)$.
The coefficient of the first-degree term is 2 less than 18. You can multiply
   $2a$ and (9) to get $18a$ leaving the factors $2a$ and (1) to get a $2a$. Use this
   information to place factors within the trinomial factor form.
                                                $(2a + 1)(2a - 9)$

Check using FOIL.
First—$(2a)(2a) = 4a^2$
Outer—$(2a)(^-9) = ^-18a$
Inner—$(1)(2a) = 2a$
Last—$(1)(^-9) = ^-9$
The result of multiplying the factors is
   $(2a + 1)(2a - 9) = 4a^2 - 18a + 2a - 9 = 4a^2 - 16a - 9.$

383. Both signs in the trinomial expression are negative. To get a negative sign
   for the numerical term, the signs within the trinomial factors must be
   + and −. $(ax + ( ))(bx - ( ))$
The factors of the second-degree term $6a^2 = (6a)(a)$ or $(2a)(3a)$.
The factors of the numerical term 15 are $(1)(15)$ or $(3)(5)$.
We can predict that $13 = 18 - 5$. The factors $(6a)(3) = 18a$. The remaining
   factors $(a)(5) = 5a$. But we need the thirteen to be negative so arrange
   the $6a$ and the (3) so their product is ^-18a.
$(6a + 5)(a - 3)$
Check using FOIL.
First—$(6a)(a) = 6a^2$
Outer—$(6a)(^-3) = ^-18a$
Inner—$(5)(a) = 5a$
Last—$(5)(^-3) = ^-15$
Combining the results of multiplying using FOIL results in
   $(6a + 5)(a - 3) = 6a^2 - 18a + 5a - 15 = 6a^2 - 13a - 15.$
The factors check out.

384. Both signs in the trinomial expression are negative. To get a negative sign for the numerical term, the signs within the trinomial factors must be + and −. $(ax + (\ ))(bx − (\ ))$
The factors of the second-degree term $6a^2 = (6a)(a)$ or $6a^2 = (2a)(3a)$.
The factors of the numerical term 6 are $(6)(1)$ or $(2)(3)$.
The trinomial looks balanced with a 6 on each end and a 5 in the middle.
Try a balanced factor arrangement. $(3a + 2)(2a − 3)$
Check using FOIL.
First—$^-(3a)(2a) = 6a^2$
Outer—$^-(3a)(^-3) = {}^-9a$
Inner—$^-(2)(a) = 2a$
Last—$^-(2)(^-3) = {}^-6$
Combining the results of multiplying using FOIL results in
$(3a + 2)(2a − 3) = 6a^2 − 9a + 4a − 6 = 6a^2 − 5a − 6.$
Didn't that work out nicely? A sense of balance can be useful.

385. This expression is the difference between two perfect squares. Using the form for the difference of two perfect squares gives you the factors $(4y + 6)(4y − 6)$.
However, there is a greatest common factor that could be factored out first to leave $4(4y^2 − 9)$. Now you need only factor the difference of two simpler perfect squares.
$4(4y^2 − 9) = 4(2y + 3)(2y − 3).$
The first factorization is equivalent to the second because you can factor out two from each of the factors. This will result in $(2)(2)(2y + 3)(2y − 3)$ or $4(2y + 3)(2y − 3)$. When factoring polynomials, watch for the greatest common factors first.

386. The terms of the trinomial have a greatest common factor of 3. So the term $3(2x^2 + 5x − 12)$ will simplify the trinomial factoring. You need only factor the trinomial within the parentheses.
The sign of the numerical term is negative. So the signs in the trinomial factor form will have to be + and −. $(ax + (\ ))(bx − (\ ))$
The factors of the second-degree term are $2x^2 = (2x)(x)$.
The factors of the numerical term 12 are $(1)(12)$ or $(2)(6)$ or $(3)(4)$.
The factors $(2x)(4) = 8x$ and the remaining factors $(x)(3) = 3x$. It's clear that $8x − 3x = 5x$. Use those factors in the trinomial factor form.
$(2x − 3)(x + 4)$
Check using FOIL.
First—$^-(2x)(x) = 2x^2$
Outer—$^-(2x)(4) = 8x$
Inner—$^-(^-3)(x) = {}^-3x$
Last—$^-(^-3)(4) = {}^-12$
The result of multiplying factors is $2x^2 + 8x − 3x − 12 = 2x^2 + 5x − 12.$
Now include the greatest common factor of 3 for the final solution.
$3(2x − 3)(x + 4) = 6x^2 + 15x − 36$

387. Each term in the polynomial has a common factor of $2b$. The resulting expression looks like this: $2b(2c^2 + 11c - 21)$

The sign of the numerical term is negative. So the signs in the trinomial factor form will have to be $+$ and $-$ because that is the only way to get a negative sign when multiplying the Last terms when checking with FOIL. $(ax + (\ ))(bx - (\ ))$

The factors of the second-degree term $2c^2 = (2c)(c)$.

The factors of the numerical term 21 are $(1)(21)$ or $(3)(7)$. The factors $(2c)(7) = 14c$ and the associated factors $(c)(3) = 3c$. Place these factors in the trinomial factor form so that the result of the Outer and Inner products when using FOIL to multiply are ^+14c and ^-3c. $(2c - 3)(c + 7)$

Check using FOIL.

First—$^-(2c)(c) = 2c^2$

Outer—$^-(2c)(7) = 14c$

Inner—$^-(^-3)(c) = ^-3c$

Last—$^-(^-3)(7) = ^-21$

The product of the factors is

$(2c - 3)(c + 7) = 2c^2 + 14c - 3c - 21 = 2c^2 + 11c - 21.$

Now include the greatest common factor term.

$2b(2c - 3)(c + 7) = 2b(2c^2 + 11c - 21 = 4bc^2 + 22bc - 42b$

388. This expression appears to be in the familiar trinomial form, but what's with those exponents? Think of $a^6 = (a^3)^2$. Then the expression becomes $2(a^3)^2 + (a^3) - 21$. Now you factor like it was a trinomial expression. The sign of the numerical term is negative. So the signs in the trinomial factor form will have to be $+$ and $-$. $(ax + (\ ))(bx - (\ ))$

The second-degree term $2(a^3)^2 = 2(a^3)(a^3)$.

The factors of the numerical term 21 are $(1)(21)$ or $(3)(7)$. The factors $(a^3)(7) = 7(a^3)$ and the factors $(2(a^3))(3) = 6(a^3)$. The difference of 7 and 6 is 1. Place these factors in the trinomial factor form so that the first degree term is $1(a^3)$.

$(a^3 - 3)(2a^3 + 7)$

Check using FOIL.

First—$^-(a^3)(2a^3) = 2a^6$

Outer—$^-(a^3)(7) = 7a^3$

Inner—$^-(^-3)(2a^3) = ^-6a^3$

Last—$^-(^-3)(7) = ^-21$

The product of the factors is

$(a^3 - 3)(2a^3 + 7) = 2a^6 + 7a^3 - 6a^3 - 21 = 2a^6 + a^3 - 21.$

The factors of the trinomial are correct.

389. The greatest common factor of the terms in the trinomial expression is $3x$.
Factoring $3x$ out results in the expression $3x(2a^2 - 13a - 24)$. Factor the
trinomial expression inside the parentheses.
The sign of the numerical term is negative. So the signs in the trinomial
factor form will have to be + and −. $(ax + (\;))(bx - (\;))$
The factors of the term $2a^2 = (2a)(a)$.
The factors of the numerical term 24 are $(1)(24)$ or $(2)(12)$ or $(3)(8)$
or $(4)(6)$.
The factors $(2a)(8) = 16a$, and the related factors $(a)(3) = 3a$. The
difference of 16 and 3 is 13. Place these numbers in the trinomial factor
form, and check the expression using FOIL.
$(2a + 3)(a - 8)$
First—$^-(2a)(a) = 2a^2$
Outer—$^-(2a)(^-8) = {^-16a}$
Inner—$^-(3)(a) = 3a$
Last—$^-(3)(^-8) = {^-24}$
The result is $(2a + 3)(a - 8) = 2a^2 - 16a + 3a - 24 = 2a^2 - 13a - 24$.
Now include the greatest common factor if $3x$.
$\underline{3x(2a + 3)(a - 8) = 3x(2a^2 - 13a - 24) = 6a^2x - 39ax - 72x}$

390. The numerical term of the trinomial has a negative sign, so the signs
within the factors of the trinomial will be a + and −. $(ax + (\;))(bx - (\;))$
The factors of the second-degree term are $8x^2 = (x)(8x)$ or $8x^2 = (2x)(4x)$.
The numerical term of the trinomial 9 has factors of $(1)(9)$ or $(3)(3)$.
What combination will result in a ^-6x when the Outer and Inner products
of the multiplication of the trinomial factors are added together?
Consider just the coefficients of x and the numerical term factors. The
numbers $2(3) = 6$, and the corresponding $4(3) = 12$. The difference
between 12 and 6 is 6. So use the second-degree term factors $(2x)(4x)$
and the numerical factors $(3)(3)$.
$(2x - 3)(4x + 3)$
Check using FOIL.
First—$^-(2x)(4x) = 8x^2$
Outer—$^-(2x)(3) = 6x$
Inner—$^-(^-3)(4x) = {^-12x}$
Last—$^-(^-3)(3) = {^-9}$
The product of the factors
$\underline{(2x - 3)(4x + 3) = 8x^2 + 6x - 12x - 9 = 8x^2 - 6x - 9.}$

391. The numerical term of the trinomial has a negative sign so the signs within
the factors of the trinomial will be a + and −. $(ax + (\;))(bx - (\;))$
The only factors of the second-degree term are $(c)(5c)$.
The numerical term of the trinomial 1 has factors of $(1)(1)$. Placing the
numbers into the trinomial factor form is easy because there really are

no choices. Just place the + and − signs in the right spot and you've got a solution. Check using FOIL to multiply terms. $(5c + 1)(c − 1)$

Check using FOIL.

First—$(5c)(c) = 5c^2$

Outer—$(5c)(^-1) = ^-5c$

Inner—$(1)(c) = c$

Last—$(1)(^-1) = ^-1$

The product of the factors $(5c + 1)(c − 1) = 5c^2 − 5c + c − 1 = 5c − 4c − 1$.

392. The terms of the expression have a greatest common factor of x. Factoring x out of the expression results in $x(9x^2 − 4)$.

The expression inside the parentheses is the difference of two perfect squares. Factor that expression using the form for the difference of two perfect squares. Include the greatest common factor to complete the factorization of the original expression.

$9x^2 = (3x)^2$

$4 = 2^2$

Using the form, the factorization of the difference of two perfect squares is $(3x − 2)(3x + 2)$.

Check using FOIL.

First—$(3x)(3x) = 9x^2$

Outer—$(3x)(2) = 6x$

Inner—$(^-2)(3x) = ^-6x$

Last—$(^-2)(2) = ^-4$

Include the greatest common factor x in the complete factorization.

$x(3x − 2)(3x + 2) = x(9x^2 − 4) = 9x^3 − 4x$

393. The terms in the trinomial expression are all positive, so the signs in the trinomial factor form will be positive. $(ax + (\ ))(bx + (\ ))$

The factors of the second-degree term are $8r^2 = (r)(8r)$ or $(2r)(4r)$.

The numerical term 63 has the factors $(1)(63)$ or $(3)(21)$ or $(7)(9)$.

You need two sets of factors that when multiplied and added will result in a 46. Let's look at the possibilities using the $2r$ and $4r$. $2r(1) + 4r(63) = 254r$ is too much. $2r(3) + 4r(21) = 87r$ is still too much. Try $2r(21)$ and $4r(3) = 54r$. Getting closer. $2r(7) + 4r(9) = 50r$. Nope. Now try $2r(9) + 4r(7) = 46r$. Bingo!

$(2r + 7)(4r + 9)$

Check using FOIL.

First—$(2r)(4r) = 8r^2$

Outer—$(2r)(9) = 18r$

Inner—$(4r)(7) = 28r$

Last—$(7)(9) = 63$

Add the result of the multiplication. $8r^2 + 18r + 28r + 63 = 8r^2 + 46r + 63$

The factors check out. $(2r + 7)(4r + 9) = 8r^2 + 46r + 63$

394. When you think of $x^4 = (x^2)^2$, you can see that the expression is a trinomial that is easy to factor.

The numerical term is positive, so the signs in the trinomial factor form will be the same. The sign of the first-degree term is negative so you will use two – signs. $(ax - (\ ))(bx - (\ ))$

The factors of the second-degree term are $4x^4 = (x^2)(4x^2)$ or $(2x^2)(2x^2)$.

The numerical term 9 has $(1)(9)$ or $(3)(3)$ as factors.

What combination will result in a total of 37 when the Outer and Inner products are determined? $4x^2(9) = 36x^2$, $1\ x^2\ (1) = 1\ x^2$ and $36\ x^2 + 1x^2 = 37x^2$. Use these factors in the trinomial factor form.

$(4x^2 - 1)(x^2 - 9)$

Check using FOIL and you will find

$(4x^2 - 1)(x^2 - 9) = 4x^4 - 36x^2 - x^2 + 9 = 4x^4 - 37x^2 + 9.$

Now you need to notice that the factors of the original trinomial expression are both factorable. Why? Because they are both the difference of two perfect squares.

Use the factor form for the difference of two perfect squares for each factor of the trinomial.

$(4x^2 - 1) = (2x + 1)(2x - 1)$

$(x^2 - 9) = (x + 3)(x - 3)$

Put the factors together to complete the factorization of the original expression.

$\underline{(4x^2 - 1)(x^2 - 9) = (2x + 1)(2x - 1)(x + 3)(x - 3)}$

395. The negative sign in front of the numerical term tells you that the signs of the trinomial factors will be + and –. $(ax + (\ ))(bx - (\ ))$

This expression has a nice balance to it with 12 at the extremities and a modest 7 in the middle. Let's guess at some middle of the road factors to plug in. Use FOIL to check.

$(4d + 3)(3d - 4)$

Using FOIL you find

$(4d + 3)(3d - 4) = 12d^2 - 16d + 9d - 12 = 12d^2 - 7d - 12.$

Those are the right terms but the wrong signs. Try changing the signs around.

$(4d - 3)(3d + 4)$

Multiply the factors using FOIL.

$\underline{(4d - 3)(3d + 4) = 12d^2 + 16d - 9d - 12 = 12d^2 + 7d - 12}$

This is the correct factorization of the original expression.

396. Each term in the expression has a common factor of $2xy$. When factored out, the expression becomes $2xy(2y^2 + 3y - 5)$. Now factor the trinomial in the parentheses.

The last sign is negative so the signs within the factor form will be a + and –.

$(ax + (\ ))(bx - (\ ))$

The factors of the second-degree term are $2y^2 = y(2y)$.

The numerical term 5 has factors $(5)(1)$.

Place the factors of the second degree and the numerical terms so that the result of the Outer and Inner multiplication of terms within the factor form of a trinomial expression results in a ^+3x.

$(2y + 5)(y - 1)$

Multiply using FOIL. $(2y + 5)(y - 1) = 2y^2 - 2y + 5x - 5 = 2y^2 + 3x - 5$

The factors of the trinomial expression are correct. Now include the greatest common factor to complete the factorization of the original expression.

$\underline{2xy(2y + 5)(y - 1) = 2xy(2y^2 - 2y + 5x - 5) - 2xy(2y^2 + 3x - 5)}$

397. The terms of the trinomial have a greatest common factor of $2a$. When factored out, the resulting expression is $2a(2x^2 - 19x - 33)$. The expression within the parentheses is a trinomial and can be factored.

The signs within the terms of the factor form will be + and − because the numerical term has a negative sign. Only a $(+)(-) = (-)$ $(ax + (\ ))(bx - (\ ))$

The factors of the second degree term are $2a^2 = a(2a)$.

The numerical term 33 has $(1)(33)$ or $(3)(11)$ as factors.

Since $2a(11) = 22a$, and $a(3) = 3a$, and $22a - 3a = 19a$, use those factors in the trinomial factor form so that the result of the multiplication of the Outer and Inner terms results in ^-19x.

$(2x + 3)(x - 11)$

Check using FOIL. $(2x + 3)(x - 11) = 2x^2 - 22x + 3x - 33 = 2x^2 - 19x - 33$

The factorization of the trinomial factor is correct. Now include the greatest common factor of the original expression to get the complete factorization of the original expression.

$\underline{2a(2x + 3)(x - 11) = 2a(2x^2 - 22x + 3x - 33) = 2a(2x^2 - 19x - 33)}$

398. The signs within the terms of the factor form will be + and − because the numerical term has a negative sign. $(ax + (\ ))(bx - (\ ))$

The factors of the second-degree term are $3c^2 = c(3c)$.

The numerical term 40 has $(1)(40)$ or $(2)(20)$ or $(4)(10)$ or $(5)(8)$ as factors.

You want the result of multiplying and then adding the Outer and Inner terms of the trinomial factor form to result in a ^+19c when the like terms are combined. Using trial and error, you can determine that $3c(8) = 24c$, and $c(5) = 5c$, and $24c - 5c = 19c$. Use those factors in the factor form in such a way that you get the result you seek.

$(3c - 5)(c + 8) = 3c^2 + 24c - 5c - 40 = 3c^2 + 19c - 40$

The complete factorization of the original expression is $\underline{(3c - 5)(c + 8)}$.

399. The signs within the terms of the factor form will be + and − because the
numerical term has a negative sign. $(ax + (\ ))(bx - (\ ))$
The factors of the second-degree term are $2a^2 = a(2a)$.
The numerical term 84 has (1)(84) or (2)(42) or (3)(28) or (4)(21) or (6)(14)
or (7)(12) as factors. You want the result of multiplying and then adding
the Outer and Inner terms of the trinomial factor form to result in a
^+17a when the like terms are combined.
$2a(12) = 24a$, and $a(7) = 7a$, and $24a - 7a = 17a$. Use the factors $2a$ and a as
the first terms in the factor form and use (12) and (7) as the numerical
terms. Place them in position so you get the result that you want.
$(2a - 7)(a + 12) = 2a^2 + 24a - 7a - 84 = 2a^2 + 17a - 84$
The complete factorization of the original expression is $\underline{(2a - 7)(a + 12)}$.

400. This expression is in trinomial form. If you think of the variable as x^2, you
can see that the expression is in the trinomial form. Use x^2 where you
usually put a first-degree variable. The trinomial you will be factoring
looks like this: $4(x^2)^2 + 2(x^2) - 30$.
The signs within the terms of the factor form will be + and − because the
numerical term has a negative sign.
$(ax + (\ ))(bx - (\ ))$
The term $(4x^2)^2$ can be factored as $(4x^2)^2 = x^2(4x^2)$ or $(2x^2)(2x^2)$.
The numerical term 30 can be factored as (1)(30) or (2)(15) or (3)(10) or
(5)(6).
The factors $(4x^2)(3) = 12x^2$ and $x^2(10) = 10x^2$ will give you $12x^2 - 10x^2 = 2x^2$ when you perform the Inner and Outer multiplications and combine
like terms using FOIL with the terms in the trinomial factor form. The
factors of the expression will be $(4x^2 - 10)(x^2 + 3$.
Check using FOIL.
$$(4x^2 - 10)(x^2 + 3) = 4x^4 + 12x^2 - 10x^2 - 30 = 4x^4 + 2x^2 - 30$$
The expression $(4x^2 - 10)(x^2 + 3)$ is the correct factorization of the original
expression. However, the first factor has a greatest common factor of 2.
So a complete factorization would be $2(2x^2 - 5)(x^2 + 3)$.
Did you notice that you could have used the greatest common factor
method to factor out a 2 from each term in the original polynomial? If
you did, you would have had to factor the trinomial expression
$2x^4 + x^2 - 15$ and multiply the result by the factor 2 to equal the original
expression. Let's see:
$\underline{2(2x^4 + x^2 - 15) = 2(2x^2 - 5)(x^2 + 3) = (4x^2 - 10)(x^2 + 3) = 4x^4 + 2x^2 - 30}$
It all comes out the same, but if you left the factor of 2 in the term $(4x^2 - 10)$, you wouldn't have done a complete factorization of the original
trinomial expression.

17
Solving Quadratic Equations

This chapter will give you practice in finding solutions to quadratic equations. Quadratic equations are those equations that can be written in the form $ax^2 + bx + c = 0$, where $a \neq 0$. While there are several methods for solving quadratic equations, solutions for all the equations presented here can be found by factoring.

In the previous chapter, you practiced factoring polynomials by using the greatest common factor method, the difference of two perfect squares method, and the trinomial factor method. Use these methods to factor the equations that have been transformed into quadratic equations. Then, using the zero product property (if $(a)(b) = 0$, then $a = 0$ or $b = 0$ or both $= 0$), let each factor equal zero and solve for the variable. There will be two solutions for each quadratic equation. (Ignore numerical factors such as the 3 in the factored equation $3(x + 1)(x + 1) = 0$ when finding solutions to quadratic equations. The solutions will be the same for equations with or without the numerical factors.)

Find the solutions to the following quadratic equations.

401. $x^2 - 25 = 0$

402. $n^2 - 121 = 0$

403. $a^2 + 12a + 32 = 0$

404. $y^2 - 15y + 56 = 0$

405. $b^2 + b - 90 = 0$

406. $4x^2 = 81$

407. $25r^2 = 144$

408. $2n^2 + 20n + 42 = 0$

409. $3c^2 - 33c - 78 = 0$

410. $100r^2 = 196$

411. $3x^2 - 36x + 108 = 0$

412. $7a^2 - 21a - 70 = 0$

413. $8y^2 + 56y + 96 = 0$

414. $2x^2 + x = 10$

415. $4x^2 + 4x = 15$

416. $9x^2 + 12x = {}^-4$

417. $3x^2 = 19x - 20$

418. $8b^2 + 10b = 42$

419. $14n^2 = 7n + 21$

420. $6b^2 + 20b = {}^-9b - 20$

421. $15x^2 - 70x - 120 = 0$

422. $7x^2 = 52x - 21$

423. $36z^2 + 78z = {}^-36$

424. $12r^2 = 192 - 40r$

425. $24x^2 = 3(43x - 15)$

Answers

Numerical expressions in parentheses like this [ ] are operations performed on only part of the original expression. The operations performed within these symbols are intended to show how to evaluate the various terms that make up the entire expression.

Expressions with parentheses that look like this ( ) contain either numerical substitutions or expressions that are part of a numerical expression. Once a single number appears within these parentheses, the parentheses are no longer needed and need not be used the next time the entire expression is written.

When two pair of parentheses appear side by side like this ( )( ), it means that the expressions within are to be multiplied.

Sometimes parentheses appear within other parentheses in numerical or algebraic expressions. Regardless of what symbol is used, ( ), { }, or [ ], perform operations in the innermost parentheses first and work outward.

The solutions are underlined.

401. The expression is the difference of two perfect squares.
  The equation factors into $(x + 5)(x - 5) = 0$
  Applying the zero product property (if $(a)(b) = 0$,
    then $a = 0$ or $b = 0$ or both $= 0$), the first factor
    or the second factor or both must equal 0. $(x + 5) = 0$
  Subtract 5 from both sides of the equation. $x + 5 - 5 = 0 - 5$
  Combine like terms on each side. $x = {}^-5$
  Let the second factor $= 0$. $x - 5 = 0$
  Add 5 to both sides of the equation. $x - 5 + 5 = 0 + 5$
  Combine like terms on each side. $x = 5$
  The solutions for the equation are $x = 5$ and $x = -5$.

402. The expression is the difference of two perfect
    squares.
  The equation factors into $(n + 11)(n - 11) = 0$
  Applying the zero product property (if $(a)(b) = 0$,
    then $a = 0$ or $b = 0$ or both $= 0$), the first factor
    or the second factor or both must equal zero. $(n + 11) = 0$
  Subtract 11 from both sides of the equation. $n + 11 - 11 = 0 - 11$
  Combine like terms on each side. $n = {}^-11$
  Let the second factor equal zero. $n - 11 = 0$
  Add 11 to both sides of the equation. $n - 11 + 11 = 0 + 11$
  Combine like terms on each side. $n = 11$
  The solutions for the equation are $n = 11$ and $n = -11$.

403. Factor the trinomial expression using the trinomial factor form.

$(a + 4)(a + 8) = 0$

Using the zero product property, subtract 4 from both sides.

$(a + 4) = 0$
$a + 4 - 4 = 0 - 4$

Combine like terms on each side. $a = -4$
Let the second factor equal zero. $(a + 8) = 0$
Subtract 8 from both sides. $a + 8 - 8 = 0 - 8$
Combine like terms on each side. $a = -8$

The solutions for the quadratic equation $a^2 + 12a + 32 = 0$ are $a = -4$ and $a = -8$.

404. Factor the trinomial expression using the trinomial factor form.

$(y - 8)(y - 7) = 0$

Using the zero product property, $(y - 8) = 0$
Add 8 to both sides. $y - 8 + 8 = 0 + 8$
Combine like terms on each side. $y = 8$
Let the second factor equal zero. $(y - 7) = 0$
Add 7 to both sides. $y - 7 + 7 = 0 + 7$
Combine like terms on each side. $y = 7$

The solutions for the equation $y^2 - 15y + 56 = 0$ are $y = 8$ and $y = 7$.

405. Factor the trinomial expression using the trinomial factor form.

$(b + 10)(b - 9) = 0$

Using the zero product property, subtract 10 from both sides.

$(b + 10) = 0$
$b + 10 - 10 = 0 - 10$

Combine like terms on each side. $b = {}^-10$
Let the second factor equal zero. $(b - 9) = 0$
Add 9 to both sides. $b - 9 + 9 = 0 + 9$
Combine like terms on each side. $b = 9$

The solutions for the quadratic equation $b^2 + b - 90 = 0$ are $b = -10$ and $b = 9$.

406. Transform the equation so that all terms are on one side and are equal to zero.

Subtract 81 from both sides. $4x^2 - 81 = 81 - 81$
Combine like terms on each side. $4x^2 - 81 = 0$

The expression is the difference of two perfect squares.

The equation factors into $(2x + 9)(2x - 9) = 0$

Applying the zero product property (if $(a)(b) = 0$, then $a = 0$ or $b = 0$ or both $= 0$), the first factor or the second factor or both must equal 0. $(2x + 9) = 0$

Subtract 9 from both sides of the equation. $2x + 9 - 9 = 0 - 9$
Combine like terms on each side. $2x = {}^-9$
Divide both sides by 2. $\frac{2x}{2} = \frac{{}^-9}{2}$

Simplify. $\qquad$ $x = {}^-4\frac{1}{2}$

Let the second factor = 0. $\qquad$ $(2x - 9) = 0$

Add 9 to both sides of the equation. $\qquad$ $2x - 9 + 9 = 0 + 9$

Combine like terms on both sides. $\qquad$ $2x = 9$

Divide both sides by 2. $\qquad$ $x = 4\frac{1}{2}$

The solutions for the quadratic equation $4x^2 = 81$ are $x = {}^-4\frac{1}{2}$
and $x = 4\frac{1}{2}$.

407. Transform the equation so that all terms are
on one side and are equal to zero.

Subtract 144 from both sides. $\qquad$ $25r^2 - 144 = 144 - 144$

Combine like terms on each side. $\qquad$ $25r^2 - 144 = 0$

The expression is the difference of two perfect
squares.

The equation factors into $\qquad$ $(5r + 12)(5r - 12) = 0.$

Applying the zero product property (if $(a)(b) = 0$,
then $a = 0$ or $b = 0$ or both $= 0$), the first factor
or the second factor or both must equal 0. $\qquad$ $(5r + 12) = 0$

Subtract 12 from both sides of the equation. $\qquad$ $5r + 12 - 12 = 0 - 12$

Combine like terms on each side. $\qquad$ $5r = {}^-12$

Divide both sides by 5. $\qquad$ $\frac{5r}{5} = \frac{{}^-12}{5}$

Simplify. $\qquad$ $r = {}^-2\frac{2}{5}$

Let the second factor = 0. $\qquad$ $(5r - 12) = 0$

Add 12 to both sides of the equation. $\qquad$ $5r - 12 + 12 = 0 + 12$

Combine like terms on each side. $\qquad$ $5r = 12$

Divide both sides by 5. $\qquad$ $\frac{5r}{5} = \frac{12}{5}$

Simplify. $\qquad$ $r = 2\frac{2}{5}$

The solution for the quadratic equation $25r^2 = 144$ is $r = \pm\, 2\frac{2}{5}$.

408. Factor the trinomial expression using the
trinomial factor form. $\qquad$ $(2n + 6)(n + 7) = 0$

Using the zero product property, subtract 6 from
both sides. $\qquad$ $(2n + 6) = 0$
$\qquad$ $2n + 6 - 6 = 0 - 6$

Combine like terms on each side. $\qquad$ $2n = {}^-6$

Divide both sides by 2. $\qquad$ $\frac{2n}{2} = \frac{{}^-6}{2}$

Simplify terms. $\qquad$ $n = {}^-3$

Let the second factor equal zero. $\qquad$ $(n + 7) = 0$

Subtract 7 from both sides. $\qquad$ $n + 7 - 7 = 0 - 7$

Combine like terms on each side. $\qquad$ $n = {}^-7$

The solutions for the quadratic equation $2n^2 + 20n + 42 = 0$ are $n = -3$
and $n = {}^-7$.

409. Use the greatest common factor method. $\qquad$ $3(c^2 - 11c - 26) = 0$
Factor the trinomial expression using the
   trinomial factor form. $\qquad$ $3(c - 13)(c + 2) = 0$
Ignore the factor 3 in the expression.
Using the zero product property, add 13 to both sides. $(c - 13) = 0$
$\qquad$ $c - 13 + 13 = 0 + 13$
Combine like terms on each side. $\qquad$ $c = 13$
Let the second factor equal zero. $\qquad$ $(c + 2) = 0$
Subtract 2 from both sides. $\qquad$ $c + 2 - 2 = 0 - 2$
Combine like terms on each side. $\qquad$ $c = {}^-2$
The solutions for the quadratic equation $3c^2 - 33c - 78 = 0$ are $c = 13$
and $c = {}^-2$.

410. Transform the equation so that all terms are on
   one side and are equal to zero.
Subtract 196 from both sides. $\qquad$ $100r^2 - 196 = 196 - 196$
Combine like terms on each side. $\qquad$ $100r^2 - 196 = 0$
The expression is the difference of two
   perfect squares.
The equation factors into $\qquad$ $(10r + 14)(10r - 14) = 0.$
Applying the zero product property (if $(a)(b) = 0$,
   then $a = 0$ or $b = 0$ or both $= 0$), the first factor
   or the second factor or both must equal 0. $\qquad$ $(10r + 14) = 0$
Subtract 14 from both sides of the equation. $\qquad$ $10r + 14 - 14 = 0 - 14$
Combine like terms on each side. $\qquad$ $10r = {}^-14$
Divide both sides by 10. $\qquad$ $\frac{10r}{10} = \frac{{}^-14}{10} = \frac{{}^-7}{5}$
Simplify terms. $\qquad$ $r = {}^-1\frac{2}{5}$
Let the second factor $= 0$. $\qquad$ $(10r - 14) = 0$
Add 14 to both sides of the equation. $\qquad$ $10r - 14 + 14 = 0 + 14$
Combine like terms on each side. $\qquad$ $10r = 14$
Divide both sides by 10. $\qquad$ $\frac{10r}{10} = \frac{14}{10} = \frac{7}{5}$
Simplify terms. $\qquad$ $r = 1\frac{2}{5}$
The solution for the quadratic equation $100r^2 = 196$ is $r = \pm 1\frac{2}{5}$.

411. Use the greatest common factor method. $\qquad$ $3(x^2 - 12x + 36) = 0$
Factor the trinomial expression using the trinomial
   factor form. $\qquad$ $3(x - 6)(x - 6) = 0$
Ignore the factor 3 in the expression.
Using the zero product property, add 6 to both sides. $(x - 6) = 0$
$\qquad$ $x - 6 + 6 = 0 + 6$
Combine like terms on each side. $\qquad$ $x = 6$
Since both factors of the trinomial expression are the same, the solution
for the quadratic equation $3x^2 - 36x + 108 = 0$ is $x = 6$.

412. Use the greatest common factor method. $\qquad$ $7(a^2 - 3a - 10) = 0$

Factor the trinomial expression using the trinomial

factor form. $\qquad$ $7(a - 5)(a + 2) = 0$

Ignore the factor 7 in the expression.

Using the zero product property, add 5 to both sides. $\quad (a - 5) = 0$

$a - 5 + 5 = 0 + 5$

Combine like terms on each side. $\qquad$ $a = 5$

Let the second factor equal zero. $\qquad$ $(a + 2) = 0$

Subtract 2 from both sides. $\qquad$ $a + 2 - 2 = 0 - 2$

Combine like terms on each side. $\qquad$ $a = {}^-2$

The solutions for the quadratic equation $7a^2 - 21a - 70 = 0$ are $a = -2$
and $a = 5$.

413. Use the greatest common factor method. $\qquad$ $8(y^2 + 7y + 12) = 0$

Factor the trinomial expression using the trinomial

factor form. $\qquad$ $8(y + 4)(y + 3) = 0$

Ignore the factor 8 in the expression.

Using the zero product property, subtract 4 from

both sides. $\qquad$ $(y + 4) = 0$

$y + 4 - 4 = 0 - 4$

Combine like terms on each side. $\qquad$ $y = {}^-4$

Let the second factor equal zero. $\qquad$ $(y + 3) = 0$

Subtract 3 from both sides. $\qquad$ $y + 3 - 3 = 0 - 3$

Simplify. $\qquad$ $y = {}^-3$

The solutions for the quadratic equation $8y^2 + 56y + 96 = 0$ are $y = -4$
and $y = {}^-3$.

414. Transform the equation into the familiar trinomial

equation form.

Subtract 10 from both sides of the equation. $\qquad$ $2x^2 + x - 10 = 10 - 10$

Combine like terms on each side. $\qquad$ $2x^2 + x - 10 = 0$

Factor the trinomial expression using the trinomial

factor form. $\qquad$ $(2x + 5)(x - 2) = 0$

Using the zero product property, subtract 5 from

both sides. $\qquad$ $(2x + 5) = 0$

$2x + 5 - 5 = 0 - 5$

Combine like terms on each side. $\qquad$ $2x = {}^-5$

Divide both sides by 2. $\qquad$ $\frac{2x}{2} = \frac{{}^-5}{2}$

Simplify terms. $\qquad$ $x = {}^-2\frac{1}{2}$

Let the second term equal 0. $\qquad$ $x - 2 = 0$

Add 2 to both sides. $\qquad$ $x - 2 + 2 = 0 + 2$

Simplify. $\qquad$ $x = 2$

The solutions for the quadratic equation $2x^2 + x = 10$ are $x = -2\frac{1}{2}$
and $x = 2$.

415. Transform the equation into the familiar
trinomial equation form.

Subtract 15 from both sides of the equation.	$4x^2 + 4x - 15 = 15 - 15$
Combine like terms on each side.	$4x^2 + 4x - 15 = 0$
Factor the trinomial expression using the trinomial factor form.	$(2x - 3)(2x + 5) = 0$
Using the zero product property, subtract 5 from both sides.	$(2x + 5) = 0$
	$2x + 5 - 5 = 0 - 5$
Simplify.	$2x = {}^-5$
Divide both sides by 2.	$\frac{2x}{2} = \frac{{}^-5}{2}$
Simplify terms.	$x = {}^-2\frac{1}{2}$
Let the second factor equal 0.	$(2x - 3) = 0$
Add 3 to both sides.	$2x - 3 + 3 = 0 + 3$
Simplify.	$2x = 3$
Divide both sides by 2.	$\frac{2x}{2} = \frac{3}{2}$
Simplify terms.	$x = 1\frac{1}{2}$

The solutions for the quadratic equation $4x^2 + 4x = 15$ are $x = {}^-2\frac{1}{2}$
and $x = 1\frac{1}{2}$.

416. Transform the equation into the familiar
trinomial equation form.

Add 4 to both sides of the equation.	$9x^2 + 12x + 4 = {}^-4 + 4$
Combine like terms on each side.	$9x^2 + 12x + 4 = 0$
Factor the trinomial expression using the trinomial factor form.	$(3x + 2)(3x + 2) = 0$
Using the zero product property, subtract 2 from both sides.	$(3x + 2) = 0$
	$3x + 2 - 2 = 0 - 2$
Simplify.	$3x = {}^-2$
Divide both sides by 3.	$\frac{3x}{3} = \frac{{}^-2}{3}$
Simplify terms.	$x = \frac{{}^-2}{3}$

Since both factors of the trinomial are the same, the solution to the
quadratic equation $9x^2 + 12x = {}^-4$ is $x = \frac{{}^-2}{3}$.

417. Transform the equation into the familiar trinomial equation form.

Subtract 19x from both sides. $\quad 3x^2 - 19x = 19x - 19x - 20$

Combine like terms. $\quad 3x^2 - 19x = {}^-20$

Add 20 to both sides. $\quad 3x^2 - 19x + 20 = {}^-20 + 20$

Combine like terms on each side. $\quad 3x^2 - 19x + 20 = 0$

Factor the trinomial expression using the trinomial factor form. $\quad (3x - 4)(x - 5) = 0$

Using the zero product property, add 4 to both sides. $\quad (3x - 4) = 0$

$\quad 3x - 4 + 4 = 0 + 4$

Simplify. $\quad 3x = 4$

Divide both sides by 3. $\quad \frac{3x}{3} = \frac{4}{3}$

Simplify terms. $\quad x = 1\frac{1}{3}$

Now let the second term equal zero. $\quad x - 5 = 0$

Add 5 to both sides. $\quad x - 5 + 5 = 0 + 5$

Simplify. $\quad x = 5$

The solutions for the quadratic equation $3x^2 = 19x - 20$ are $x = 1\frac{1}{3}$ and $x = 5$.

418. Transform the equation into the familiar trinomial equation form.

Subtract 42 from both sides of the equation. $\quad 8b^2 + 10b - 42 = 42 - 42$

Simplify. $\quad 8b^2 + 10b - 42 = 0$

Use the greatest common factor method to factor out 2. $\quad 2(4b^2 + 5b - 21) = 0$

Factor the trinomial expression using the trinomial factor form. $\quad 2(4b - 7)(b + 3) = 0$

Ignore the factor 2 in the expression.

Using the zero product property, add 7 to both sides. $\quad (4b - 7) = 0$

$\quad 4b - 7 + 7 = 0 + 7$

Simplify. $\quad 4b = 7$

Divide both sides by 4. $\quad \frac{4b}{4} = \frac{7}{4}$

Simplify terms. $\quad b = 1\frac{3}{4}$

Now let the second term equal zero. $\quad (b + 3) = 0$

Subtract 3 from both sides. $\quad b + 3 - 3 = 0 - 3$

Simplify. $\quad b = {}^-3$

The solutions for the quadratic equation $8b^2 + 10b = 42$ are $b = 1\frac{3}{4}$ and $b = {}^-3$.

419. Transform the equation into the familiar
trinomial equation form.

Subtract $7n$ from both sides of the equation.	$14n^2 - 7n = 7n - 7n + 21$
Simplify and subtract 21 from both sides.	$14n^2 - 7n - 21 = 21 - 21$
Simplify the equation.	$14n^2 - 7n - 21 = 0$
Factor the greatest common factor from each term.	$7(2n^2 - n - 3) = 0$
Factor the trinomial expression using the trinomial factor form.	$7(2n - 3)(n + 1) = 0$
Ignore the factor 7 in the expression.	
Using the zero product property, add 3 to both sides.	$(2n - 3) = 0$
	$2n - 3 + 3 = 0 + 3$
Simplify.	$2n = 3$
Divide both sides by 2.	$\frac{2n}{2} = \frac{3}{2}$
Simplify terms.	$n = 1\frac{1}{2}$
Now set the second equal to zero.	$n + 1 = 0$
Subtract 1 from both sides.	$n + 1 - 1 = 0 - 1$
Simplify.	$n = {}^-1$

The solutions for the quadratic equation $14n^2 = 7n + 21$ are $n = 1\frac{1}{2}$
and $n = {}^-1$.

420. Transform the equation into the familiar
trinomial equation form.

Add $9b$ to both sides of the equation.	$6b^2 + 20b + 9b = {}^-9b + 9b - 20$
Simplify and add 20 to both sides of the equation.	$6b^2 + 29b + 20 = 20 - 20$
Simplify.	$6b^2 + 29b + 20 = 0$
Factor the trinomial expression using the trinomial factor form.	$(6b + 5)(b + 4) = 0$
Using the zero product property, subtract 5 from both sides.	$(6b + 5) = 0$
	$6b + 5 - 5 = 0 - 5$
Simplify.	$6b = {}^-5$
Divide both sides by 6.	$\frac{6b}{6} = \frac{{}^-5}{6}$
Simplify terms.	$b = \frac{{}^-5}{6}$
Now set the second factor equal to zero.	$b + 4 = 0$
Subtract 4 from both sides.	$b + 4 - 4 = 0 - 4$
Simplify.	$b = {}^-4$

The solutions for the quadratic equation $6b^2 + 20b = {}^-9b - 20$ are
$b = \frac{{}^-5}{6}$ and $b = -4$.

421. Factor the greatest common factor from
  each term. $5(3x^2 - 14x - 24) = 0$

Now factor the trinomial expression using the
  trinomial factor form. $5(3x + 4)(x - 6) = 0$

Using the zero product property, subtract 4 from
  both sides. $(3x + 4) = 0$
                 $3x + 4 - 4 = 0 - 4$

Simplify. $3x = {}^-4$

Divide both sides by 3. $\frac{3x}{3} = \frac{-4}{3}$

Simplify terms. $x = \frac{-4}{3}$

Add 6 to both sides. $x - 6 + 6 = 0 + 6$

Simplify. $x = 6$

The solutions for the quadratic equation $15x^2 - 70x - 120 = 0$ are

$x = \frac{-4}{3}$ and $x = 6$.

422. Transform the equation into the familiar
  trinomial equation form.

Subtract $52x$ from both sides of the equation. $7x^2 - 52x = 52x - 52x - 21$

Simplify and add 21 to both sides of the
  equation. $7x^2 - 52x + 21 = 21 - 21$

Simplify. $7x^2 - 52x + 21 = 0$

Factor the trinomial expression using the
  trinomial factor form. $(7x - 3)(x - 7) = 0$

Using the zero product property, add 3
  to both sides. $(7x - 3) = 0$
                 $7x - 3 + 3 = 0 + 3$

Simplify. $7x = 3$

Divide both sides by 7. $\frac{7x}{7} = \frac{3}{7}$

Simplify terms. $x = \frac{3}{7}$

Now set the second factor equal to zero. $x - 7 = 0$

Add 7 to both sides of the equation. $x - 7 + 7 = 0 + 7$

Simplify. $x = 7$

The solutions for the quadratic equation $7x^2 = 52x - 21$ are $x = \frac{3}{7}$

and $x = 7$.

423. Transform the equation into the familiar
   trinomial equation form.

Add 36 to both sides of the equation. $\quad 36z^2 + 78z + 36 = {}^-36 + 36$

Combine like terms. $\quad 36z^2 + 78z + 36 = 0$

Factor out the greatest common factor from
   each term. $\quad 6(6z^2 + 13z + 6) = 0$

Factor the trinomial expression into
   two factors. $\quad 6(2z + 3)(3z + 2) = 0$

Ignore the numerical factor and set the first
   factor equal to zero. $\quad (2z + 3) = 0$

Subtract 3 from both sides. $\quad 2z + 3 - 3 = 0 - 3$

Simplify terms. $\quad 2z = {}^-3$

Divide both sides by 2. $\quad \frac{2z}{2} = \frac{{}^-3}{2}$

Simplify terms. $\quad z = {}^-1\frac{1}{2}$

Now let the second factor equal zero. $\quad (3z + 2) = 0$

Subtract 2 from both sides. $\quad 3z + 2 - 2 = 0 - 2$

Simplify terms. $\quad 3z = {}^-2$

Divide both sides by 3. $\quad \frac{3z}{3} = \frac{{}^-2}{3}$

Simplify terms. $\quad z = \frac{{}^-2}{3}$

The solutions for the quadratic equation $36z^2 + 78z = {}^-36$ are $z = -1\frac{1}{2}$
and $z = \frac{{}^-2}{3}$.

424. Transform the equation into the
   familiar trinomial equation form.

Add $(40r - 192)$ to both sides
   of the equation. $\quad 12r^2 + 40r - 192 = 192 - 40r + 40r - 192$

Combine like terms. $\quad 12r^2 + 40r - 192 = 0$

Factor the greatest common
   factor, 4, out of each term. $\quad 4(3r^2 + 10r - 48) = 0$

Now factor the trinomial
   expression. $\quad 4(r + 6)(3r - 8) = 0$

Ignoring the numerical factor,
   set one factor = 0. $\quad (r + 6) = 0$

Subtract 6 from both sides. $\quad r + 6 - 6 = 0 - 6$

Simplify. $\quad r = {}^-6$

Now set the second factor = 0. $\quad 3r - 8 = 0$

Add 8 to both sides. $\quad 3r - 8 + 8 = 0 + 8$

Simplify. $\quad 3r = 8$

Divide both sides by 3. $\quad \frac{3r}{3} = \frac{8}{3}$

Simplify terms. $\quad r = 2\frac{2}{3}$

The solutions for the quadratic equation $12r^2 = 192 - 40r$ are $r = -6$
and $r = 2\frac{2}{3}$.

425. Divide both sides of the equation by 3.

$$\frac{24x^2}{3} = \frac{3(43x - 15)}{3}$$

Simplify terms.

$$8x^2 = 43x - 15$$

Add $(15 - 43x)$ to both sides of the equation.

$$8x^2 + 15 - 43x = 43x - 15 + 15 - 43x$$

Combine like terms.

$$8x^2 + 15 - 43x = 0$$

Use the commutative property to move terms.

$$8x^2 - 43x + 15 = 0$$

Factor the trinomial expression.

$$(8x - 3)(x - 5) = 0$$

Using the zero product property, add 3 to both sides and divide by 8.

$$8x - 3 = 0$$

$$\frac{8x}{8} = \frac{3}{8}$$

Simplify terms.

$$x = \frac{3}{8}$$

Now let the second factor $= 0$.

$$x - 5 = 0$$

Add 5 to both sides.

$$x = 5$$

The solutions for the quadratic equation $24x^2 = 3(43x - 15)$ are $x = \frac{3}{8}$ and $x = 5$.

Simplifying Radicals

This chapter will give you practice in operating with radicals. You will not always be able to factor polynomials by factoring whole numbers and whole number coefficients. Nor do all trinomials with whole numbers have whole numbers for solutions. In the last chapters, you will need to know how to operate with radicals.

The radical sign $\sqrt{}$ tells you to find the root of a number. The number under the radical sign is called the *radicand*. Generally, a number has two roots, one positive and one negative. It is understood in mathematics that $\sqrt{}$ or $+\sqrt{}$ is telling you to find the positive root. The symbol $-\sqrt{}$ tells you to find the negative root. The symbol $\pm\sqrt{}$ asks for both roots.

Tips for Simplifying Radicals

Simplify radicals by completely factoring the radicand and taking out the square root. The most thorough method for factoring is to do a prime factorization of the radicand. Then you look for square roots that can be factored out of the radicand.

e.g., $\sqrt{28} = \sqrt{2 \cdot 2 \cdot 7} = \sqrt{2 \cdot 2} \cdot \sqrt{7} = 2\sqrt{7}$

or $\sqrt{4x^3} = \sqrt{2 \cdot 2 \cdot x \cdot x \cdot x} = \sqrt{2 \cdot 2} \cdot \sqrt{x \cdot x} \cdot \sqrt{x} = 2x\sqrt{x}$

You may also recognize perfect squares within the radicand. Then you can simplify their roots out of the radical sign.

It is improper form for the radicand to be a fraction. If you get rid of the denominator within the radical sign, you will no longer have a fractional radicand. This is known as *rationalizing* the denominator.

e.g. $\sqrt{\frac{2x}{5}} = \sqrt{\frac{2x}{5} \cdot \frac{5}{5}} = \sqrt{\frac{10x}{5^2}} = \sqrt{\frac{1}{5^2} \cdot 10x} = \frac{1}{5}\sqrt{10x}$

When there is a radical in the denominator, you can rationalize the expression as follows:

$\frac{3}{\sqrt{6}} = \frac{3}{\sqrt{6}} \cdot \frac{\sqrt{6}}{\sqrt{6}} = \frac{3\sqrt{6}}{6} = \frac{1}{2}\sqrt{6}$

If the radicands are the same, radicals can be added and subtracted as if the radicals were variables.

e.g., $3\sqrt{3} + 2\sqrt{3} = 5\sqrt{3}$ or $5\sqrt{x} - 2\sqrt{x} = 3\sqrt{x}$

Product property of radicals

When multiplying radicals, multiply the terms in front of the radicals, then multiply the radicands and put that result under the radical sign.

e.g., $4\sqrt{3} \cdot 7\sqrt{5} = 4 \cdot 7\sqrt{3 \cdot 5} = 28\sqrt{15}$

Quotient property of radicals

When dividing radicals, first divide the terms in front of the radicals, and then divide the radicands.

e.g., $\frac{6\sqrt{10}}{3\sqrt{2}} = \frac{6}{3}\sqrt{\frac{10}{2}} = 2\sqrt{5}$

Simplify the following radical expressions.

426. $\sqrt{12}$

427. $\sqrt{300}$

428. $\sqrt{3n^2}$

429. $\sqrt{24x^5}$

430. $\sqrt{\dfrac{3x^2}{4}}$

431. $\sqrt{50a^2b}$

432. $\sqrt{\dfrac{5}{4}}$

433. $\dfrac{3}{\sqrt{7}}$

434. $\dfrac{\sqrt{12xy}}{\sqrt{x}}$

435. $3\sqrt{3} + 7\sqrt{3} + 2\sqrt{5}$

436. $2\sqrt{7} - 3\sqrt{28}$

437. $(9\sqrt{a^2b})(3a\sqrt{b})$

438. $2\sqrt{5} \cdot 3\sqrt{15}$

439. $\sqrt{\dfrac{16}{9} \cdot 32}$

440. $\sqrt{\dfrac{56}{4}}$

441. $\dfrac{\sqrt{160}}{\sqrt{2}}$

442. $\dfrac{\sqrt{150}}{\sqrt{3}}$

443. $5\sqrt{\dfrac{8}{64}}$

444. $\dfrac{^-2\sqrt{98}}{\sqrt{2}}$

445. $\dfrac{\sqrt{27}}{\sqrt{72}}$

446. $^-4\sqrt{3} \cdot \sqrt{27}$

447. $\sqrt{\dfrac{4}{3}} \cdot \sqrt{\dfrac{10}{3}}$

448. $\dfrac{\sqrt{15} \cdot \sqrt{105}}{^-3}$

449. $3\sqrt{24} \cdot \sqrt{6}$

450. $\dfrac{6\sqrt{126}}{\sqrt{18}}$

Answers

Numerical expressions in parentheses like this [ ] are operations performed on only part of the original expression. The operations performed within these symbols are intended to show how to evaluate the various terms that make up the entire expression.

Expressions with parentheses that look like this ( ) contain either numerical substitutions or expressions that are part of a numerical expression. Once a single number appears within these parentheses, the parentheses are no longer needed and need not be used the next time the entire expression is written.

When two pair of parentheses appear side by side like this ( )( ), it means that the expressions within are to be multiplied.

Sometimes parentheses appear within other parentheses in numerical or algebraic expressions. Regardless of what symbol is used, ( ), { }, or [ ], perform operations in the innermost parentheses first and work outward.

<u>Underlined</u> expressions show simplified result.

426. First, factor the radicand.
Now take out the square root of any pair of factors or any perfect squares you recognize.

$$\sqrt{12} = \sqrt{2 \cdot 2 \cdot 3}$$
$$\underline{\sqrt{2 \cdot 2 \cdot 3} = 2\sqrt{3}}$$

427. First, factor the radicand.
Now take out the square root.

$$\sqrt{300} = \sqrt{3 \cdot 10 \cdot 10}$$
$$\underline{\sqrt{3 \cdot 10 \cdot 10} = 10\sqrt{3}}$$

428. First, factor the radicand.
Now take out the square root.

$$\sqrt{3n^2} = \sqrt{3 \cdot n \cdot n}$$
$$\underline{\sqrt{3 \cdot n \cdot n} = n\sqrt{3}}$$

429. First, factor the radicand and look for squares.
Now take out the square root.

$$\sqrt{24x^5} = \sqrt{6 \cdot 2 \cdot 2 \cdot x \cdot x \cdot x \cdot x \cdot x}$$
$$\underline{\sqrt{6 \cdot 2 \cdot 2 \cdot x \cdot x \cdot x \cdot x \cdot x} = 2x \cdot x\sqrt{6x} = 2x^2\sqrt{6x}}$$

430. Although it looks complex, you can still begin by factoring the terms in the radical sign.

$$\sqrt{\tfrac{3x^2}{4}} = \sqrt{\tfrac{3 \cdot x \cdot x}{2 \cdot 2}} = \sqrt{3 \cdot \tfrac{x \cdot x}{2 \cdot 2}}$$

Factoring out the squares leaves

$$\sqrt{3 \cdot \tfrac{x \cdot x}{2 \cdot 2}} = \tfrac{x}{2}\sqrt{3}.$$

This result can be written a few different ways.

$$\tfrac{x}{2}\sqrt{3} = \tfrac{\sqrt{3}x}{2} = \tfrac{\sqrt{3}}{2}x = \tfrac{1}{2}x\sqrt{3}$$

431. First, factor the radicand and look for squares.

Take out the square roots.

$$\sqrt{50a^2b} = \sqrt{2 \cdot 5 \cdot 5 \cdot a \cdot a \cdot b}$$
$$\underline{\sqrt{2 \cdot 5 \cdot 5 \cdot a \cdot a \cdot b} = 5a\sqrt{2b}}$$

432. Use the quotient property of radicals and rationalize the denominator.

$$\sqrt{\frac{5}{4}} = \frac{\sqrt{5}}{\sqrt{4}} = \frac{\sqrt{5}}{\sqrt{2 \cdot 2}} = \frac{\sqrt{5}}{2}$$

433. For this expression, you must rationalize the denominator. Use the identity property of multiplication and multiply the expression by 1 in a form useful for your purposes. In this case, that is to get the radical out of the denominator.

$$\frac{3}{\sqrt{7}} = \frac{3}{\sqrt{7}} \cdot \frac{\sqrt{7}}{\sqrt{7}} = \frac{3\sqrt{7}}{7}$$

434. First, rationalize the denominator for this expression. Then see if it can be simplified any further. As in the previous problem, multiply the expression by 1 in a form suitable for this purpose.

$$\frac{\sqrt{12xy}}{\sqrt{x}} = \frac{\sqrt{12xy}}{\sqrt{x}} \cdot \frac{\sqrt{x}}{\sqrt{x}}$$

Use the product property of radicals to combine the radicands in the numerator. In the denominator, a square root times itself is the radicand by itself.

$$\frac{\sqrt{12xy}}{\sqrt{x}} \cdot \frac{\sqrt{x}}{\sqrt{x}} = \frac{\sqrt{12xyx}}{x}$$

Now factor the radicand.

$$\frac{\sqrt{12xyx}}{x} = \frac{\sqrt{3 \cdot 4x^2y}}{x}$$

Factoring out the square roots results in
The x in the numerator and the denominator divides out, leaving

$$\frac{\sqrt{3 \cdot 4x^2y}}{x} = \frac{2x\sqrt{3y}}{x}$$

$$2\sqrt{3y}.$$

435. In this expression, add the "like terms" as if the similar radicals were similar variables.

$$3\sqrt{3} + 7\sqrt{3} + 2\sqrt{5} = 10\sqrt{3} + 2\sqrt{5}$$

The radical terms cannot be added further because the radicands are different.

436. Simplify the second term of the expression by factoring the radicand.

$$2\sqrt{7} - 3\sqrt{28} = 2\sqrt{7} - 3\sqrt{4 \cdot 7}$$

Now simplify the radicand.

$$2\sqrt{7} - 3\sqrt{4 \cdot 7} = 2\sqrt{7} - 3 \cdot 2\sqrt{7}$$

Finally, combine like terms.

$$2\sqrt{7} - 6\sqrt{7} = {}^-4\sqrt{7}$$

437. For this expression, use the product property of radicals and combine the factors in the radicand and outside the radical signs.

$$(9\sqrt{a^2b})(3a\sqrt{b}) = 9 \cdot 3a\sqrt{a^2b \cdot b} = 27a\sqrt{a^2b^2} = 27a \cdot ab = \underline{27a^2b}$$

438. Use the product property of radicals to simplify the expression.

$$2\sqrt{5} \cdot 3\sqrt{15} = 2 \cdot 3\sqrt{5 \cdot 15}$$

Now look for a perfect square in the radicand.
You can multiply and
then factor or just
factor first. $\quad 6\sqrt{5 \cdot 15} = 6\sqrt{75} = 6\sqrt{25 \cdot 3} = 6 \cdot 5\sqrt{3} = 30\sqrt{3}$
Or if you just factor the
radicand, you will see the
perfect square as 5 times 5. $\quad 6\sqrt{5 \cdot 15} = 6\sqrt{5 \cdot 5 \cdot 3} = 6 \cdot 5\sqrt{3} = \underline{30\sqrt{3}}$

439. You can start by using the product property
to simplify the expression.

$$\sqrt{\frac{16}{9} \cdot 32} = \sqrt{\frac{16}{9}} \cdot \sqrt{32}$$

Now use the quotient property to simplify
the first radical.

$$\sqrt{\frac{16}{9}} \cdot \sqrt{32} = \frac{\sqrt{16}}{\sqrt{9}} \cdot \sqrt{32}$$

You should recognize the perfect squares 9
and 16. Simplify the fraction and factor
the radicand of the second radical term.

$$\frac{\sqrt{16}}{\sqrt{9}} \cdot \sqrt{32} = \frac{4}{3}\sqrt{16 \cdot 2} = \frac{4}{3} \cdot 4\sqrt{2} = \frac{16\sqrt{2}}{3}$$

440. Use the quotient property to get the
denominator out of the radicand.

$$\sqrt{\frac{56}{4}} = \frac{\sqrt{56}}{\sqrt{4}} = \frac{\sqrt{56}}{2}$$

Now simplify the radicand by factoring so
that any perfect squares will come out of
the radical sign.

$$\frac{\sqrt{56}}{2} = \frac{\sqrt{4 \cdot 14}}{2} = \frac{2\sqrt{14}}{2}$$

The common factor in both the numerator and
denominator divides out, and you are left with

$$\underline{\sqrt{14}.}$$

441. For this term, factor the radicand in the
numerator and look for perfect squares.

$$\frac{\sqrt{160}}{\sqrt{2}} = \frac{\sqrt{4 \cdot 4 \cdot 2 \cdot 5}}{\sqrt{2}} = \frac{4\sqrt{2 \cdot 5}}{\sqrt{2}}$$

Use the product property in the numerator.
Divide out the common factor in the numerator
and the denominator.

$$\frac{4\sqrt{2 \cdot 5}}{\sqrt{2}} = \frac{4\sqrt{2} \cdot \sqrt{5}}{\sqrt{2}}$$

$$\frac{4\sqrt{2} \cdot \sqrt{5}}{\sqrt{2}} = 4\sqrt{5}$$

442. You could proceed in the same way as the previous
solution, but let's try another way.
Rationalize the denominator.

$$\frac{\sqrt{150}}{\sqrt{3}} \cdot \frac{\sqrt{3}}{\sqrt{3}} = \frac{\sqrt{150} \cdot \sqrt{3}}{\sqrt{3} \cdot \sqrt{3}} = \frac{\sqrt{150} \cdot \sqrt{3}}{3}$$

Use the product property to simplify
the numerator.

$$\frac{\sqrt{150} \cdot \sqrt{3}}{3} = \frac{\sqrt{150 \cdot 3}}{3}$$

Factor the radicand seeking perfect
squares.

$$\frac{\sqrt{150 \cdot 3}}{3} = \frac{\sqrt{25 \cdot 2 \cdot 3 \cdot 3}}{3}$$

Simplify the numerator.

$$\frac{\sqrt{25 \cdot 2 \cdot 3 \cdot 3}}{3} = \frac{5 \cdot 3\sqrt{2}}{3}$$

Divide out the common factor in the
numerator and denominator and you're done.

$$\frac{5 \cdot 3\sqrt{2}}{3} = 5\sqrt{2}$$

443. You use the quotient property to begin rationalizing the denominator.

$$5\sqrt{\frac{8}{64}} = 5\frac{\sqrt{8}}{\sqrt{64}}$$

The 5 becomes part of the numerator. Factor the numerator and simplify the perfect square in the denominator.

$$5\frac{\sqrt{8}}{\sqrt{64}} = \frac{5\sqrt{4 \cdot 2}}{8}$$

Simplify the numerator.

$$\frac{5\sqrt{4 \cdot 2}}{8} = \frac{5 \cdot 2\sqrt{2}}{8}$$

Factor 2 out of the numerator and denominator.

$$\frac{5 \cdot 2\sqrt{2}}{8} = \frac{5\sqrt{2}}{4}$$

444. Begin simplifying this term by rationalizing the denominator.

$$\frac{^-2\sqrt{98}}{\sqrt{2}} \cdot \frac{\sqrt{2}}{\sqrt{2}} = \frac{^-2\sqrt{98} \cdot \sqrt{2}}{\sqrt{2} \cdot \sqrt{2}}$$

Using the product property, simplify the numerator and write the product of the term in the denominator.

$$\frac{^-2\sqrt{98} \cdot \sqrt{2}}{\sqrt{2} \cdot \sqrt{2}} = \frac{^-2\sqrt{98 \cdot 2}}{2}$$

Divide out the common factor in the numerator and denominator. Then factor the radicand looking for perfect squares.

$$\frac{^-2\sqrt{98 \cdot 2}}{2} = {}^-\sqrt{49 \cdot 2 \cdot 2} = {}^-7 \cdot 2 = \underline{{}^-14}$$

445. You will have to rationalize the denominator, but first factor the radicands and look for perfect squares.

$$\frac{\sqrt{27}}{\sqrt{72}} = \frac{\sqrt{9 \cdot 3}}{\sqrt{36 \cdot 2}} = \frac{3\sqrt{3}}{6\sqrt{2}}$$

You can simplify the whole numbers in the numerator and denominator by a factor of 3.

$$\frac{3\sqrt{3}}{6\sqrt{2}} = \frac{\sqrt{3}}{2\sqrt{2}}$$

Now rationalize the denominator.
Simplify terms by using the product property in the numerator and multiplying terms in the denominator.

$$\frac{\sqrt{3}}{2\sqrt{2}} \cdot \frac{\sqrt{2}}{\sqrt{2}} = \frac{\sqrt{3} \cdot \sqrt{2}}{2 \cdot \sqrt{2} \cdot \sqrt{2}}$$

$$\frac{\sqrt{3} \cdot \sqrt{2}}{2 \cdot \sqrt{2} \cdot \sqrt{2}} = \frac{\sqrt{3 \cdot 2}}{2 \cdot 2} = \frac{\sqrt{6}}{4}$$

446. Factor the radicand in the last radical.

$${}^-4\sqrt{3} \cdot \sqrt{27} = {}^-4\sqrt{3} \cdot \sqrt{9 \cdot 3}$$

Simplify the perfect square.

$${}^-4\sqrt{3} \cdot \sqrt{9 \cdot 3} = {}^-4\sqrt{3} \cdot 3\sqrt{3}$$

Use the commutative property of multiplication.

$${}^-4\sqrt{3} \cdot 3\sqrt{3} = {}^-4 \cdot 3 \cdot \sqrt{3} \cdot \sqrt{3}$$

Now simplify terms.

$${}^-4 \cdot 3 \cdot \sqrt{3} \cdot \sqrt{3} = {}^-12 \cdot 3 = \underline{{}^-36}$$

447. Using the product property, put all terms in one radical sign.

$$\sqrt{\frac{4}{3}} \cdot \sqrt{\frac{10}{3}} = \sqrt{\frac{4 \cdot 10}{3 \cdot 3}}$$

Now use the quotient property to continue simplifying.

$$\sqrt{\frac{4 \cdot 10}{3 \cdot 3}} = \frac{\sqrt{4 \cdot 10}}{\sqrt{9}}$$

Simplify the perfect squares in the numerator and denominator.

$$\frac{\sqrt{4 \cdot 10}}{\sqrt{9}} = \frac{2\sqrt{10}}{3}$$

The expression is fine the way it is, or it could be written as

$$\frac{2}{3}\sqrt{10}.$$

448. Begin by factoring the radicand of the second radical.

$$\frac{\sqrt{15} \cdot \sqrt{105}}{^-3} = \frac{\sqrt{15} \cdot \sqrt{15 \cdot 7}}{^-3}$$

Now use the product property to separate the factors of the second radical term into two radical terms. Why? Because you will then have the product of two identical radicals.

$$\frac{\sqrt{15} \cdot \sqrt{15 \cdot 7}}{^-3} = \frac{\sqrt{15} \cdot \sqrt{15} \cdot \sqrt{7}}{^-3} = \frac{15\sqrt{7}}{^-3}$$

Now simplify the whole numbers.

$$\frac{15\sqrt{7}}{^-3} = {}^-5\sqrt{7}$$

449. There is more than one way to simplify an expression. Start this one by using the product property to combine the radicands.

$$3\sqrt{24} \cdot \sqrt{6} = 3\sqrt{24 \cdot 6}$$

Now factor the terms in the radicand and look for perfect squares.

$$3\sqrt{24 \cdot 6} = 3\sqrt{4 \cdot 6 \cdot 6} = 3\sqrt{2 \cdot 2 \cdot 6 \cdot 6}$$

Simplify the radical.

$$3\sqrt{2 \cdot 2 \cdot 6 \cdot 6} = 3 \cdot 2 \cdot 6 = 36$$

Another way is to multiply 6 and 24 to get 144, another perfect square. Then 3 times 12 equals 36.

450. Begin by rationalizing the denominator.

$$\frac{6\sqrt{126}}{\sqrt{18}} \cdot \frac{\sqrt{18}}{\sqrt{18}} = \frac{6\sqrt{126} \cdot \sqrt{18}}{18}$$

Use the product property to simplify the numerator.

$$\frac{6\sqrt{126} \cdot \sqrt{18}}{18} = \frac{6\sqrt{126 \cdot 18}}{18}$$

Simplify the whole numbers in the numerator and denominator. Then factor the radicand and look for perfect squares.

$$\frac{6\sqrt{126 \cdot 18}}{18} = \frac{\sqrt{9 \cdot 7 \cdot 2 \cdot 2 \cdot 9}}{3} = \frac{\sqrt{9 \cdot 9 \cdot 2 \cdot 2 \cdot 7}}{3}$$

Simplify the numerator and divide out common factors in the numerator and denominator.

$$\frac{\sqrt{9 \cdot 9 \cdot 2 \cdot 2 \cdot 7}}{3} = \frac{9 \cdot 2\sqrt{7}}{3} = \frac{18\sqrt{7}}{3} = 6\sqrt{7}$$

Solving Radical Equations

This chapter will give you more practice operating with radicals. However, the focus here is to use radicals to solve equations. An equation is considered a *radical equation* when the radicand contains a variable. When you use a radical to solve an equation, you must be aware of the positive and negative roots. You should always check your results in the original equation to see that both solutions work. When one of the solutions does not work, it is called an *extraneous solution*. When neither solution works in the original equation, there is said to be no solution.

Tips for Solving Radical Equations

- Squaring both sides of an equation is a valuable tool when solving radical equations. Use the following property: When a and b are algebraic expressions, if $a = b$, then $a^2 = b^2$.
- Isolate the radical on one side of an equation before using the squaring property.
- Squaring a radical results in the radical symbol disappearing, e.g., $(\sqrt{x+5})^2 = x + 5$.

- For second degree equations, use the radical sign on both sides of the equation to find a solution for the variable. Check your answers.

Solve the following radical equations. Watch for extraneous solutions.

451. $x^2 = 64$

452. $x^2 = 135$

453. $\sqrt{n} = 13$

454. $2\sqrt{a} = 24$

455. $\sqrt{2x} - 4 = 4$

456. $\sqrt{4x + 6} = 6$

457. $\sqrt{3x + 4} + 8 = 12$

458. $\sqrt{5x - 4} + 3 = 12$

459. $\sqrt{4x + 9} = {}^-13$

460. $\sqrt{5x - 6} + 3 = 11$

461. $\sqrt{9 - x} + 14 = 25$

462. $3\sqrt{3x + 1} = 15$

463. $3\sqrt{-x} + 7 = 22$

464. $3 = 10 - \sqrt{100x - 1}$

465. $\sqrt{3x + 46} + 24 = 38$

466. ${}^-7 = 10 - \sqrt{25x + 39}$

467. $3\sqrt{13x + 43} - 4 = 29$

468. $\frac{28}{\sqrt{5x + 1}} = 7$

469. $x = \sqrt{8 - 2x}$

470. $x = \sqrt{2x + 3}$

471. $x = \sqrt{x + 12}$

472. $x = \sqrt{7x - 10}$

473. $\sqrt{4x + 3} = 2x$

474. $\sqrt{2 - \frac{7}{2}x} = x$

475. $x = \sqrt{\frac{3}{2}x + 10}$

Answers

Numerical expressions in parentheses like this [ ] are operations performed on only part of the original expression. The operations performed within these symbols are intended to show how to evaluate the various terms that make up the entire expression.

Expressions with parentheses that look like this ( ) contain either numerical substitutions or expressions that are part of a numerical expression. Once a single number appears within these parentheses, the parentheses are no longer needed and need not be used the next time the entire expression is written.

When two pair of parentheses appear side by side like this ( )( ), it means that the expressions within are to be multiplied.

Sometimes parentheses appear within other parentheses in numerical or algebraic expressions. Regardless of what symbol is used, ( ), { }, or [ ], perform operations in the innermost parentheses first and work outward.

The solution is underlined.

451. Use the radical sign on both sides of the equation. $\sqrt{x^2} = \sqrt{64}$
Show both solutions for the square root of 64. $x = \pm 8$
Check the first solution in the original equation. $(8)^2 = 64$
$$64 = 64$$
Check the second solution in the original equation. $(^-8)^2 = 64$
$$64 = 64$$

Both solutions, $\underline{x = \pm 8}$, check out.

452. Use the radical sign on both sides of the equation.
$$\sqrt{x^2} = \sqrt{135}$$
Simplify the radical. $x = \sqrt{135} = \sqrt{9 \cdot 15} = \pm 3\sqrt{15}$
Check the first solution in the original equation.
$$(3\sqrt{15})^2 = 135$$
$$3^2(\sqrt{15})^2 = 135$$
$$9(15) = 135$$
$$135 = 135$$
Check the second solution in the original equation.
$$(^-3\sqrt{15})^2 = 135$$
$$(^-3)^2(\sqrt{15})^2 = 135$$
$$(9)(15) = 135$$
$$135 = 135$$

Both solutions, $\underline{x = \pm 3\sqrt{15}}$, check out.

453. First, square both sides of the equation. $(\sqrt{n})^2 = 13^2$
Simplify both terms. $n = 169$
Check by substituting in the original equation. $\sqrt{169} = 13$
The original equation asks for only the positive root of n. So when you substitute 169 into the original equation, only the positive root $\underline{\sqrt{n} = 13}$ is to be

considered. 13 = 13 checks out. Although this may seem trivial at this point, as the radical equations become more complex, this will become important.

454. Isolate the radical on one side of the equation. Divide both sides by 2.

$$\frac{2\sqrt{a}}{2} = \frac{24}{2}$$

Simplify terms. $\sqrt{a} = 12$

Now square both sides of the equation. $(\sqrt{a})^2 = 12^2$

Simplify terms. $a = 144$

Check the solution in the original equation.
$$2\sqrt{144} = 24$$
$$2(12) = 24$$

The solution $\underline{a = 144}$ checks out. $24 = 24$

455. Begin by adding 4 to both sides to isolate the radical. $\sqrt{2x} - 4 + 4 = 4 + 4$

Combine like terms on each side. $\sqrt{2x} = 8$

Square both sides of the equation. $(\sqrt{2x})^2 = 8^2$

Simplify terms. $2x = 64$

Divide both sides by 2. $x = 32$

Check the solution in the original equation.
$$\sqrt{2(32)} - 4 = 4$$
$$\sqrt{64} - 4 = 4$$

The solution $\underline{x = 32}$ checks out. $8 - 4 = 4, \ 4 = 4$

456. Square both sides of the equation.
$$(\sqrt{4x + 6})^2 = 6^2$$
$$4x + 6 = 36$$

Subtract 6 from both sides of the equation. $4x = 30$

Divide both sides by 4 and simplify. $x = \frac{30}{4} = 7.5$

Check the solution in the original equation. $\sqrt{4(7.5) + 6} = 6$

Simplify terms. $\sqrt{36} = 6$

The solution $\underline{x = 7.5}$ checks out. $6 = 6$

457. Subtract 8 from both sides in order to isolate the radical.

$$\sqrt{3x + 4} = 4$$

Square both sides of the equation. $(\sqrt{3x + 4})^2 = 4^2$

Simplify terms. $3x + 4 = 16$

Subtract 4 from both sides and divide by 3. $x = 4$

Check your solution in the original equation. $\sqrt{3(4) + 4} + 8 = 12$

Simplify terms. $\sqrt{16} + 8 = 12$

$$4 + 8 = 12$$

The solution $\underline{x = 4}$ checks out. $12 = 12$

458. Subtract 3 from both sides of the equation isolating the radical.

$\sqrt{5x-4} = 9$

Square both sides of the equation.

$(\sqrt{5x-4})^2 = 9^2$

Simplify terms on both sides.

$5x - 4 = 81$

Add 4 to both sides and then divide by 5.

$x = \frac{85}{5} = 17$

Check your solution in the original equation.

$\sqrt{5(17)-4} + 3 = 12$

Simplify terms under the radical sign.

$\sqrt{81} + 3 = 12$

Find the positive square root of 81.

$9 + 3 = 12$

Simplify.

$12 = 12$

The solution $\underline{x = 17}$ checks out.

459. Square both sides of the equation.

$(\sqrt{4x+9})^2 = (^-13)^2$

Simplify terms on both sides of the equation.

$4x + 9 = 169$

Subtract 9 from both sides and then divide by 4.

$x = 40$

Substitute the solution in the original equation.

$\sqrt{4(40+9)} = {^-13}$

Simplify the expression under the radical sign.

$\sqrt{169} = {^-13}$

The radical sign calls for the positive square root.

$13 \neq {^-13}$

The solution does **not** check out.

There is **no** solution for this equation.

460. Subtract 3 from both sides isolating the radical.

$\sqrt{5x-6} = 8$

Square both sides of the equation.

$(\sqrt{5x-6})^2 = 8\,2$

Simplify terms.

$5x - 6 = 64$

Add 6 to both sides and divide the result by 5.

$x = 14$

Check the solution in the original equation.

$\sqrt{5(14)-6} + 3 = 11$

Simplify the expression under the radical.

$\sqrt{64} + 3 = 11$

Find the positive square root of 64 and add 3.

$8 + 3 = 11$

The solution $\underline{x = 14}$ checks out.

$11 = 11$

461. Subtract 14 from both sides to isolate the radical.

$\sqrt{9-x} = 11$

Now square both sides of the equation.

$9 - x = 121$

Subtract 9 from both sides.

${^-x} = 112$

Multiply both sides by negative 1 to solve for x.

$x = {^-112}$

Check the solution in the original equation.

$\sqrt{9-(^-112)} + 14 = 25$

Simplify the expression under the radical sign.

$\sqrt{121} + 14 = 25$

The square root of 121 is 11. Add 14 and the solution $\underline{x = {^-112}}$ checks.

$25 = 25$

462. To isolate the radical, divide both sides by 3.

$\sqrt{3x + 1} = 5$

Square both sides of the equation.

$(\sqrt{3x + 1})^2 = 5^2$

Simplify terms.

$3x + 1 = 25$

Subtract 1 from both sides of the equation and divide by 3.

$x = 8$

Check the solution in the original equation.

$3\sqrt{3(8) + 1} = 15$

Simplify the expression under the radical sign.

$3\sqrt{25} = 15$

Multiply 3 by the positive root of 25.

$3(5) = 15$

The solution $x = 8$ checks out.

$15 = 15$

463. Subtract 7 from both sides of the equation.

$3\sqrt{^-x} = 15$

Divide both sides by 3 to isolate the radical.

$\sqrt{^-x} = 5$

Square both sides of the equation.

$(\sqrt{^-x})^2 = 5^2$

Simplify terms.

$^-x = 25$

Multiply both sides by negative 1.

$x = ^-25$

Check the solution in the original equation.

$3\sqrt{^-(^-25)} + 7 = 22$

Simplify terms under the radical.

$3\sqrt{25} + 7 = 22$

Use the positive square root of 25.

$3(5) + 7 = 22$

$15 + 7 = 22$

The solution $x = ^-25$ checks out.

$22 = 22$

464. Add $\sqrt{100x - 1}$ to both sides of the equation.

$$3 + \sqrt{100x - 1} = 10 - \sqrt{100x - 1} + \sqrt{100x - 1}$$

Combine like terms and simplify the equation.

$3 + \sqrt{100x - 1} = 10$

Now subtract 3 from both sides.

$\sqrt{100x - 1} = 7$

Square both sides of the equation.

$100x - 1 = 49$

Add 1 to both sides of the equation and divide by 100.

$x = 0.5$

Check the solution in the original equation.

$3 = 10 - \sqrt{100(0.5) - 1}$

Simplify the expression under the radical sign.

$3 = 10 - \sqrt{49}$

The equation asks you to subtract the positive square root of 49 from 10.

$3 = 10 - 7$

The solution $x = 0.5$ checks out.

$3 = 3$

465. Subtract 24 from both sides to isolate the radical.

$\sqrt{3x + 46} = 14$

Square both sides of the equation.

$3x + 46 = 196$

Subtract 46 from both sides of the equation and divide by 3.

$x = 50$

Check the solution in the original equation.

$\sqrt{3(50) + 46} + 24 = 38$

Simplify the expression under the radical sign.

$\sqrt{196} + 24 = 38$

$14 + 24 = 38$

The solution $x = 50$ checks out.

$38 = 38$

466. Add $\sqrt{25x + 39}$ to both sides of the equation.
$$\sqrt{25x + 39} - 7 = 10 - \sqrt{25x + 39} + \sqrt{25x + 39}$$
Combine like terms and simplify the equation. $\quad \sqrt{25x + 39} - 7 = 10$
Add 7 to both sides of the equation. $\quad \sqrt{25x + 39} = 17$
Square both sides. $\quad 25x + 39 = 289$
Subtract 39 from both sides and divide
   the result by 25. $\quad x = 10$
Check the solution in the original equation. $\quad {}^-7 = 10 - \sqrt{25(10) + 39}$
Simplify the expression under the radical sign. $\quad {}^-7 = 10 - \sqrt{289}$
The equation asks you to subtract the positive
   square root of 289 from 10. $\quad {}^-7 = 10 - 17$
The solution $\underline{x = 10}$ checks out. $\quad {}^-7 = {}^-7$

467. To isolate the radical on one side of the equation,
   add 4 to both sides and divide the result by 3. $\quad \sqrt{13x + 43} = 11$
Square both sides of the equation. $\quad 13x + 43 = 121$
Subtract 43 from both sides and divide by 13. $\quad x = 6$
Check the solution in the original equation. $\quad 3\sqrt{13(6) + 43} - 4 = 29$
Simplify the expression under the radical sign. $\quad 3\sqrt{121} - 4 = 29$
Evaluate the left side of the equation. $\quad 3(11) - 4 = 29$
The solution $\underline{x = 6}$ checks out. $\quad 29 = 29$

468. To isolate the radical on one side of the equation,
   multiply both sides by $\sqrt{5x + 1}$. $\quad 28 = 7\sqrt{5x + 1}$
Divide both sides of the equation by 7. $\quad 4 = \sqrt{5x + 1}$
Square both sides of the equation. $\quad 16 = 5x + 1$
Subtract 1 from both sides and divide the result by 5. $\quad 3 = x$

Check the solution in the original equation. $\quad \dfrac{28}{\sqrt{5(3) + 1}} = 7$

Simplify the expression under the radical sign. $\quad \dfrac{28}{\sqrt{16}} = 7$

Divide the numerator by the positive square root of 16. $\quad \dfrac{28}{4} = 7$
The solution $\underline{3 = x}$ checks out. $\quad 7 = 7$

469. The radical is alone on one side. Square
   both sides. $\quad x^2 = 8 - 2x$
Transform the equation by putting all terms
   on one side. $\quad x^2 + 2x - 8 = 0$
The result is a quadratic equation. Solve
   for x by factoring using the trinomial
   factor form and setting each factor equal
   to zero and solving for x. (Refer to
   Chapter 16 for practice and tips for

factoring quadratic equations.) It will be important to check each solution. $x^2 + 2x - 8 = (x + 4)(x - 2) = 0$

Let the first factor equal zero and solve for x. $x + 4 = 0$

Subtract 4 from both sides. $x = {}^-4$

Check the solution in the original equation. $({}^-4) = \sqrt{8 - 2({}^-4)}$

Evaluate the expression under the radical sign. ${}^-4 = \sqrt{16}$

The radical sign calls for a positive root. ${}^-4 \neq 4$

Therefore, x cannot equal ${}^-4$. $x = {}^-4$ is an example of an *extraneous root*.

Let the second factor equal zero and solve for x. $x - 2 = 0$

Subtract 2 from both sides. $x = 2$

Check the solution in the original equation. $(2) = \sqrt{8 - 2(2)}$

Evaluate the expression under the radical sign. $2 = \sqrt{4}$

The positive square root of 4 is 2. $2 = 2$

Therefore, the only solution for the equation is $\underline{x = 2}$.

470. With the radical alone on one side of the equation, square both sides. $x^2 = 2x + 3$

The resulting quadratic equation may have up to two solutions. Put it into standard form and factor the equation using the trinomial factor form to find the solutions. Then check the solutions in the original equation. $x^2 - 2x - 3 = (x - 3)(x + 1) = 0$

Letting each factor equal zero and solving for x results in two possible solutions, $x = 3$ and/or ${}^-1$. Check the first possible solution in the original equation. $(3) = \sqrt{2(3 + 3)} = \sqrt{9} = 3$

The solution checks out. Now check the second possible solution in the original equation. $({}^-1) = \sqrt{2({}^-1) + 3} = \sqrt{1} = 1$

${}^-1 \neq 1$

Therefore $x \neq {}^-1$. $x = {}^-1$ is an *extraneous root*. The only solution for the original equation is $\underline{x = 3}$.

471. Square both sides of the equation. $x^2 = x + 12$

Subtract $(x + 12)$ from both sides of the equation. $x^2 - x - 12 = 0$

The resulting quadratic equation may have up to two solutions. Factor the equation to find the solutions and check in the original equation. $x^2 - x - 12 = (x - 4)(x + 3) = 0$

Let the first factor equal zero and solve for x. $x - 4 = 0 \quad x = 4$

Let the second factor equal zero and solve for x. $x + 3 = 0 \quad x = {}^-3$

Check each solution in the original equation to rule out an extraneous solution. $(4) = \sqrt{(4) + 12}$

Simplify the expression under the radical sign. $4 = \sqrt{16}$

The solution $\underline{x = 4}$ checks out.

Now check the second possible solution in the original equation. $({}^-3) = \sqrt{({}^-3) + 12}$

You could simplify the expression under the radical sign to get the square root of 9. However, the radical sign indicates that the positive solution is called for, and the left side of the original equation when $x = {}^-3$ is a negative number. So, $x = {}^-3$ is **not** a solution.

472. Square both sides of the equation. $x^2 = 7x - 10$

Subtract $(7x - 10)$ from both sides of the equation. $x^2 - 7x + 10 = 0$

Factor the quadratic equation to find the solutions, and check each in the original equation to rule out any extraneous solution. $x^2 - 7x + 10 = (x - 5)(x - 2) = 0$

The first factor will give you the solution $x = 5$. The second factor will give the solution $x = 2$. Check the first solution for the quadratic equation in the original equation. $(5) = \sqrt{7(5) - 10}$

Simplify the expression under the radical sign. $5 = \sqrt{25}$ or $5 = 5$

The solution $\underline{x = 5}$ is a solution to the original equation.

Now check the second solution to the quadratic equation in the original. $(2) = \sqrt{7(2) - 10}$

Simplify the expression under the radical sign. $2 = \sqrt{4}$ or $2 = 2$

There are two solutions to the original equation, $\underline{x = 2 \text{ and } x = 5}$.

473. Square both sides of the radical equation.

$$4x + 3 = 4x^2$$

Transform the equation into a quadratic equation.

$$4x^2 - 4x - 3 = 0$$

Factor the result using the trinomial factor form.

$$4x^2 - 4x - 3 = (2x + 1)(2x - 3) = 0$$

Let the first factor equal zero and solve for x.

$$2x + 1 = 0, x = {}^-0.5$$

Let the second factor equal zero and solve for x.

$$2x - 3 = 0, x = 1.5$$

When you substitute $^-0.5$ for x in the original equation, the result will be $\sqrt{1} = {}^-1$. That cannot be true for the original equation, so $x \neq {}^-0.5$.

Substitute 1.5 for x in the original equation.

$$\sqrt{4(1.5) + 3} = 2(1.5)$$

Simplify the terms on each side of the equal sign.

$$\sqrt{9} = 3 \text{ or } 3 = 3$$

The only solution for the original equation is $x = 1.5$.

474. Square both sides of the equation.

$$2 - \tfrac{7}{2}x = x^2$$

Subtract $(2 - \tfrac{7}{2}x)$ from both sides of the equation.

$$0 = x^2 + \tfrac{7}{2}x - 2$$

Multiply both sides of the equation by 2 to simplify the fraction.

$$0 = 2x^2 + 7x - 4$$

Factor using the trinomial factor form.

$$2x^2 + 7x - 4 = (2x - 1)(x + 4) = 0$$

Let the first factor equal zero and solve for x.

$$2x - 1 = 0, \text{ so } x = \tfrac{1}{2}$$

Let the second factor equal zero and solve for x.

$$x + 4 = 0, \text{ so } x = {}^-4$$

Check the first possible solution in the original equation.

$$\sqrt{2 - \tfrac{7}{2}(\tfrac{1}{2})} = (\tfrac{1}{2})$$

Simplify the expression under the radical sign.

$$\sqrt{2 - \tfrac{7}{4}} = \sqrt{2 - 1\tfrac{3}{4}} = \sqrt{\tfrac{1}{4}} = \tfrac{1}{2}$$

$$\tfrac{1}{2} = \tfrac{1}{2}$$

So $x = \tfrac{1}{2}$ is a solution.

Check the solution $x = {}^-4$ in the original equation.

$$\sqrt{2 - \tfrac{7}{2}({}^-4)} = ({}^-4)$$

Simplify the expression.

$$\sqrt{16} = ({}^-4) \text{ or } 4 = {}^-4$$

This is not true. There is one solution for the original equation, $x = \tfrac{1}{2}$.

475. Square both sides of the equation. $x^2 = \frac{3}{2}x + 10$

Add $(\frac{-3}{2x} - 10)$ to both sides of
the equation. $x^2 - \frac{3}{2}x - 10 = 0$

Multiply the equation by 2 to
eliminate the fraction. $2x^2 - 3x - 20 = 0$

Factor using the trinomial factor form. $2x^2 - 3x - 20 = (x - 4)(2x + 5) = 0$

Letting each factor of the trinomial
factors equal zero results in two
possible solutions for the original
equation, $x = 4$ and/or $x = {}^-2\frac{1}{2}$.

Check the first possible solution in
the original equation. $4 = \sqrt{\frac{3}{2}(4) + 10}$

Simplify the radical expression. $4 = \sqrt{16}$ or $4 = 4$

The solution $x = 4$ checks out as a
solution for the original equation.

Check the second possible solution
in the original equation. ${}^-2\frac{1}{2} = \sqrt{\frac{3}{2}({}^-2\frac{1}{2}) + 10}$

A negative number cannot be equal to
a positive square root as the radical
sign in the original expression calls for.
Therefore, $x = {}^-2\frac{1}{2}$ is **not** a solution
to the original equation. The only
solution for this equation is $\underline{x = 4}$.

20

Solving Equations with the Quadratic Formula

In this chapter, you will have the opportunity to practice solving equations using the quadratic formula. In Chapter 17 you practiced using factoring to solve quadratic equations, but factoring is useful only for those equations that can easily be factored. The quadratic formula will allow you to find solutions for any quadratic equation that can be put in the form $ax^2 + bx + c = 0$, where a, b, and c are numbers.

The quadratic formula tells you that for any equation in the form $ax^2 + bx + c = 0$, the solution will be $x = \frac{-b \pm \sqrt{b^2 - 4ac}}{2a}$. The solutions found using the quadratic formula are also called the roots of the equation. Some solutions will be in the form of whole numbers or fractions. Some will be in the form of a radical. Some will be undefined, as when the radicand is equal to a negative number. The $\pm$ in the quadratic equation tells you that there will be two solutions, one when you add the radical and one when you subtract it.

Tips for Solving Equations with the Quadratic Formula

- Transform the equation into the form $ax^2 + bx + c = 0$. Use the values for a, b, and c in the quadratic equation to determine the solution for the original equation.
- For solutions that contain a radical, be sure to simplify the radical as you practiced in Chapter 18.
- When you are asked to find the solution to the nearest hundredth, you can use a calculator to find the value of the radical.

Solve the following equations using the quadratic formula. Reduce answers to their simplest form or to the simplest radical form. Use of a calculator is recommended.

476. $x^2 + 2x - 15 = 0$

477. $2x^2 - 7x - 30 = 0$

478. $6x^2 + 13x - 28 = 0$

479. $18x^2 + 9x + 1 = 0$

480. $6x^2 + 17x = 28$

481. $14x^2 = 12x + 32$

482. $3x^2 + 5x = 0$

483. $2x^2 = 27$

484. $5x^2 = 18x - 17$

485. $3x^2 + 11x - 7 = 0$

486. $5x^2 + 52x + 20 = 0$

487. $x^2 = \frac{-5x - 2}{2}$

488. $x^2 + 7x = 5$

489. $x^2 = 20x - 19$

490. $23x^2 = 2(8x - 1)$

491. $x^2 + 10x + 12 = 0$

492. $24x^2 + 18x - 6 = 0$

493. $7x^2 = 4(3x + 1)$

494. $\frac{1}{3}x^2 + \frac{3}{4}x - 3 = 0$

495. $5x^2 - 12x + 1 = 0$

Find the solution to the following equations to the nearest hundredth.

496. $11r^2 - 4r - 7 = 0$

497. $3m^2 + 21m - 8 = 0$

498. $4y^2 = 16y - 5$

499. $5s^2 + 12s - 1 = 0$

500. $4c^2 - 11c + 2 = 0$

501. $11k^2 - 32k + 10 = 0$

Answers

Numerical expressions in parentheses like this [ ] are operations performed on only part of the original expression. The operations performed within these symbols are intended to show how to evaluate the various terms that make up the entire expression.

Expressions with parentheses that look like this ( ) contain either numerical substitutions or expressions that are part of a numerical expression. Once a single number appears within these parentheses, the parentheses are no longer needed and need not be used the next time the entire expression is written.

When two pair of parentheses appear side by side like this ( )( ), it means that the expressions within are to be multiplied.

Sometimes parentheses appear within other parentheses in numerical or algebraic expressions. Regardless of what symbol is used, ( ), { }, or [ ], perform operations in the innermost parentheses first and work outward.

The solutions are underlined.

476. The equation is in the proper form.
First, list the values for a, b, and c.
$a = 1 \quad b = 2 \quad c = {}^-15$
Substitute the values into the quadratic equation.
$$x = \frac{{}^-(2) \pm \sqrt{(2)^2 - 4(1)({}^-15)}}{2(1)}$$

Simplify the expression under the radical sign.
$$x = \frac{{}^-2 \pm \sqrt{4 - ({}^-60)}}{2} = \frac{{}^-2 \pm \sqrt{64}}{2}$$

Evaluate the square root of 64.
$$x = \frac{{}^-2 \pm 8}{2}$$

Find the two solutions for x by simplifying terms. First add the terms in the numerator, and then subtract them.
$$x = \frac{{}^-2 + 8}{2} = \frac{6}{2} = 3 \text{ and}$$
$$x = \frac{{}^-2 - 8}{2} = \frac{{}^-10}{2} = {}^-5$$

The two solutions for the variable x are $\underline{x = 3}$ and $\underline{x = {}^-5}$.

477. The equation is in the proper form.
First, list the values for a, b, and c.
$a = 2 \quad b = {}^-7 \quad c = {}^-30$
Substitute the values into the quadratic equation.
$$x = \frac{{}^-({}^-7) \pm \sqrt{({}^-7)^2 - 4(2)({}^-30)}}{2(2)}$$

Simplify the expression.
$$x = \frac{7 \pm \sqrt{49 - ({}^-240)}}{4} = \frac{7 \pm \sqrt{289}}{4} = \frac{7 \pm 17}{4}$$

Find the two solutions for x by adding and then subtracting in the numerator.
$$x = \frac{7 + 17}{4} = \frac{24}{4} = 6 \text{ and}$$
$$x = \frac{7 - 17}{4} = \frac{{}^-10}{4} = {}^-2.5$$

The two solutions for the variable x are $\underline{x = 6}$ and $\underline{x = {}^-2.5}$.

478. The equation is in the proper form.
First, list the values for a, b, and c.

$$a = 6 \quad b = 13 \quad c = {}^-28$$

Substitute the values into the quadratic equation.

$$x = \frac{{}^-(13) \pm \sqrt{(13)^2 - 4(6)({}^-28)}}{2(6)}$$

Simplify the expression.
Find the two solutions for x by adding and then subtracting in the numerator.

$$x = \frac{{}^-13 \pm \sqrt{169 + 672}}{12} = \frac{{}^-13 \pm \sqrt{841}}{12} = \frac{{}^-13 \pm 29}{12}$$

$$x = \frac{{}^-13 + 29}{12} = \frac{16}{12} = 1\tfrac{1}{3} \text{ and}$$

$$x = \frac{{}^-13 - 29}{12} = \frac{{}^-42}{12} = {}^-3\tfrac{1}{2}$$

The two solutions for the variable x are $x = 1\tfrac{1}{3}$ and $x = {}^-3\tfrac{1}{2}$.

479. The equation is in the proper form.
First, list the values for a, b, and c.

$$a = 18 \quad b = 9 \quad c = 1$$

Substitute the values into the quadratic equation.

$$x = \frac{{}^-(9) \pm \sqrt{(9)^2 - 4(18)(1)}}{2(18)}$$

Simplify the expression.
Find the two solutions for x by adding and then subtracting in the numerator.

$$x = \frac{{}^-9 \pm \sqrt{81 - 72}}{36} = \frac{{}^-9 \pm \sqrt{9}}{36} = \frac{{}^-9 + 3}{36}$$

$$x = \frac{{}^-9 + 3}{36} = \frac{{}^-6}{36} = \frac{{}^-1}{6} \text{ and}$$

$$x = \frac{{}^-12}{36} = \frac{{}^-1}{3}$$

The two solutions for the variable x are $x = \frac{{}^-1}{6}$ and $x = \frac{{}^-1}{3}$.

480. First transform the equation into the proper form. Subtract 88 from both sides of the equation.

$$6x^2 + 17x - 28 = 28 - 28$$

Combine like terms on both sides.

$$6x^2 + 17x - 28 = 0$$

Now list the values for a, b, and c.

$$a = 6 \quad b = 17 \quad c = {}^-28$$

Substitute the values into the quadratic equation.

$$x = \frac{{}^-(17) \pm \sqrt{(17)^2 - 4(6)({}^-28)}}{2(6)}$$

Simplify the expression.
Find the two solutions for x by adding and then subtracting in the numerator.

$$x = \frac{{}^-17 \pm \sqrt{289 + 672}}{12} = \frac{{}^-17 \pm \sqrt{961}}{12} = \frac{{}^-17 \pm 31}{12}$$

$$x = \frac{{}^-17 + 31}{12} = \frac{14}{12} = 1\tfrac{1}{6} \text{ and}$$

$$x = \frac{{}^-17 - 31}{12} = \frac{{}^-48}{12} = {}^-4$$

The two solutions for the variable x are $x = 1\tfrac{1}{6}$ and $x = {}^-4$.

481. First transform the equation into
the proper form. Add ($^-12x - 32$)
to both sides of the equation. $14x^2 - 12x - 32 = 12x + 32 - 12x - 32$
Combine like terms. $14x^2 - 12x - 32 = 0$
Now list the values for a, b,
and c. $a = 14 \quad b = ^-12 \quad c = ^-32$
Substitute the values into the
quadratic equation.

$$x = \frac{^-(^-12) \pm \sqrt{(^-12)^2 - 4(14)(^-32)}}{2(14)}$$

Simplify the expression.

$$x = \frac{12 \pm \sqrt{144 + 1792}}{28} = \frac{12 \pm \sqrt{1936}}{28} = \frac{12 \pm 44}{28}$$

Find the two solutions for x by
adding and then subtracting
in the numerator.

$$x = \frac{12 + 44}{28} = \frac{56}{28} = 2 \text{ and}$$
$$x = \frac{12 - 44}{28} = \frac{^-32}{28} = ^-1\frac{1}{7}$$

The two solutions for the variable x are $\underline{x = 2}$ and $\underline{x = ^-1\frac{1}{7}}$.

Yes, you could have divided both sides of the equation
by 2 before listing your a, b, and c values. However,
the solution would have been the same. Try it yourself.

482. The equation may not appear to be in proper
form because there is no value for c. But you
could write it as $3x^2 + 5x + 0 = 0$, and then
your values would be $a = 3$, $b = 5$, and $c = 0$.
Substitute the values into the quadratic equation. $x = \frac{^-(5) \pm \sqrt{(5)^2 - 4(3)(0)}}{2(3)}$

Simplify the expression. $x = \frac{^-5 \pm \sqrt{25 - 0}}{6} = \frac{^-5 \pm 5}{6}$
Find the two solutions for x by adding and then
subtracting in the numerator.

$$x = \frac{^-5 + 5}{6} = \frac{0}{6} = 0 \text{ and}$$
$$x = \frac{^-5 - 5}{6} = \frac{^-10}{6} = ^-1\frac{2}{3}$$

The two solutions for the variable x are $\underline{x = 0}$ and $\underline{x = ^-1\frac{2}{3}}$.

483. Subtract 27 from both sides of the
equation. $2x^2 - 27 = 27 - 27 \text{ or } 2x^2 - 27 = 0.$
In this equation, there appears to be
no coefficient for the x term unless
you realize that $0x = 0$.
So you could write the equation in
the proper form like this: $2x^2 + 0x - 27 = 0$
Now list the values for a, b, and c. $a = 2 \quad b = 0 \quad c = ^-27$
Substitute the values into the
quadratic equation. $x = \frac{^-(0) \pm \sqrt{(0)^2 - 4(2)(^-27)}}{2(2)}$

Simplify the expression. $x = \frac{\pm \sqrt{216}}{2(2)} = \frac{\pm \sqrt{9 \cdot 4 \cdot 6}}{2(2)} = \frac{\pm 3 \cdot 2\sqrt{6}}{2(2)} = \frac{\pm 3\sqrt{6}}{2}$

Simplify the radical.

$$\frac{\pm 3\sqrt{6}}{2} = \pm 1\tfrac{1}{2}\sqrt{6}$$

The two solutions for the variable x are $\underline{x = \pm 1\tfrac{1}{2}\sqrt{6}}$.

484. Transform the equation into the
desired form. Subtract $18x$ and
add 17 to both sides.
$$5x^2 - 18x + 17 = 18x - 18x - 17 + 17$$
Combine like terms on both sides. $\quad 5x^2 - 18x + 17 = 0$
Now list the values for a, b, and c. $\quad a = 5 \quad b = {}^-18 \quad c = 17$
Substitute the values into the
quadratic equation.
$$x = \frac{{}^-({}^-18) \pm \sqrt{({}^-18)^2 - 4(5)(17)}}{2(5)}$$

Simplify the expression.
$$x = \frac{18 \pm \sqrt{324 - 340}}{10} = \frac{18 \pm \sqrt{{}^-16}}{10}$$
Since there is no rational number
equal to the square root of a
negative number, there are
no solutions for this equation.

485. List the values of a, b,
and c.
$$a = 3 \quad b = 11 \quad c = {}^-7$$
Substitute the values into
the quadratic equation.
$$x = \frac{{}^-(11) \pm \sqrt{(11)^2 - 4(3)({}^-7)}}{2(3)}$$

Simplify the expression.
$$x = \frac{{}^-11 \pm \sqrt{121 + 84}}{6} = \frac{{}^-11 \pm \sqrt{205}}{6} = {}^-1\tfrac{5}{6} + \tfrac{1}{6}\sqrt{205}$$

The solutions for the variable x are $\underline{x = {}^-1\tfrac{5}{6} \pm \tfrac{1}{6}\sqrt{205}}$.

486. List the values of a, b, and c. $\quad a = 5 \quad b = 52 \quad c = 20$
Substitute the values into the
quadratic equation.
$$x = \frac{{}^-(52) \pm \sqrt{(52)^2 - 4(5)(20)}}{2(5)}$$

Simplify the expression.
$$x = \frac{{}^-52 \pm \sqrt{2704 - 400}}{10} = \frac{{}^-52 \pm \sqrt{2304}}{10} = \frac{{}^-52 \pm 48}{10}$$

Find the two solutions for x by
adding and then subtracting
in the numerator.
$$x = \frac{{}^-52 + 48}{10} = \frac{{}^-4}{10} = {}^-0.4 \text{ and}$$
$$x = \frac{{}^-52 - 48}{10} = \frac{{}^-100}{10} = {}^-10$$

The two solutions for the variable x are $\underline{x = {}^-0.4}$ and $\underline{x = {}^-10}$.

487. First, multiply both sides of
the equation by 2. $\qquad$ $2x^2 = {}^-5x - 2$
Then add $5x + 2$ to both
sides of the equation. $\qquad$ $2x^2 + 5x + 2 = 0$
List the values of a, b, and c. $\quad$ $a = 2 \quad b = 5 \quad c = 2$
Substitute the values into
the quadratic equation. $\quad$ $x = \frac{{}^-(5) \pm \sqrt{(5)^2 - 4(2)(2)}}{2(2)} = \frac{{}^-5 \pm \sqrt{25 - 16}}{2(2)} = \frac{{}^-5 \pm 3}{4}$
Find the two solutions for
x by adding and then sub-
tracting in the numerator. $\quad$ $x = \frac{{}^-5 + 3}{4} = \frac{{}^-2}{4} = \frac{{}^-1}{2}$ and $x = \frac{{}^-5 - 3}{4} = \frac{{}^-8}{4} = {}^-2$

The two solutions for the variable x are $\underline{x = -\frac{1}{2}}$ and $\underline{x = {}^-2}$.

488. Transform the equation by
subtracting 5 from both sides. $\quad$ $x^2 + 7x - 5 = 0$
List the values of a, b, and c. $\quad$ $a = 1 \quad b = 7 \quad c = {}^-5$
Substitute the values into the
quadratic equation. $\qquad$ $x = \frac{{}^-(7) \pm \sqrt{(7)^2 - 4(1)({}^-5)}}{2(1)}$

Simplify the expression. $\qquad$ $x = \frac{{}^-7 \pm \sqrt{49 + 20}}{2} = \frac{{}^-7 \pm \sqrt{69}}{2} = {}^-3\frac{1}{2} \pm \frac{1}{2}\sqrt{69}$

The solution for the variable x is $\underline{x = {}^-3\frac{1}{2} \pm \frac{1}{2}\sqrt{69}}$.

489. Transform the equation by subtracting
$20x$ and adding 19 to both sides
of the equation. $\qquad$ $x^2 - 20x + 19 = 0$
List the values of a, b, and c. $\quad$ $a = 1 \quad b = {}^-20 \quad c = 19$
Substitute the values into the
quadratic equation. $\qquad$ $x = \frac{{}^-({}^-20) \pm \sqrt{({}^-20)^2 - 4(1)(19)}}{2(1)}$

Simplify the expression. $\qquad$ $x = \frac{20 \pm \sqrt{400 - 76}}{2} = \frac{20 \pm \sqrt{324}}{2} = \frac{20 \pm 18}{2}$
Find the two solutions for x by adding
and then subtracting in the
numerator. $\qquad$ $x = \frac{20 + 18}{2} = \frac{38}{2} = 19$ and
$\qquad$ $x = \frac{20 - 18}{2} = \frac{2}{2} = 1$

The two solutions for the variable x are $\underline{x = 19}$ and $\underline{x = 1}$.

490. Transform the equation into proper form.
Use the distributive property of multiplica-
tion on the right side of the equation. $\quad$ $23x^2 = 16x - 2$
Subtract $16x$ and add 2 to both sides. $\quad$ $23x^2 - 16x + 2 = 0$
List the values of a, b, and c. $\quad$ $a = 23 \quad b = {}^-16 \quad c = 2$
Substitute the values into the
quadratic equation. $\qquad$ $x = \frac{{}^-({}^-16) \pm \sqrt{({}^-16)^2 - 4(23)(2)}}{2(23)}$
Simplify the expression.

$$x = \frac{16 \pm \sqrt{256 - 184}}{2(23)} = \frac{16 \pm \sqrt{72}}{2(23)} = \frac{16 \pm \sqrt{4 \cdot 9 \cdot 2}}{2(23)} = \frac{2 \cdot 8 \pm 2 \cdot 3\sqrt{2}}{2(23)} = \frac{8 \pm 3\sqrt{2}}{23} = \frac{8}{23} \pm \frac{3}{23}\sqrt{2}$$

The solution for the variable x is $x = \frac{8}{23} \pm \frac{3}{23}\sqrt{2}$.

491. List the values of a, b, and c. $a = 1 \quad b = 10 \quad c = 12$

Substitute the values into the quadratic equation.

$$x = \frac{-(10) \pm \sqrt{(10^2 - 4(1)(12)}}{2(1)}$$

Simplify the expression.

$$x = \frac{-10 \pm \sqrt{100 - 48}}{2} = \frac{-10 \pm \sqrt{52}}{2} = \frac{-10 \pm \sqrt{4 \cdot 13}}{2} = \frac{-10 \pm 2\sqrt{13}}{2} = -5 \pm \sqrt{13}$$

The two solutions for the variable x are $x = -5 + \sqrt{13}$ and $x = -5 - \sqrt{13}$.

492. List the values of a, b, and c. $a = 24 \quad b = 18 \quad c = -6$

Substitute the values into the quadratic equation.

$$x = \frac{-(18) \pm \sqrt{(18)^2 - 4(24)(-6)}}{2(24)}$$

Simplify the expression.
Find the two solutions for x by adding and then subtracting in the numerator.

$$x = \frac{-18 \pm \sqrt{324 + 576}}{48} = \frac{-18 \pm \sqrt{900}}{48} = \frac{-18 \pm 30}{48}$$

$$x = \frac{-18 + 30}{48} = \frac{12}{48} = \frac{1}{4} \text{ and}$$

$$x = \frac{-18 - 30}{48} = \frac{-48}{48} = -1$$

The two solutions for the variable x are $x = \frac{1}{4}$ and $x = -1$.

493. Transform the equation into the proper form. First use the distributive property of multiplication.

$$7x^2 = 4(3x) + 4(1) = 12x + 4$$

Then subtract $(12x + 4)$ from both sides.

$$7x^2 - 12x - 4 = 0$$

List the values of a, b, and c. $a = 7 \qquad b = -12 \quad c = -4$

Substitute the values into the quadratic equation.

$$x = \frac{-(-12) \pm \sqrt{(-12)^2 - 4(7)(-4)}}{2(7)}$$

Simplify the expression.

$$x = \frac{12 \pm \sqrt{144 + 112}}{14} = \frac{12 \pm \sqrt{256}}{14} = \frac{12 \pm 16}{14}$$

Find the two solutions for x by adding and then subtracting in the numerator.

$$x = \frac{12 + 16}{14} = \frac{28}{14} = 2 \text{ and}$$

$$x = \frac{12 - 16}{14} = \frac{-4}{14} = \frac{-2}{7}$$

The two solutions for the variable x are $x = 2$ and $x = \frac{-2}{7}$.

494. You could use the fractions as values for a and b, but it might be easier to first transform the equation by multiplying it by 12.

$$12(\tfrac{1}{3}x^2 + \tfrac{3}{4}x - 3 = 0)$$

Using the distributive property, you get

$$12(13x^2) + 12(\tfrac{3}{4}x) - 12(3) = 12(0).$$

Simplify the terms.

$$4x^2 + 9x - 36 = 0$$

List the values of a, b, and c.

$$a = 4 \quad b = 9 \quad c = {}^{-}36$$

Substitute the values into the quadratic equation.

$$x = \frac{{}^{-}(9) \pm \sqrt{(9)^2 - 4(4)({}^{-}36)}}{2(4)}$$

Simplify the expression.

$$x = \frac{{}^{-}9 \pm \sqrt{81 + 576}}{8} = \frac{{}^{-}9 \pm \sqrt{657}}{8}$$
$$= \frac{{}^{-}9 \pm \sqrt{9 \cdot 73}}{8} = \frac{{}^{-}9 \pm 3\sqrt{73}}{8}$$

The two solutions for the variable x are $x = \underline{\frac{{}^{-}9 + 3\sqrt{73}}{8}}$ and $x = \underline{\frac{{}^{-}9 - 3\sqrt{73}}{8}}$.

495. List the values of a, b, and c.

$$a = 5 \quad b = {}^{-}12 \quad c = 1$$

Substitute the values into the quadratic equation.

$$x = \frac{{}^{-}({}^{-}12) \pm \sqrt{({}^{-}12)^2 - 4(5)(1)}}{2(5)}$$

Simplify the expression.

$$x = \frac{12 \pm \sqrt{144 - 20}}{2(5)} = \frac{12 \pm \sqrt{124}}{2(5)} = \frac{12 \pm \sqrt{4 \cdot 31}}{2(5)} = \frac{12 \pm 2\sqrt{31}}{2(5)} = \frac{6 \pm \sqrt{31}}{5}$$

The two solutions for the variable x are $x = \underline{\frac{6 + \sqrt{31}}{5}}$ and $x = \underline{\frac{6 - \sqrt{31}}{5}}$.

496. List the values of a, b, and c.

$$a = 11 \quad b = {}^{-}4 \quad c = {}^{-}7$$

Substitute the values into the quadratic equation.

$$x = \frac{{}^{-}({}^{-}4) \pm \sqrt{({}^{-}4)^2 - 4(11)({}^{-}7)}}{2(11)}$$

Simplify the expression.

$$r = \frac{4 \pm \sqrt{16 + 308}}{22} = \frac{4 \pm \sqrt{324}}{22} = \frac{4 \pm 18}{22}$$

Find the two solutions for r by adding and then subtracting in the numerator.

$$r = \frac{4 + 18}{22} = \frac{22}{22} = 1 \text{ and}$$
$$r = \frac{4 - 18}{22} = \frac{{}^{-}14}{22} = {}^{-}0.64$$

The two solutions for the variable r are $r = \underline{1}$ and $r = \underline{{}^{-}0.64}$.

497. List the values of a, b, and c.

$$a = 3 \quad b = 21 \quad c = {}^{-}8$$

Substitute the values into the quadratic equation.

$$m = \frac{{}^{-}(21) \pm \sqrt{(21)^2 - 4(3)({}^{-}8)}}{2(3)}$$

Simplify the expression.

$$m = \frac{{}^{-}21 \pm \sqrt{441 + 96}}{6} = \frac{{}^{-}21 \pm \sqrt{537}}{6}$$

The square root of 537 rounded to the nearest hundredth is 23.17. Substitute into the expression and simplify.

$$m = \frac{{}^{-}21 + 23.17}{6} = \frac{2.17}{6} = 0.36 \text{ and}$$
$$m = \frac{{}^{-}21 - 23.17}{6} = \frac{{}^{-}44.17}{6} = {}^{-}7.36$$

The two solutions for the variable m are $m = \underline{0.36}$ and $m = \underline{{}^{-}7.36}$.

498. Transform the equation by subtracting
16y from and adding 5 to both sides. $4y^2 - 16y + 5 = 16y - 5 - 16y + 5$
Combine like terms. $4y^2 - 16y + 5 = 0$
List the values of a, b, and c. $a = 4 \quad b = {}^-16 \quad c = 5$
Substitute the values into the
quadratic equation. $y = \frac{{}^-({}^-16) \pm \sqrt{({}^-16)^2 - 4(4)(5)}}{2(4)}$
Simplify the expression.

$$y = \frac{16 \pm \sqrt{256 - 80}}{8} = \frac{16 \pm \sqrt{176}}{8} = \frac{16 \pm \sqrt{16 \cdot 11}}{8} = \frac{16 \pm 4\sqrt{11}}{8}$$

The square root of 11 rounded to the
nearest hundredth is 3.32. Substitute
into the expression and simplify. $y = \frac{16 + 4\,(3.32)}{8} = \frac{29.28}{8} = 3.66$ and

$$y = \frac{16 - 4(3.32)}{8} = \frac{2.72}{8} = 0.34$$

The two solutions for the variable y are $\underline{y = 3.66}$ and $\underline{y = 0.34}$.

499. List the values of a, b, and c. $a = 5 \quad b = 12 \quad c = {}^-1$
Substitute the values into the
quadratic equation $s = \frac{{}^-(12) \pm \sqrt{(12)^2 - 4(5)({}^-1)}}{2(5)}$

Simplify the expression. $s = \frac{{}^-12 \pm \sqrt{144 + 20}}{10} = \frac{{}^-12 \pm \sqrt{164}}{10}$
The square root of 164 rounded to the
nearest hundredth is 12.81. Substitute
into the expression and simplify. $s = \frac{{}^-12 + 12.81}{10} = \frac{0.81}{10} = 0.081$

and $s = \frac{{}^-12 - 12.81}{10} = \frac{{}^-24.81}{10} = 2.48$

The two solutions for the variable s are $\underline{s = 0.08}$ and $\underline{s = {}^-2.48}$.

500. List the values of a, b, and c. $a = 4 \quad b = {}^-11 \quad c = 2$
Substitute the values into the
quadratic equation. $c = \frac{{}^-({}^-11) \pm \sqrt{({}^-11)^2 - 4(4)(2)}}{2(4)}$

Simplify the expression. $c = \frac{11 \pm \sqrt{121 - 32}}{8} = \frac{11 \pm \sqrt{89}}{8} = \frac{11 \pm 9.43}{8}$

$$c = \frac{11 + 9.43}{8} = \frac{20.43}{8} = 2.55 \text{ and}$$

$$c = \frac{11 - 9.43}{8} = \frac{1.57}{8} = 0.20$$

The two solutions for the variable c are $\underline{c = 2.55}$ and $\underline{c = 0.20}$.

501. List the values of a, b, and c. $a = 11 \quad b = {}^-32 \quad c = 10$
Substitute the values into the
quadratic equation. $k = \frac{{}^-({}^-32) \pm \sqrt{({}^-32)^2 - 4(11)(10)}}{2(11)}$

Simplify the expression. $k = \frac{32 \pm \sqrt{1024 - 440}}{22} = \frac{32 \pm \sqrt{584}}{22} = \frac{32 \pm 24.17}{22}$

$$k = \frac{32 + 24.17}{22} = \frac{56.17}{22} = 2.55 \text{ and}$$

$$k = \frac{32 - 24.17}{22} = 7.8322 = 0.36$$

The two solutions for the variable k are $\underline{k = 2.55}$ and $\underline{k = 0.36}$.